EXPLORING COMPLEX ORGANIZATIONS

This book is about making sense of how people in organizations that do not make sense try to make sense of what they do.

EXPLORING COMPLEX ORGANIZATIONS

A Cultural Perspective

Barbara
CZARNIAWSKA-JOERGES

SAGE PUBLICATIONS
International Educational and Professional Publisher
Newbury Park   London   New Delhi

For information address:

SAGE Publications, Inc.
2455 Teller Road
Newbury Park, California 91320

SAGE Publications Ltd.
6 Bonhill Street
London EC2A 4PU
United Kingdom

SAGE Publications India Pvt. Ltd.
M-32 Market
Greater Kailash I
New Delhi 110 048 India

Printed in the United States of America

Library of Congress Cataloging-in-Publication Data

Czarniawska-Joerges, Barbara.
    Exploring complex organizations: a cultural perspective / Barbara
Czarniawska-Joerges.
        p.   cm.
    Includes bibliographical references (p.   ) and index.
    ISBN 0-8039-4454-3.—ISBN (invalid) 0-8039-4455-1 (pbk.)
    1. Complex organizations.   I. Title.
HM131.C97   1992
302.3'5—dc20
                                                        91-36605

92 93 94 95 10 9 8 7 6 5 4 3 2 1

Sage Production Editor: Chiara C. Huddleston

Contents

1

Introduction in a Form of Self-Explanation

The Need to Study Large Organizations

Large organizations are one of the most characteristic signs of our times, together with such phenomena as large technical systems, global markets, and mass communication. This does not mean that small organizations are unimportant, only that they have been with us for a long time now, and we know relatively much about them. This does not mean, either, that large organizations arrived here yesterday. The armies, the state bureaucracies, and the churches have been with us since time immemorial, but most people lived their lives and came in contact with them only sporadically. Today, this is no longer possible. On the one hand, modern, multiunit business enterprises replaced small and traditional enterprises in many sectors of the economy, altering the structure of these sectors and of the economy as a whole (Chandler, 1977). On the other hand, the welfare state, in its many forms, is filling greater and greater parts of its citizens' lives with various types of large organizations.

Life for most people today is shaped by one or another form of organization. As employees, we spend at least 8 out of 16 waking hours in work organizations. The primary source of power experienced by most people in ordinary situations resides there. It often happens that the main source of meaning is there, also. Organizations are, for many people, a main source of their identity. Not only that—in the hours that are left, we encounter other organizations as customers, patients, pupils, or clients.

Although many of these organizations are still small, and although the recurring waves of nostalgia remind us that "small is beautiful" (Schumacher, 1973), the reality of multinational, state-sponsored projects, and the growing complexity of local administration is manifest. Be it an institutional response to changes in the environment (mostly technological, as Chandler explains it), the power-seeking force of capitalism (Sabel & Piore, 1984), American business, or the European bureaucracies (not to speculate about the remnants of feudalism in the Orient), large organizations are with us and will be for a long time yet.

Yet we do not know much about large organizations. Their complexity defies many of the traditional approaches. In the first place, we lack good methods that allow us to describe and understand the complexity of such organizations. Neither macroeconomics, which operates on a different scale, nor the theory of the firm, which reduces organization to a hypothetical decision-maker, can do much in this respect. These approaches were designed with the aim of tackling the problems of simple (sometimes simplified) organizations. And although small organizations can also be complex, large organizations always are.

In the following text, *large* and *complex* are often used synonymously, with the assumption that it is large and complex organizations that are the central element of our culture. If large organizations are seen as a part of culture, anthropology seems to be the discipline to turn to for help. Simple loans, however, rarely pay off in interdisciplinary approaches. We need, then, to disregard the disciplinary boundaries and definitions in order to search for methods that can be molded, shaped, and adapted for the best use on the object of study—complex organizations. The present text is no more than an attempt in this direction. Its form and content might be more understandable, though, and therefore easier to judge, if the author abandons her objectivist disguise and presents herself at the outset.

A Piece of Autobiography

This book is not written by an anthropologist, but by a student of organizations looking for a method. All of my professional life, I have been greatly interested in what adult people, in my own and in other societies, do for most of their time and why. Literature of the *belles lettres* type told me a great deal, but not everything. It does not take any outstanding perceptiveness to notice that people spend most of their working time in groups, which are to a large extent formalized in the shape of organizations—and yet the literature tackles this phenomenon only infrequently, preferring its heroes and heroines to be free individuals.

Prompted by this unsatisfied interest, I earned a degree in social psychology under the illusion that this discipline explores the mysteries of group experience. I learned many fascinating things that might happen in a laboratory to a person who imagines the company of another person, but I also knew that I had to continue my search elsewhere. Economics seemed to be most promising in the face of the fact that economic organizations are dominant, both in terms of time and importance, in the lives of most people. I graduated with a degree in economic sciences with a comforting awareness that economics too, and for its own reasons, is interested in what real people do when they act in real groups and why. But this knowledge was not yet very advanced compared to the knowledge of behavior of theoretical variables in theoretical models. At least there seemed to be a shared interest. All that remained was to find a method of investigation—if possible, an empirical one.

Business administration was a first beacon in my journey—not because it has a method, but because it does not have one. Therefore, an open search was not seen as an iconoclastic rebellion against old masters, an irreverence toward the holy tradition, but as a legitimate task. The second step was the methodological revolution of the social sciences in the 1970s, which gradually widened the scope of options, even within traditional disciplines.

After having searched, tried, experimented, failed, succeeded, and tried again, I arrived at a harbor that seemed promising to me and also attracted many other boats uncertain where to anchor. But the idea is not to compete with ports that already exist and are in full operation. Organization theory has an important topic; anthropology has a promising method. If the two can be put together more systematically and consistently, maybe the result would help us understand what we experience during the major part of our adult lives. An anthropologically inspired organization theory would be, then, an interpretation of organizational processes from the standpoint of the actors involved, collected and retold by a researcher (also representing a certain standpoint). It would be a polyphony of voices from inside rather than an aerial picture taken from the outside.

Having said earlier that I am not an anthropologist, I might now add that I am not an epistemologist either. In terms of theory, the present text is a plea for concentrating dispersed effects more clearly. In terms of method, it is a plea for a closer-to-ground treatment of methodology, somewhere between the ivory towers of science and the adobe huts of research techniques. As I was watching new generations of researchers wandering on wide plains—created among the multiple realities of Alfred Schütz, the social structures of Talcott Parsons, and the instructions for the use of Sony's *Walkman Professional*—in search of a solid and unpretentious shelter, the idea of sharing my similar wandering experience came to mind. If this book is of any help to anybody who feels at a loss, it has achieved its goal.

On This Book's Method

The book starts by establishing the aim of the search by reminding the reader of the most important and best known attempts to tackle the subject of complex organizations. With the focus thus sharpened, the search begins in the field of social anthropology, with the purpose of finding possibilities and indicating hindrances. It then moves on to traditional empirical studies of complex organizations. The contrast of the two disciplines makes for a clearer understanding of historical developments and current needs concerning their possible combination.

Attention is then focused on contemporary attempts to combine ethnomethodology with political anthropology and organizational culture studies. The book ends with a cumulative account of the possibilities of studying and understanding complex organizations.

The book does not contain a review of the literature—there are quite a few of those—but it does contain a thesis, or rather, a plea based on a confrontation between the field experience of the author and the theoretical recommendations of the literature. Examples were chosen from the vast array of sources on the basis of their relevance to this plea. This book is not designed to prove anything, but to propose; as such, it should be tempting rather than convincing. The final result of the search is individual: It could be an enthusiastic will to prove one's hand at an anthropological study of a complex organization, or a certainty that this is not the way to achieve desired research results.

The form that best suits such aims is that of a literary collage. Like all authors, my intention in writing this text is to convey a message of my own, to which other texts are instrumental. At the same time, I would like the reader to have a look into the original texts, to be encouraged to reach for them if only to challenge my interpretation. A collage distorts the original sources—this lies in the nature of every interpretation—but it also reveals relatively unprocessed fragments that might give an intimation of the original whole.

An additional warning is due, one that came to me not at the beginning, but at the end of the process of composing the present text. This is a collage of texts, not of authors. The mistake is easy to make, as most of the authors quoted tend to put a visible "signature" on their texts (on differences between authoring and writing see Geertz, 1988). However, all of them developed and changed their insights over years of work. "Early Selznick" can be seen as being sometimes in sharp opposition to "late Selznick"; "Geertz, 1973" is different from "Geertz, 1988," and so on. This phenomenon is easier to tackle where the authors explicitly reflected on changes in their writing (see Leach, 1976; Perrow, 1980). In all remaining cases, the reader should bear in mind that any given text is less than its author, but more than just a text or my interpretation of it. It exemplifies a certain period in the life of the academic community; it evokes contemporary social and political contexts; it reflects trends and fashions.

The collection of sources might seem unorthodox, but it is by no means incidental. A "telephone directory" style of referencing is avoided on the assumption that it hampers reasoning and does not do justice to the authors quoted. The criterion for choosing the sources was not "as many as possible," but "the most relevant." Such a choice is, of necessity, arbitrary and can be questioned on many accounts. Readers are wholeheartedly encouraged to improve on my choices in building methodologies of their own.

Relevance to the aim, that is, the search for methods of studying complex organizations, served not only as a criterion for the choice of sources, but also for the way they were presented. At this point it may be most appropriate to say, along with Berger and Luckmann (1966/ 1971):

> We are fully aware that, in various places, we do violence to certain thinkers by integrating their thought into a theoretical formation that some of them might have found quite alien. We would say in justification that historical gratitude is not in itself a scientific virtue. (p. 29)

Finally, it must be added that the judgments pronounced (an activity that is inevitable, if only by inference, when building an argument) are not meant to express more than the author's opinion. To avoid even unconscious attempts at donning the cloak of scientific authority, a subjective rhetoric has been chosen to remind readers that the aim of this book is to encourage them to make judgments of their own and to construct methodologies for their own use. The present text does not aspire to be more than a source of inspiration.

Affiliations and Allegiances

It is not humanly possible to be free from biases, but it is possible to attempt to account for them. I have already mentioned my research interests, but I feel that there are at least two other factors that are significant from the point of view of writing this book, and to those reading it. One is that I am a woman, and although not counted among organized feminists, I take it for granted that women deserve all the rights and options accessible to humans in their lives, and I consider it deplorable that this is not so.

Another is my somewhat complicated cultural affiliation. I am Polish; I was educated within the U.S. tradition of social sciences and worked on a study in the United States; I live and work in Sweden, and publish mostly in European journals. I fully acknowledge my debt to the U.S. research tradition, but it does not prevent me from considering it a burden as well. Until recently it was often taken for granted that complex organizations are U.S. organizations. The proposed anthropology is not, however, to be an anthropology of European organizations, but a study of complex organizations in their proper cultural contexts.

After gender and cultural affiliations, it is time to say something about my research affinities. I am a realist; I believe in the existence of reality independent of our cognition. However, the only means accessible to us in apprehending this reality is human cognition, and therefore we must strive for intersubjectivity rather than objectivity. The notion of *conventional realism* (Manicas & Rosenberg, 1988) illustrates this rather well. To borrow their example, if I see a panda, it is obvious to me that something is standing in my field of vision, but in order to know that this something is a panda, I must know the appropriate convention (otherwise I might see a yeti, for instance). R. H. Brown (1977) calls such perspective, with an ironic twist, *symbolic realism,* a very fitting name indeed.

Finally, as a researcher I am both a determinist and a voluntarist, but as a person I lean toward the latter. I believe that neither God nor nature, but humankind itself, gives sense to existence, and that this sense-finding is its main occupation.

Self-labeling is, of course, a risky enterprise. It gives an appearance of a static picture to something that is basically an ongoing process. I am all the things mentioned above when writing this book, but I used to be a functionalist positivist, and do not know who I shall become by the time this book is in print. The only safe position, then, is that of a methodological pluralist who tries to be tolerant toward all traditions, knowing that one might need this tolerance oneself.

2

Complex Organizations:
Looking for Definitions and Metaphors

In this chapter I wish to establish a starting point by sharpening the focus of discussion. What do we know about complex organizations and what more do we want know about them? In order to answer this question, I will examine two classics, by Etzioni and Perrow, and then move to more recent approaches to the topic.

The Analysis of Complex Organizations

The comparative study of organization is a much neglected field. Its development requires "middle range" organizational theory, falling between high-level abstractions about the characteristics of organizations in general and detailed observations about single cases. (Etzioni, 1961, p. xi)

Thus begins the book *The Analysis of Complex Organizations: On Power, Involvement, and Their Correlates,* written by Amitai Etzioni in 1961. The appeal remains valid, even if at present the comparative study of organization is not so much neglected as still not fully satisfactory. Researchers try to avoid traps of complexity by concentrating on a single organizational problem cut out of its organizational context (aiming at the abstract characteristics mentioned above), or they limit themselves to only a few cases. The persistence of this unsatisfactory conduct should be attributed not so much to stubbornness on the part of the researchers themselves as to the shortage of methods that permit alternative approaches.

What did Etzioni propose in this respect? "Models for the analysis of various organizational types must be constructed" (1961, p. xi). To be able to understand the results this postulate has produced, we must start with a review of Etzioni's basic concepts: What are complex organizations? Which phenomena should one study? Which methods should be applied? What results should one aim for? Which results already exist?

Starting Point and Desired Results

The treatise opens with a definition of its subject:

> By *organization* we mean, following Parsons . . . social units devoted primarily to attainment of specific goals. Organizations discussed in this volume are complex and have many of the characteristics Weber specified as "bureaucratic." Thus in this volume *organization* stands for "complex bureaucratic organization." (1961, p. xi)

This definition tells us two important things about Etzioni's approach to complex organizations: first, that it was functionalist (social units devoted to the attainment of goals); and second, that at the time the book was written, it was taken for granted that organizations were complex. It was also assumed that in order to be compared, complex organizations must reside in a constant sociocultural context—more specifically, the contemporary (late 1950s) United States.

These assumptions were explicit; I would like to add two more that I see as implicit: first, that the sociocultural context is an entity separate from the organization; and second, that the sociocultural context of the United States was homogeneous in character.[1]

As to method—within the deductive, theory-testing, explanatory approach, one hypothesizes the result first and then looks for an appropriate verification method.[2] Thus the desired outcome of the comparative study of organizations is to:

1. establish the truly universal propositions of organizational theory;
2. reduce overgeneralized propositions to middle-range (specific) statements, specifying the categories of organizations to which they apply; and
3. develop new middle-range propositions so that knowledge of universals will be supplemented with statements concerning analytical types of organizations. (Etzioni, 1961, p. xiv)

This can be achieved by comparing all organizations on the basis of one central variable—*compliance*.

Compliance is a relationship consisting of the power employed by superiors to control subordinates and the orientation of the subordinates to this power. (p. xv)

Thus compliance permitted the combination of structural (type and distribution of power) and motivational (individual commitment) aspects of complex organizations, thereby creating the hope of overcoming the traditional gap between micro- (individual, psychological) and macro-level (structural, sociological, and economic) approaches.[3]

Compliance, it must be stressed, is a theoretical construct introduced a priori, and as such it lacks empirical justification, and therefore needs a theoretical one. This justification was found in the fact that compliance can be seen as connected to many other organizational variables, such as organizational goals, power elites, consensus, communication and socialization, recruitment, and charisma. During the past 20 years of organizational research, however, almost all of these variables have been problematized. It is doubtful whether organizations pursue specific goals, whether power elites and charisma can be observed, and whether they are at all important, and if so, how much consensus is really needed to accomplish a collective action. Nevertheless, the issue of compliance remains. It is often called *control* in descriptive terms, and *power* in analytical terminology. Semantics aside, the persistence of this focus seems to indicate that compliance is a crucial issue for complex organizations.

According to Etzioni, the ultimate justification for specific research goals lies in their contribution to a specific theory. In his case, the choice was guided by disciplinary attachment. Etzioni is a sociologist, and according to many sociologists, sociology was born as an intellectual search for an explanation of social order. An explanation of compliance should therefore contribute to an explanation of social order.

At this juncture, one should point out that, in contrast, organizational theory was born out of a pragmatic wish to establish conditions for the successful functioning of organizations in order to improve existing ones. This hardly intellectual aim has undergone a series of dramatic changes in the course of its development. Although the mainstream still follows the functionalist approach, at least two new trends have emerged: critical and interpretive. Critical organization theories aim at disclosing organizational deceptions in defense of the people in organizations—who are there for their own interests, not for organizational survival. The interpretive approaches share the humanistic ideals of the critical approach (organizations for people, not people for organizations), but do not assume any a priori evaluations of a given organizational reality. Instead a milder assumption is posited: People not only are *in* organizations (which both functionalists and critical theorists assume), but they also *create* organizations. Consequently, the increased understanding of organizational phenomena should enable people to create more benevolent organizations and to fight against nonbenevolent ones.

Increased understanding is therefore the ultimate goal of organizational research. Disciplinary considerations should be of secondary interest, just as explaining the sources of social order is important only if it contributes to increased understanding (which, undoubtedly, it does). This shift in goals, however, happened long after Etzioni wrote his treatise on complex organizations; and, indeed, its impact is distinctly seen in his latest book, *The Moral Dimension* (1988). The goal behind the theory determines the methodology chosen; therefore we must consider the recommended method of analysis in light of the author's goal.

The Analytical Scheme

With the concept of compliance at its core, a skeleton theory was built by examining other concepts in the existing body of literature in light of the core concept.[4] This resulted in a typology of compliance relationships that juxtaposed three types of power (coercive, remunerative, and normative) against three kinds of involvement (alienative, calculative, and moral). The result was congruent (e.g., coercive power and alienative involvement) or incongruent (e.g., normative power and calculative involvement) compliance relationships. Etzioni concluded that congruent relationships, that is, those in which the kind of power exercised was consistent with the kind of existing involvement, were more frequent. On this basis, he then postulated that congruent compliance relationships were more functional.[5]

This exercise in typology building was meant to provide answers to the following questions concerning U.S. organizations: Why do people enter them? Why do they stay? Why are they doing what they are doing? These questions can easily be extended to non-U.S. and non-complex organizations, and the difference in answers may well be pivotal in determining the phenomenon of complex organizations. The problem is that the questions are uncomfortably general and some specification seems necessary. Etzioni's typology is a way of dealing with this requirement. It builds a system of categories (forms, labeled boxes) into which unruly organizational behavior can be packed. These boxes, when full, have concrete attributes, just like things. *Coercive compliance* is everything that fits certain descriptions of power (which in itself is a package-type concept), of involvement, and of the relationship between the two. Organization, then, is not a process, or something that happens while we watch it (or created while we act), but a set of elements that can be properly classified according to a previously constructed set of categories. What does not fit into the assigned categories is either cut to measure or left aside; if many elements are left on one side, a new package can be constructed.

Who decides on the classification scheme? Who does the classifying? Organizational actors do it continuously; they objectify their experience by categorizing it (Berger & Luckmann, 1966/1971). But their classifications are unsatisfactory—illogical, contradictory, shifting, and poorly explained. The task, then, is left to researchers. But why should researchers' classifications be any better? Because they have a forum in which to negotiate their classifications? What is more, how can we be assured that the organizations we are going to compare do indeed possess elements that can be packaged in our boxes? If we know this from the start, the point of doing the study seems somewhat redundant.

This does not mean that all classifications are reifying or redundant. It is easy and legitimate to classify people according to the month they were born, to their declared allegiance to a given creed, or, as Etzioni did in relation to lower participants, according to their formal allegiance to an organization (inmates, clients, customers, members, employees). We classify time into days of the week, geographic directions according to their relation to the North Pole, and so on.[6] The problem starts when we begin classifying human and social action, forgetting that sense making is at its core, and therefore meddle with it by a premature attribution of sense.[7]

But even the classification based on a declared creed or organizational allegiance is at best a snapshot taken at a given moment. People convert, become heretics, or feel like inmates when they are employees. Therefore, the next step proposed, classifying organizations according to the type of involvement (coercive, utilitarian, and normative), is even more risky or, at best, tautological. In trying to fit the categories with the contents, Etzioni reviewed many interesting examples of organizational action but his choices were limited by his own definition. The result is that, such studies as Milgram's (1963) and Zimbardo, Haney, Banks, and Jaffe's (1974), while perhaps the most revealing as to the mechanisms that guide coercive action, cannot be included in a discussion of coercion because an experimental setup (i.e., researchers and voluntary or paid subjects) is not a "coercive organization." Similarly, to accommodate the fact that ideological control is used in business organizations, an entirely new category is required—*dual organizations*. This spoils the elegance of the analytical scheme (if categories overlap, where are the boundaries?) and revives the question of the utility of thing-like categories in promoting understanding.

After having accomplished the classification of compliance relationships, Etzioni related it to other organizational variables. I shall pass over *organizational goals* and *organizational effectiveness* as abstract constructs that have some importance as discussion topics in organizations, but whose physical existence cannot be empirically established. *Consensus* can be disputed, but communication and socialization undoubtedly relate to certain observable organizational actions. Let us concentrate on these.

Etzioni, quoting Parsons, assumed that each collective had a cultural system that included sets of values and cognitive perspectives that were, to varying degrees, shared by organizational actors. (This is probably the best definition of organizational culture so far!) One can say, therefore, that the communication that takes place in a collective shapes a commonly recognized or accepted worldview based on a common set of values. If these worldviews and values are to be called *culture,* then actors who join the interaction have to be *acculturated,* which is usually called *socialization,* and the more experienced actors must constantly reconfirm the shared worldview, which is usually called *negotiation.*

But by attempting these translations, I am departing from Etzioni, whose primary aim was to include the above phenomena into the extended classification scheme. His next step was to turn to the environment, and, for a change, Etzioni rejected a reifying approach (an organization and an environment) in order to see organization as an action varying in range. *Recruitment* was turning nonorganizational actors into organizational actors, *scope* was including "extraorganizational life" into organizational action, and *pervasiveness* was creating norms for nonorganizational actors. If we look for names of processes rather than states or attributes, we might speak of recruitment, inclusion, and external control.

This was the main analytical scheme to be used in comparing complex organizations. Because the scheme was basically static, it required a specific approach to organizational dynamics. Organizational change meant that an organization moved from one state (a given content of a box) to another, applying specific mechanisms to achieve it. I stress this in order to contrast it with a different perspective (see the section "Looking for Metaphors of Complex Organizations")—that of organization as continuous change, where some patterns can be only temporarily discerned. Etzioni's view (and that of many other change theorists) imposed movement on a basically static structure; the *organization as flux and transformation* perspective attempts to introduce tentative static into continuous movement.

Let us now turn to how this scheme can be applied to comparisons of existing organizations.

Methods for Studying Complex Organizations

Comparative analysis was a necessity, as Etzioni frequently stressed. Interestingly enough, he noted in passing that anthropologists had been the first to appreciate the merits of a comparative approach, which could free us from the limits of our previous patterns of thought and reveal a broader scale of human interaction patterns. The problem, then, is how to make the comparison.

The research tradition to which Etzioni subscribed required that the elements of the analytical scheme become operational, that is, that their empirical indicators be found and turned into measures. Next, to establish the inclusion of a given organization in a given category, the relative primacy of certain analytical elements over others (e.g., coercive over normative compliance) had to be proved. The introduction of continua in place of polar extremes should have eased this endeavor. In addition, measurement in more transparent situations, such as conflict, was recommended. These recommendations are well worth remembering because some categorization is needed sooner or later, if only to present an emergent theory, and because in some situations, such as open conflict, organizations become more transparent. (It is not by accident that most organizations do not wish to have researchers on the premises while they are in a state of an open conflict.) The problem is that it is hard to say what the subsequent comparison could contribute to Etzioni's theory. The explanatory strength of his model resides in its analytical scheme—the empirical research could consist only of making correct classifications.

This explains Etzioni's hesitations about studying organizations situated in sociocultural contexts outside the United States. His theory was practically closed: It had been built on the foundations of existing research in U.S. organizations; therefore, the correct classifications could be made only within the same population. With due respect to Amitai Etzioni, I think that the theory of complex organizations is still in its crib, and, therefore, opening rather than closing seems to be proper action at this point in time.

Where Do We Go From Here?

Etzioni's powerful classic attracted research attention to complex organizations and formulated a list of important issues pertaining to organizational life that should be studied. The usefulness of his theoretical constructs in actual interpretations remains to be seen, but there is no doubt that organizational phenomena such as recruitment, socialization, control, and development of personal relationships should be of interest to any student of organizations.

Etzioni concluded that complex organizations were promising study subjects because problems of social order could be empirically studied there. Complex organizations could indeed be seen as strategic sites for such studies because social order in modern societies is to a great extent revealed in organizational interactions.

Fully agreeing with this conclusion, I would like to reverse its premise. A complex organization is a phenomenon in itself, a major form of social life in modern societies (both quantitatively—in terms of the number of people involved and the number of hours spent, and qualitatively—in terms of their impact on individual, social, and societal life). The difficulty with Etzioni's theory is in its character, which requires that existing organizations be compared to the theory, and not to each other, making it doubtful that new concepts and insights can be generated. In that sense, the book's main contribution lies in formulating the research appeal rather than answering it. Since its publication, a great many researchers have expressed interest in complex organization, among them, Charles Perrow.

A Critical Essay on Complex Organizations

The first edition of Perrow's *Complex Organization* appeared in 1972; the edition I used as a basis for this section appeared in 1986. The period between the two editions is long, and indeed, even if the gist remains the same, many things have changed. The author accounted for these changes in an autobiographical article entitled "Zoo Story, or Life in the Organizational Sandpit" (1980b). I think his reflections are important not only because they shed light on his own perspective, but also because they are strongly relevant to the present text.

Organizations are beasts, said Perrow, which we as organization students see only on our visits to the zoo. We do not know much about their habitat and only slightly more about their behavior. What is more, we tend to visit only certain cages, and we believe that whatever we happen to see represents the whole of the animal world.

So much for organizations! Organization researchers, on the other hand, build their theories like children build sand castles. This metaphor has many consequences. Although sand building has an enormous influence on children's development and a paramount significance in the world of children, it occupies only a minor place in the wider scheme of things and events—castle building is much more play than a serious construction business. Another consequence is that the social processes involved are analogous—children tend to play in groups, and each group considers their castle to be truly beautiful. For a passer-by, however, all are just mounds of the same sand, shaped somewhat differently.

If we are to learn from Perrow's experience, which he generously shares with us, the lessons would be three: relativity, pluralism, and modesty. Pictures of complex organizations change depending on the standpoint. No matter how attached one is to one's own standpoint, it would be naive and arrogant not to acknowledge the usefulness of others. And, finally:

> Since we live in an organizational society, almost anything we can learn about them will help us survive among and in them. . . (p. 272). But given our small population in the sandpit, our toddler age, and the variety

and power of the beasts in the zoo, it would be unrealistic to expect much more than another unstable sandpile to emerge from all this work. (Perrow, 1980b, p. 277)

Thus warned, we can start examining Perrow's sandpile in detail.

Complex Organizations as Bureaucracies

Perrow built his definition of bureaucracy along developmental lines. He started with the example of General Gypsum Corporation, described by Alvin Gouldner in his *Patterns of Industrial Bureaucracy* (1954). The gypsum plant was a simple, traditional organization, community- rather than profit-oriented, where collective action was based on interpersonal relationships, not a system of formal rules. The times had changed, however, and the gypsum plant had to open its gates to the "rational-legal bureaucracy," whose elements are so well known to us:

1. Equal treatment for all employees.
2. Reliance on expertise, skills, and experience relevant to the position.
3. No extraorganizational prerogatives of the position.
4. Specific standards of work and output.
5. Extensive record keeping dealing with the work and output.
6. Establishment and enforcement of rules and regulations that serve the interests of the organization.
7. Recognition that rules and regulations bind managers as well as employees; thus, employees can hold management to the terms of the employment contract. (Perrow, 1972/1986, p. 3)

All complex organizations in the United States are bureaucracies, claimed Perrow, thereby joining Etzioni in his definition. Their existence as bureaucracies is not, however, unproblematic. Problems stem from two different sources. First, organizations are not bureaucratic enough—extraorganizational actors, the unpredictable natural and social environment, and the bounded rationality of actors prevent achievement of the bureaucratic ideal. But insofar as this ideal can be attained, it constitutes a second source of trouble: rigidity and stifled creativity, which are traditional complaints. To these, Perrow added a third:

> [B]ureaucracy has become a means, both in capitalist and noncapitalist countries, of centralizing power in society and legitimating or disguising that centralization. (1972/1986, p. 5)

This is a more powerful restatement of Etzioni's claim concerning compliance and presents a real challenge to people who deal with complex organizations. Before we move on to a possible list of phenomena worth studying, let us stay with this definition for a while.

Suppose there are no impediments to total bureaucratization. The result would be a simple, although nontraditional, machine-like organization. The army used to be a good case of such an organization, although the example seems to be rather inflated in the case of the modern army. What does seem to be the case is that bureaucracies became aware of the inevitability of failures, and, led by the torch of human relations, attempted to incorporate what they could not remove. Although there are some bastions of pure bureaucratic rationality left, still fighting, most modern organizations attempt to combine a traditional organization with a rational-legal one, and this, in my opinion, contributes to their complexity significantly.

Perrow also addressed a more universal problem of the *raison d'etre* of all organizations. In his definition, "Organizations are tools for shaping the world as one wishes it to be shaped" (1972/1986, p. 11). This definition is interesting because it allows us to analyze jointly actions and notions such as goal setting, multiple goals, conflicting interests, and so on. Perrow's definition reduces the strict teleology of organizations to goal-directed, and it removes the anthropomorphic metaphor of organizations as purposeful actors. People certainly create and join organizations with the idea of shaping the world—and their lives—in a certain manner. Whether this involves a desire to build an empire or simply to earn enough to support a family, it can still be subsumed under Perrow's definition, making it easier to understand how those disparate individual visions can be united in collective action. It helps us understand how the oppressed help to legitimate oppression by compliance, or even by resistance, and other similar paradoxes of complex organization. If organizations are everybody's tools, then it is easier to understand how they are daily recreated in organizational practice.

Perrow's definition contains a definitive metaphor—organization as a tool, an instrument. It is therefore necessary to observe the limits of such a metaphor. Physical tools do not have to be recreated daily—they exist independently from their organizational use. Social tools—such as organizations—also have a relatively stable existence, but it depends on their use. To follow Etzioni's advice, and to avoid dichotomies, one should think of a continuum of tools, with a *perpetuum mobile* at one extreme and ad hoc groups at the other. Choosing metaphors is an important task to be undertaken in any study of complex organizations.

Phenomena Under Study

The definition employed by Perrow indicates the major phenomena that should be examined when studying complex organization.[8] The first question, How do they become complex?, queries the historical processes behind new cultural formations, the next chapter to Chandler's *Visible Hand* (1977). The ruling hand becomes invisible again, but this time by putting on a glove. Perrow's book is in large part dedicated to the analysis of this development, tracing it through changes in managerial ideologies as reflected in organizational theory and against the background of historical changes. Another phenomenon is rationalization as the main drive, and formal rationality as the main value behind this drive. Related to this phenomenon are several others: centralization of control, legitimation of centralized control, and norm-building (which can be seen as a more economical form of legitimation).

These basic phenomena permit interpretation, from the outside, of a number of actions or processes that are visible in organizations, such as decision-making, socialization, and motivation. Unlike Etzioni's "boxes," these are not categories to be filled in with examples, but theoretical constructs that give meaning to a great variety of observations collected in accumulated research on organizations and societies. These constructs are the result of social science's attempt to make sense of social phenomena. They exclude the possibility of a *tabula rasa* access to the study site; instead they assume a generalized knowledge that researchers, as members of modern Western culture with a specific status ("universe-maintenance," to use Berger & Luckmann's terms, 1966/1971), quite naturally possess. But this does not necessitate an a priori structure imposed on the object in question. We may know all about legitimation as an important social process, and still be curious as to why some accountants indulge in double bookkeeping—one set of accounts in their computers and one in their old black notebooks. We know quite a lot about how complex organizations act in public because we can all see that, but we still do not understand why. The problem is how to use existing knowledge to promote further knowledge without stifling it. There have been many attempts to "operationalize," thus reifying the concepts of power, rationalization, and legitimation. The task should be reversed to consist of using our theoretical constructs in the hope that they might be useful in the everyday organizational construction of meaning. The next question is which method to use.

Studies of Complex Organizations

Charles Perrow approached methodological problems through a review of the main schools of thought in organizational theory. The *human relations* school of thought can be seen as favoring the experimental method. A change is introduced, and resultant changes are expected. This line of thought survives today in the tradition of action research. Now as before, however, the theoretical basis for action research is a source of difficulty. An answer to the question, What causes what? is expected. Was it better work organization or special attention that caused the productivity increase in the Hawthorne plant? The first reaction was to search for labels, and that is how notions such as leadership, performance, and job satisfaction were introduced. Not surprisingly, these variables and their labels came from a small field, psychological research, because this was where the researchers came from. If sociologists had undertaken the study, we should expect terms such as class allegiance, interest, and alienation. Labeling has a great impact not only on organizational theory but also on organizational practice, and once successfully accomplished, stays in place for a long time.

Leadership is still one of the hottest issues in organizations, although if one were to soberly distance oneself from the notion and ask for the basis of the analogy between leadership (as in a class exercise on team building) and a manager's action in a complex organization, a convincing answer would require some effort. Henry Mintzberg (1973) attempted to show what managers really did (which had little if anything to do with leadership); but even if his results were absorbed, they did not damage the notion of leadership in the least.

In addition, there was the question of what the statement "X causes Y" really meant. It was solved, somewhat unsatisfactorily, by substituting "Changes in X correlate with changes in Y," which continues to be attacked on the basis that X and Y are usually situationally defined, that changes in X and Y are defined insofar as the accessible measures permit, and that correlations, in themselves, demand interpretation.

The micro-character of postulated variables aroused anxiety within the human relations school itself. This was amended by introducing group variables, as in the models of Likert, McGregor, Tannenbaum, and others. The improvement was minimal, however, and at this point I would like to quote Perrow's criticism: "One cannot explain organizations by explaining the attitudes and behavior of individuals or even small groups within them. We learn a great deal about psychology and social psychology but little about organizations per se in this fashion" (1972/1986, p. 114).

I call the next school, the neo-Weberian, *cognitive* because it builds organization theory around studies of decision-making. Organization is a collective choice making, following a bounded rationality; that is, utility-maximizing within limits set by imperfect human cognition. All the principal concepts relate to cognition and information processing; studies vary from descriptive to simulative tests of the rational decision-making model. Perhaps due to the cognitive bias, this school seems to be the most perceptive in relation to actual organizational events.

The theory of bounded rationality (March & Simon, 1958) was a great revolution compared to previous models. Further observations of the unruly character of organizational life led to the conclusion that not only do individuals suffer from bounded rationality, but also decision-making as a group process suffers from conflicting goals, resembling more of a garbage can than an orderly intellectual process. As Perrow noted, the introduction of the garbage can model (and I would add, of bounded rationality in the first place) was an important event, deconstructive in character (with deconstruction considered as part of the construction of social reality). "Yet the theory remains a primitive digging tool," says Perrow (1972/1986, p. 138), meaning that it has not been applied to "normal" organizations (it was built to describe the functioning of a university), or on the macro-level. I would like to concur with his criticism, but only by changing the argument somewhat.

The cognitive school of thought did not stop at the garbage can. Computer simulations of decision processes were paralleled by a wide collection of empirical findings meant to be an exploration of reality rather than a test of the theory. James G. March and Johan P. Olsen (1976), and later Nils Brunsson (1985), came to a point that can be interpreted as an almost total deconstruction of their starting point—the rational decision-making model. Decisions are not necessarily rational; it is very likely that they do not exist, or are something else, for example, legitimating actions already taken (Brunsson, 1985). Yet, equally surprising, the authors remain faithful to the cognitive perspective, whereas their results seem to indicate the necessity and usefulness of a social or social-constructionist viewpoint. It may be that I am reading their intentions wrongly. In fact, I tend to wonder whether their theory is a final blow to the rationality myth or ultimately an attempt to save it by making it more sophisticated (Czarniawska-Joerges, in press). As it is now, I see the results of cognitively informed studies as extremely important to an anthropology of complex organizations, but find their method less convincing. As long as rationality is treated as a transcendental value, it cannot be properly analyzed.[9]

Charles Perrow himself borrowed a loosened rationality model from the cognitive school, enriched it with technology-contingent models, and added political elements in order to analyze high-risk technologies. This analytic scheme is, in fact, one possibility for those who are interested in studies of complex organizations. To put it simply, Perrow's model assumed satisfied individuals who are trying to shape the world by handling complicated technologies within power-created social structures, and used a sophisticated *systems* approach to analyze the resulting processes. The problem is that the systems approach still cuts the social tissue into separate elements, even if it does so in order to put them back again in a theoretical explanation. Thus the social character of cognition remains neglected (it is represented as an aggregate of individual cognitions, even if shaped by a social and political frame), and even more important, the social construction of technology is not properly acknowledged. Yet the physical world we build and the physical world we use are mediated by the social meaning given to them. This aspect can be deduced only from processes, or from action itself, not from the structure that results. The cognitive view takes structures—cognitive, technical, and political—as a point of departure. Avoiding the unpromising question of which comes first, one could still begin by analyzing organizational action as a producer of structures, even if it is constrained by its own product.

According to Perrow, the school that took the most sociological perspective of organization was the institutionalist, whose approach may be called *functional-evolutionary*. Perrow's own approach to the study of large technological systems can be seen as a cross between the cognitive and institutional schools, but recently he takes only the system-structural approach from the institutional school, rejecting its main foundation, the biological metaphor. Within this metaphor, organizations are seen as structures that have come to serve certain functions, and their survival proves their utility.

This assumption leads to certain normative and methodological implications. Institutionalists, according to Perrow, insist on analyzing organizations as whole entities (or their individual elements, at least, as parts of a meaningful whole) in order to grasp their organic character and at the same time propose historical (evolutionary) studies of organizations. Both tendencies lead to a preference for case studies. They emphasize the importance of organic adaptations as opposed to planned changes and attempt to look beyond the surface, aware of the role self-presentation plays in survival. Finally, intentionally or by default, institutionalists see organizations as blending with the environment rather than as separated and contradictory to it.

The institutionalists, in terms of methodological recommendations, seem to promise a more interesting picture of complex organizations than do earlier approaches. Yet, the first of their two postulates, case studies of whole organizations in a historical perspective, may prove somewhat impractical. Indeed, with the possible exception of Selznick's *TVA and the Grass Roots* (1949/1966, Chapter 4), institutionalists prefer not-so-complex organizations, or else simple institutions. Perrow interpreted this as a fascination with triviality. I would see it, rather, as a more technical matter—that of the near-impossibility of grasping the whole of the history and the nature of a truly complex organization.

The question is whether if we embrace a methodology we then have to embrace the ideology—or lack of one—that lies behind it. Perrow exposed the moral ambiguity of functionalism to the light, and, although not the first to do so, he did it more convincingly than many others due to his nonaggressive argument. Institutionalization, after all, takes place in a situation of conflicting interests; not all actions become institutions. Somebody must be helping the evolution. While looking for the culprit, Perrow (1972/1986, p. 170) quoted his teacher, Selznick, wondering at the latter's easy enthusiasm: "Creative men are needed . . . who know how to transform a neutral body of men into a committed policy. These men are called leaders; their profession is politics" (Selznick, 1957, p. 61). This vision, cheery for some and terrifying for others, is again at our door, as a new generation of leaders is out for our souls. Whether we applaud leaders' intervention or detest it, the fact remains that social evolution was and is being meddled with, and survival no longer can be seen as a simple proof of fitness. In this way, it is much like evolution theory, which started to doubt its own original version as oversimplified.[10]

Perrow's second line of attack, which concerns the naive view that organizations adapt to their environment, has since been defended by neoinstitutionalists. Organizations are their own environment (see organizational fields, DiMaggio & Powell, 1983). Network studies, population ecology, and professional systems studies tend to see complex organizations as small cogs in an enormously complex system that, willingly, can be extended to the global economy as a whole. But here we leave the meso-level and enter the macro-level, which as such is beyond the present discussion.[11]

The Result: A Theory of Organizational Power

Having reviewed a great many phenomena and an equal number of approaches, Perrow concluded that a theory of power would result from studies of complex organization. His definition of "organization as a tool for shaping the world as *one* wishes it" (1972/1986, p. 11, emphasis added) changed into that of a tool "that *masters* use to generate valued outputs that they can then appropriate" (p. 260, emphasis added). The theory was thus closed: It is a theory of power as oppression, and an a priori model of analysis. This is an eclectic scheme, joining Weber's theory of bureaucracy, Simon and March's theory of bounded rationality, Pfeffer and Salancik's theory of external control, and Clegg and Dunkerley's theory of internal control. The result is an impressive, postmodernist machinery that needs a giant such as Perrow to be applied to the study of complex organizations (which may seem simple in comparison).

Organizations under study should be analyzed within the contexts of their networks, the state, and the cultural system. Again, it is hard not to agree wholeheartedly with this postulate; however, what seems to be humanly possible is to trace some of the ties that bind organization to its wider contexts, where it belongs. Analyses of whole contexts, if this is what Perrow meant, are possible only at once- or twice-removed levels of abstraction; thus it is impossible to do such analysis in the same fiat as the organization studies.

Perrow gave the unrestrained functionalism of the Meyer and Rowan (1977/1980) variety a serious battle, which he triumphantly won. But successes tend to carry the seed of failure; my impression is that Perrow's dominant power model is in danger of another functionalistic fallacy. It seems that power must be effective, and that we should know who the "masters" and the "serfs" are. We certainly do when we compare a Rockefeller with an unemployed female, but in between there is a grey and immense "neutral body of men" who sometimes facilitate and sometimes hinder the exercise of power in and through complex organizations. Not all that exists fulfills a predetermined function for good or bad.

Contributions and Conclusions

Perrow's essay reconfirmed the importance of studying complex organizations. Their definition did not change much: Complex organizations are U.S. organizations and bureaucratic in character. It has been proposed here to extend this definition by considering the fact that modern organizations try to combine traditional ways of organizing with those based on rational-legal grounds as an important aspect that contributes considerably to organizational complexity.

From the point of view of the list of phenomena to be studied, a combination of Etzioni's and Perrow's proposals seems to accentuate the significance of compliance. Etzioni listed processes that were important to any organization, but that were born in simple, traditional ones. Perrow presented an overview of processes born and developed together with the modern, bureaucratic organization. In addition, he offered a very interesting historical analysis of this development.

As for the method, Perrow offered us a very complicated systems-theory, with power at its core. The fact, however, that power seemed to be definitely attributed to a specific group (i.e., masters) closed the theory, relatively speaking. This closure led, as in Etzioni's work, to a corresponding typology of organizations.

Still, the task that Perrow (1972/1986) set for himself—"rewriting the history of bureaucracy with an expanded vision of the environment and externalities"—is very promising to the eventual understanding of complex organizations, "because it is through organizations . . . that classes are constituted and reproduced, stratification systems created and stabilized (and changed in some cases), political processes tamed and guided, and culture itself shaped and molded" (p. 278). And, we may add, it is largely through organizations that life in modern societies acquires its meaning, for better or for worse.

Looking for Metaphors of Complex Organizations

The examples of the two classic approaches to complex organizations were meant to illustrate the fact that definitions and methods change with authors and schools. Instead of continuing, with the hope of exhausting the list of possibilities, we will adopt a meta-approach in order to see what builds such a list. Hidden behind definitions, lists of phenomena worth studying, and methods are *metaphors of organizations,* sometimes single, sometimes multiple; sometimes consistent, sometimes mixed. Morgan's (1986) review of major organizational metaphors directs us further toward an anthropology of complex organization. Which metaphor(s) are most promising for understanding this phenomenon? Morgan, for the most part, analyzed the consequences of organization designers' adoption of various metaphors. I shall look at these consequences from a research point of view.

Organizations as machines is a very tempting metaphor for at least two reasons. One is that the creators of bureaucracy—and according to Etzioni and Perrow, complex organizations are bureaucracies—had the model of the machine in mind when building their organizational design. The machine, to them, incorporated most fully the idea of formal rationality. The other reason is that the static character of the metaphor promises a satisfactory way of dealing with complexity—even the most complicated machine avoids the organic anarchy of social systems.

There are two quite serious drawbacks, however. The first is that, as Hofstede (1978) convincingly argues, it is misleading to use analogies to more primitive systems in order to understand more complex ones. Thus organizations as organisms is a more appropriate metaphor than organizations as machines. The second drawback is well known; it is the mechanical character of the perspective. What I want to stress, however, is not the mechanical perspective on organizations but the mechanical perspective on machines. If we had a proper approach to machines, they could, perhaps, serve as a very useful metaphor for organizations. But as we see them now, they are "out there," in some objective reality, immune to our thoughts and determining our relationship to them once they have been created.

If, however, we accept reality as socially constructed, there is no reason to make a sharp distinction between physical and social reality (Joerges, 1988). True, physical reality exists independently of our will, but so does the stock exchange. It is not physicality that we construct socially (even if we confirm it by our actions), but our relationship to physicality. For the time being, therefore, it is probably more appropriate to use organizations as metaphors for machines.

The next possibility is also a classic: organizations as organisms. I discussed the advantages of this possibility while presenting, after Perrow, the institutional school. Its main problem is the danger of sanctifying every status quo on the assumption that it is "functional." A shot of the political metaphor would be appropriate here—functional for whom? Such a political injection would also be helpful in straightening out the evolutionary-ecological view. We should think about Mendel, who meddled with evolution inadvertently via his dedicated helpers, and also about Lysenko, who meddled with it on purpose in order to receive the Medal of the Republic. Humankind has frequently influenced the course of evolution—accidentally, and on purpose.

Despite all these difficulties, organizations as organisms seems to be a very useful metaphor, especially because it stresses the unplanned, uncontrollable character of many organizational processes. And for that very reason, the next metaphor, organizations as brains, can be misleading. It not only gives organizations an independent existence, but also anthropomorphizes them, creating the image of a mastermind. If, in the previous metaphor, people feel helpless vis-à-vis organizations (as when they feel helpless vis-à-vis weeds covering their garden), there is always the possibility of a fight. If, however, organizations are like Dr. Mabuse, our chances are slim.[12]

Formally speaking, the brain should be a good metaphor for organization because it lies precisely beneath the level of the organization in a hierarchy of systems (Hofstede, 1978). Unfortunately, it seems that we know less about brains than about organizations. Explaining *ignotum per ignotum* is not a very promising perspective.

As for organizations as cultures, the metaphor is not powerful enough in the context of the present book, simply because I accept this metaphor as a part of the definition, a label. Organizations, to me, *are* cultural phenomena, not only *like* cultural phenomena. The strength of the metaphor lies in its power to bridge two different worlds, two different domains. Therefore, if I say that strategy making is like a rain dance, I speak metaphorically (I am comparing two different cultures); but I speak literally when I repeat, after Gareth

Morgan, that "[w]hether in Japan, Germany, Hong Kong, Britain, Russia, the United States, or Canada, large organizations are likely to influence most of our waking hours in a way that is completely alien to life in a remote tribe in the jungles of South America" (1986, p. 112). This defective distinction between labels and metaphors (Czarniawska-Joerges & Joerges, 1988) has led to many misunderstandings in the application of anthropological concepts to organizational studies, as we shall see later.

Organizations as political systems is another literal metaphor. Organizations *are* political systems, whereas they are only *like* organisms. If we trust Perrow's first definition—organizations as tools for shaping the world—then, considering the existing number of world visions, political processes are inevitable. The metaphor emphasizes the multiplicity of rationalities (tools) and functions (organic parts) in each and every organization. An organization is a political system in that it constantly negotiates pluralistic meanings and forms coalitions.

Morgan warned us that the permeation of this metaphor might lead to a somewhat paranoiac picture of organization. I would say that it depends more on the ideal of social relationships (harmony versus conflict)[13] than the vision of organization. Within the harmony perspective, all conflicts are terrifying; within the conflict perspective, only those that are detrimental to the parties involved are frightening. The latter perspective leads to a use of the political metaphor in a descriptive rather than normative way. Interests do not have to be conflicting; conflicting interests can be negotiated, and those that cannot be negotiated can be openly stated and become an object of bargaining or even fighting. Manipulation is not the only way of promoting one's interest; people are altruistic even in political systems.

The truly terrifying metaphor is organizations as psychic prisons. The image is very powerful, and the metaphor very apt, especially in grasping people's feelings in situations of helplessness and undesired ambiguity—dark walls of a prison that I built for myself with the help of my mates. But if we take the metaphor more psychoanalytically and assume that it is our subconsciousness that is the mason, we would have to conclude that the solution lies in individual therapy. But is this really so? We are certainly unaware of many of the things we do, but that is due more to lack of reflection than subconscious strains. Besides, organizational action is much more often *a*-rational (that is, undertaken without consideration of rationality criteria) than irrational. Consequently, organizations as psychic prisons seems to be a more useful metaphor if applied to social and not individual processes.

Organizations as flux and transformation is a very tempting metaphor if organizations are seen as processes of organizing, following the idea of Karl E. Weick (1969), or structures of events (Allport, 1962). This metaphor helps to fight back reification and to understand change as a continuous process, rather than as sudden efforts of planned reorganization. It permits the possibility of taking static pictures at any given moment, like the photographing of a flood. In addition, and paradoxically enough, the metaphor helps us to put "organizational change" among everyday phenomena, therefore depriving it of its implicit positive undertone. Things are continually moving and transforming, but this does not automatically mean progress. *Plus ça change, plus c'est la meme chose.* By saying this, however, I depart seriously from the intentions of Morgan, who saw the metaphor as much more value laden than I do.

Finally, there is the metaphor organizations as instruments of domination. Its main strength, as I see it, has to do with the undisputed fact that there is much oppression in organizations and that it reaches much higher hierarchical levels than we tend to believe. Morgan emphasized that the domination metaphor "shows us a way of creating an organizational theory *for* the exploited" (1986, p. 316). Its main weakness lies, to me, in its black-and-white typification of villains and victims. We know who dominates and who is oppressed. Consequently, it is unthinkable that union executives would exploit union members or that managing directors might be victims. This oversimplification is understandable because domination tends to dress its ugly head in the rosy wreath of public good: caring for community interests or investing in human resources. But these stereotypes dampen the metaphor's analytical power.

Complex organizations, therefore, are cultural phenomena that are political in character. They can be seen as tools, rationally designed to shape the world, or as webs of "organically" growing interconnections. These webs can prove to be suffocating—be it by chance or due to the fact that somebody is pulling the strings. Nevertheless, the strings are in continuous movement.

Complex Organizations as Socially Constructed

We also come upon many useful metaphors as we go further and visit anthropology. But before we depart, I should try to summarize what we have learned in order to better describe the goal of our journey.

On Organizations in General

Who has not tried his hand at framing a one-sentence (or even one-paragraph) definition of organization has denied himself an educational experience of high value. (Waldo, 1961, p. 218)

Thus fortified, I can start on an enterprise that does not make me enthusiastic. I would not risk approaching such a general definition if common sense did not make such a task necessary. In order to show that anthropology is a good way to study complex organizations, I must first reveal what I want to study. Let me try:

Organizations are nets of collective action, undertaken in an effort to shape the world and human lives. The contents of the action are meanings and things (artifacts). One net of collective action is distinguishable from another by the kind of meanings and products socially attributed to a given organization.

Such a distinction is, however, situational, temporary, and fragile. First, these nets do not have definite boundaries; they are constantly being made. To wit, the actions undertaken by the General Director of the Swedish National Board of Education and his department heads do not belong to the same net of collective action as the actions undertaken by the General Director of the Health and Welfare Board and her staff. But what happens when both general directors sit on the same governmental committee? Second, any attempt to ascribe a stable set of attributes to a given net is bound to fail. It is easy to characterize the rules of conduct for the National Bar Association as an organization, but it is not easy to distinguish between the National Bar Association and the legal profession as such. "Organizations" and "environments" merge into one another, and our attempts at delineation are mostly of situational use; both rules of conduct and principles of organizing differentiate and unify various nets of action. Third, meanings are not sharply distinct from artifacts and vice versa. Meanings can be reified and become artifacts, whereas artifacts may be or may become pure symbols.

It is often assumed that collective action requires shared meaning. This is true to a certain extent (to carry a table together we must agree about what is up and what is down, what is forward and what is back). The plural form in the definition, however, suggests that a collective action is possible in the face of many meanings that are only partly shared. It is the experience of a collective action that is shared, more than its meaning. My two colleagues went to hear a speech given by a well-known businessman. One "participated in a most exciting encounter between the wisdom of practice and curiosity of theory," whereas the other "took part in an extremely boring meeting with an elderly gentleman who told old jokes." They are each, nevertheless, members of the same organization, and what was common for them was that they went to the same room at the same hour, sharing only the idea that their bosses expected it.[14]

Organizations, and their environments (Smircich & Stubbart, 1985), therefore, are enacted daily and socially constructed, due to the fact that any collective action requires a shared element of meaning. Meanings are thus created (both in social interactions as well as in interactions with artifacts and nature), deconstructed, negotiated, and elaborated. Reality, as we experience it daily, is socially constructed. Every building is socially constructed. It consists of bricks, mortar, human labor, building regulations, architectural design, aesthetic expression, and so on; each of them, in turn, socially constructed and put together by a socially constructed concept of a building.

This means that reality exists independently of human perception, but it is not "out there," behind a wall of human distortion that must be overcome, but rather "in here," where human perception is a part of it, a maker of it, and the only tool for its cognition. These limits of our cognition may be lamentable, but only from a transcendental point of view; otherwise, because human perception is the basis for human praxis, it is sufficient in terms of this praxis, and as perception continues to evolve, technologically and maybe psychologically, helping praxis to evolve.

This means that while rain would still fall down on the earth if there were no humans to watch it, it would then be irrelevant for the human species because it could not be socially (re)constructed. The reverse is also true. Shutting one's eyes and living entirely on illusions and wishful thinking do not stop people from being killed daily as the villains and heroes continue their contribution to social construction. Solipsism is no more promising a route for social science to follow than is positive realism.

Therefore, reality is a quality appertaining to phenomena that "we recognize as having a being, independent of our own volition (we cannot 'wish them away')" (Berger & Luckmann, 1966/1971, p. 13). Hence, social construction does not mean a solipsistic imagery.

Organizations, therefore, are socially constructed—and reconstructed—in everyday actions. Organizations can be also deconstructed by action, but it would again be a case of social deconstruction. This does not mean that organizations exist only in our imagination. But, if nobody came to work anymore, a factory would become "that old factory building." Do organizations cease to exist on Sundays? No, because their rules of construction currently entail not coming to work on Sundays. Thus they are not enacted on Sundays but exist, nevertheless, as a memory of Friday and in anticipation of Monday. What about things, then? What do things do on Sundays? They (most likely) exist even if we do not enact them. On Monday, however, they help us to reconstruct our system of collective action, reminding us of its rules. They survive the period of nonenactment (that is, when we do not focus our attention on them) and can therefore be used as a kind of organizational memory.

Does enactment mean that all action, even physical, is only an "as if" action? No, a stone exists independently of our cognition; but we enact it by a *cognitive bracketing,* by concentrating our attention on it. Thus "called to life," or to attention, the stone must be socially constructed with the help of the concept of stone, its properties, and uses. We can base a physical action that might annihilate the stone on this social construction. (Reconstruction is simplified in the sense that it assumes a linear development of events; actually, we cannot enact something that has not been previously socially constructed.)

To summarize briefly my ontology and epistemology: Reality, also social reality, exists independently of human cognition; yet, it is cognizable and accessible only and ultimately through human cognition. This means, on the one hand, that we *really* can change the physical and social world; but, on the other, the concepts of "truth" and "objectivity" are irrelevant unless they are qualified as relative to experience and intersubjectivity.

Discussing organizations as socially constructed inevitably brings social construction's most prominent propagators, Peter L. Berger and Thomas Luckmann (1966/1971), into focus. Therefore, it is necessary to relate—and distinguish between—the proposed *anthropology of complex organizations* and their *sociology of knowledge*. Similarities are quite obvious; differences call for more elaboration. An anthropology of complex organizations is, on the one hand, much narrower in scope than a sociology of knowledge. A sociology of knowledge encompasses the whole of everyday life and reality; anthropology encompasses only its organizational part. Berger and Luckmann, on the other hand, sketch something that might be more correctly called a social psychology of knowledge, concentrating on personal, phenomenological knowledge of reality, whereas I propose to move on to a level of intersubjectively experienced reality, objectified in the process of construction. To put it differently, Berger and Luckmann propose to have a look at reality in order to understand the process of construction; in contrast, I propose to have a look at construction in order to better understand the reality. The difference will become even clearer when ethnomethodological approaches are discussed. There is, of course, no contradiction between the two, only a difference in emphasis due to the difference in goals. Consequently, in their book, Berger and Luckmann deal with a generalized everyday life ("an exemplary male living in a big city"), whereas my research tackles specific organizational life ("director X in organization Y").

On Complexity

Conventionally, size is related to complexity, thus my initial commonsense assumption that large organizations are complex and vice versa. But the wisdom of using size as a differentiating criterion has often been challenged—size of what? When does an organization stop being small and become large? Does size really equal complexity? These issues have been addressed before, sometimes jokingly, sometimes solemnly. David Brown, in his book *Managing the Large Organization*, said the following:

> Size . . . is a relative thing and the elephant is small when compared to the whale. Organizations are certainly large when procedures need to be committed to writing and regularly updated; when systems of selection and promotion are standardized; when relationships between those at higher managerial levels and those at operational ones have become depersonalized; and when communications must be conducted through channels. Beyond this, I am satisfied to leave the definition of largeness to the reader. Size is primarily a matter of point of view, and one probably does not need to be more specific than that. (1982, p. 5)

Eric J. Miller (1959) rejected size as a direct indicator of complexity and concentrated on differentiation in terms of technology, territory, and time. Although convincing enough, it, as usual, provokes the question, Who is going to establish the scale for this 3T differentiation? In social constructivist terms, one can say that an organization becomes complex *when no one can sensibly and comprehensibly account for all of it.*[15] But, as already mentioned, an historical interpretation would point to the fact that constructors of contemporary organizations do not hesitate to intentionally blend and combine different organizing principles, of which "rationality" and "tradition" are good examples, if not the best.[16]

This is a concept that has a hard core and extremely fuzzy edges. But to defend it, I might quote another interesting utterance:

> It is easier, and probably more useful, to give examples of formal organizations than to define the term. . . . But for present purposes we need not trouble ourselves about the precise boundaries to be drawn around an organization. . . . We are dealing with empirical phenomena, and the world has an uncomfortable way of not permitting itself to be fitted into neat classifications. (March & Simon, 1958, p. 1)

In other words, the booming, buzzing world does not lend itself to neat, sharp-edged definitions; also, in the absence of explicit definitions, some implicit ones can usually be located. The way out, then, is fuzzy-edged concepts!

Concepts that have a clear core and fuzzy edges have the advantage of not rejecting doubtful cases because of a need for purity and elegance. The clarity of the core is, however, best achieved empirically, as March and Simon noted. Large and 3*T*-differentiated organizations are always confusing for the actors and spectators alike, so it might be safe to start with them.

The nonaccountability or impossibility of comprehension stems from the fact that complex organizations embody many meanings that are not commonly shared (not because, as is the case with private opinions, they are essentially nonorganizational). To use Berger and Luckmann's expression again, they contain "subuniverses of meaning," and this pluralism is not something to be fought against, but taken for granted: "In advanced industrial societies . . . pluralistic competition between subuniverses of meaning of every conceivable sort becomes the normal state of affairs" (1966/1971, p. 103). To a lesser degree, the same phenomenon characterizes complex organizations. The reality of jet conferences at the board of director level cannot be translated to the reality of shop-floor workers, and yet both recognize each other as belonging to the same set of collective action, the corporation.

At this point, it is perhaps necessary to say that both the definition of complex organizations and the direction of research that follows this definition is based on an actor perspective. It is organizational actors who create organizations, and therefore they are the main resource for understanding what organizations truly are and what they are like. The main question that should be put to the organizational actor is, How are meanings and artifacts produced and reproduced in complex nets of collective action?

Notes

1. This is emphasized in order to contrast it with my later assumptions, that organizing is a process that both results from and produces a sociocultural context.

2. Within the inductive, theory-generating, interpretive approach that I myself use, the first step would be to locate the phenomena of interest, and then look for appropriate methods, with only a vague idea of eventual results.

3. This ambition is also present in this text.

4. In doing this, Etzioni was very close to the strategy for theory generation recommended by Glaser and Strauss (1974). The main difference is that Etzioni started with compliance, an a priori construct, to guide his search, and he used other research not as a source of insights (a text to be interpreted), but as building blocks for his emerging theory. The main similarity is that the concepts were accepted or rejected on the basis of their utility in an emerging analytical scheme. This analogy is drawn to attract attention to similarities between apparently disparate methodologies; an exaggerated tendency to classify methodologies into opposing "camps" does not serve well, in my opinion, to promote methodological development.

5. If, however, we adopt an interpretive stance, congruence is a matter of logical consistency of definition, and functionality becomes an attribute of classification (which makes sense in certain combinations but not in others) rather than organizational action.

6. More on "taxonomic groupings" in Chapter 8.

7. Henry Mintzberg (1987) presented a beautiful analogy between strategy making and pottery making. In both, the product is uncertain until it is finished; the action can be labeled only when it becomes a thing.

8. In fact, all definitions determine both focus and scope of further studies—although the explicitness may differ.

9. All theories "contaminate" their method, so to speak. Therefore, theories and methods that are particularly attractive are those that allow for analysis of themselves, in other words, self-reflection.

10. On historical contingency in evolution, see Gould (1990).

11. Perrow ended his review with economic theories of organization, but since his book's publication, the proponents of the economic approach have launched their own attack, which is best presented in Jay B. Barney and William G. Ouchi's *Organizational Economics* (1986).

12. Dr. Mabuse was the master criminal hero-villain of two films by Fritz Lang (1923, 1932). Stanley Kubrick's *Dr. Strangelove* (1963) stars Peter Sellers as his comic version. James Bond films usually host such a character.

13. I use the term *harmony* rather than the term *consensus*, which is often employed, because consensus can be seen as a result of conflict resolution rather than a natural state of affairs. Accordingly, consensus can be said to characterize organizations that continue their activities in spite of being conflict-ridden. The harmony perspective assumes that harmony is a natural state and conflicts are deviations from it.

14. For a similar view on shared meanings, see Weick (1969) and Donnellon, Gray, and Bougan (1986). Berger (1989) discusses a set of notions borrowed from a hermeneutist philosopher, Charles Taylor, that might be of relevance here. Inter-subjective meanings, which constitute shared practices, are "self-definitions of social agents, implicit in the underlying language, which involve visions of self and relation to others and society" (p. 211). These interrelate in order to create networks whose most stable parts become common meanings, that is, common reference points in a given thought world.

15. The organizational lore confirms that my concerns are well timed. One of the most recent office epigrams states, "Anybody who isn't confused here does not understand what is going on."

16. There is no reason to doubt that all these organizing principles were mixed at all times. My intention here is to emphasize the normative and not the descriptive aspects of large organizations at different points in time. From this point of view, Taylorism can be seen as an attempt to purify organizations from the sediments of tradition. Contemporary large organizations implement rationalistic reforms, while enforcing intricate ceremonies and sending their executives to transcendental meditation courses.

3

Anthropology:
The Original Sin and the New Sin

Why Anthropology?

If the meaning of words were to be found in their etymology then anthropology should be "the study of man," a monstrous universal form of inquiry which all the books in the world could not suffice to cover, so it is not surprising that most laymen find it difficult to understand just what it is that anthropologists do or why. (Leach, 1982, p. 13)

Edmund Leach, whom I have chosen as one of my guides to the field, begins his book on social anthropology with these words. However, first I would like to say a little about why guides are needed at all, and on what basis they were chosen among many anthropologists.

An excursion into another discipline, no matter how close to one's own, generates numerous occasions for confusion as different schools of thought and approaches are paraded in front of the newcomer's eyes. It takes a while to understand that "structuralism" is apparently the opposite of "structural functionalism," because the first focuses on structures of ideas, and the second on societal structures. Similarly, it is revealed that "rationalism" stands in opposition to "empiricism," in that it postulates a poetic mode of thought instead of linear logic. "Poststructuralism" turns out to be much closer to "structuralism" than the name might suggest—or at least closer to structuralism than to any other school of thought. After a while, one begins to understand that not only are the divisions arbitrary, but also that the corresponding classification of authors and works is even more so.[1] In fact, as Leach (1976) himself points out, all those approaches are complementary, and allegiances are constantly shifting. To be able to make sense of this self-rearranging landscape, then, it is best to employ a guide, but with a full awareness of the relativity of standpoints and interpretations.

Leach attracted me because of his readiness to use accessible approaches rather than to subscribe to them. This is, I think, due to the fact that he is an ironist,[2] that is, an author who realizes that no formulation—neither his own, nor that of others— is ever final or should claim to be so. Ironists make better guides than the reverent, because they understand the importance of perspective. Because they are self-ironical as well, they do not demand as much reverence for themselves, and therefore make it easier to attempt unwarranted extensions of their thought, partial acceptance of their opinions, and free interpretations of their definitions, as in what follows.

Social anthropology is, according to Leach, *a study of the unity of humankind through a study of its diversity.* This statement sounds pretty obvious; yet it can be interpreted in at least two contradictory ways. According to one interpretation, which is perhaps more traditional, the unity of humankind is something that *exists* and should be found. Its proper name may vary—from human nature to the structure of the human mind. Nevertheless, it exists, and the task of an anthropologist is to prove it—through and despite the diversity of humankind.

Another interpretation would see it the other way around: The unity of humankind is something to be *created,* and one of the ways it is created is through the study of its diversity. Within this perspective, Rorty (1989) says,

[N]ovels and ethnographies which sensitize one to the pain of those who do not speak our language must do the job which demonstrations of a common human nature were supposed to do. Solidarity has to be constructed out of little pieces, rather than found already waiting, in the form of an ur-language which all of us recognize when we hear it. (p. 94)

The common language spoken in the Tower of Babel was a myth, but, like all myths, it reflected a human dream that can be realized in its contemporary version by creating a common language. Ethnographic descriptions help this endeavor by producing translations. They retell, in our language, stories that were told by people speaking in other languages.

But what kind of a study could hope to achieve such a result? According to Leach, social anthropology is a study that should be *historical but not historicist*. Historical determinism should be avoided and, I wish to add, preferably any other variation of positively laden evolutionary metaphors. The existing forms of social life are not, by virtue of their existence, a proof of their superiority over forms that are extinct, nor are they proofs of their own functionality. Leach proposes to part with functionalism (of which Malinowski [1926] was perhaps the most interesting exponent), "even if this might sometimes mean giving a very peculiar tribute to the notion of utility" (Leach, 1982, p. 29).[3]

Not historicist, but historical: This means that anthropological studies must be firmly anchored in time and space, providing a proper context for analysis; and also indicates the lines along which comparative studies can be conducted. Leach is very much against reifying cultures into separate entities that can then be independently compared (the same applies to elements of a culture).[4] By a society, he says, we conventionally mean a political unit of some kind that is defined territorially, even if boundaries tend to be rather imprecise. But there are operational agreements as to what makes these boundaries "objective." By the same token, the members of a society are individuals who at any given time can be found within these boundaries and are supposed to share common interests, primarily related to their common territory. Therefore, continues Leach, who wants to be seen as a purist? We can speak about the society of China and the society of Tikopia (the latter being 1,300 people living on a microscopic island), as long as we do not include them as units of the same comparative analysis.

It becomes even worse when dealing with cultures. More or less explicitly, it is assumed that the boundaries of cultures are subjective equivalents to the boundaries of societies. The result is that an anthropologist studying four North American tribes is apparently discussing the same topic as an analyst of "American culture," that all Balinese supposedly share the same beliefs (Leach commented dryly that Geertz's assertion to that effect was "categorical but quite unverifiable" [1982, p. 43]), and that, generally, societies are culturally homogenous. Therefore, cultures could be compared as such, and indeed, this "culture-as-one-thing" assumption is very strong and has made its way into organizational studies, as we shall see later on.

Regarding method, anthropology is a form of *art,* or a "science" unlike natural sciences. It should be empirical, but not empiricist (behaviorism is rejected). Fieldwork should be the main source of information, but observers are and must be "part of the system" (Leach, 1985), not simply outsiders watching a rat race and counting the numbers of revolutions of the wheel in order to feed data into a computer and wonder about its significance.

> Social anthropologists should not see themselves as seekers after objective truth; their purpose is to gain insight into other people's behaviour or, for that matter, into their own. (Leach, 1982, p. 52)

And further:

> Social anthropologists are bad novelists rather than bad scientists. But I hold that the insights of the social anthropologist have a special quality because of the arena in which he characteristically exercises his artistic imagination. That arena is the living space of some quite small community of people who live together in circumstances where most of their day-to-day communications depend upon face-to-face interaction. This does not embrace the whole of human social life, still less does it embrace the whole of human history. But all human beings spend a great deal of their lives in contexts of this kind. (pp. 53-54)

The spirit is all here, if not the letter. More and more human beings spend a great deal of their lives in not-so-small communities where communication, central as it is, takes place through other interfaces than face-to-face interaction. McLuhan's global electronic village might be a useful, if limited, metaphor here. Organizational communication, either face-to-face or electronic, is the binder of those particular "communities," and this is where I propose that organizational anthropologists exercise their artistic imagination, rather than in small, exotic communities.

If Leach intended to stay faithful to the traditional domain of anthropology, his approach was, nevertheless, most accommodating to what could be called an empirical, social constructivist version of anthropology. He proposed to understand the whole of what he called "a way of life" of a people under study, who were seen as acting out a repeated social drama. People act in this drama and reflect on their actions. Therefore, we study both social (or individual) action and the account of it (in the form of plans, ideologies, rationalizations, or symbolic representations). Actions and accounts tie together the practical and the expressive, or, as Leach put it, the physical and the metaphysical. The strength of anthropology, as professed by Leach, lies in the fact that it has not become greatly influenced by natural sciences (due perhaps to its early separation from physical anthropology) and yet has never lost touch with material reality (with the exception of some exceedingly idealistic and/or symbolic variations). As a result, I believe it is best suited for grasping the essence of organizational action—the inherent dialectics of matter and ideas.

Apart from specific traits that make different variations of anthropological research attractive to different organization researchers, there are two traits that are common to all anthropological pursuits: *the holistic approach* to the subject matter and *the direct, intensive, and prolonged contact* with the reality studied (Janowitz, 1963). The two are obviously related—an intensive and extensive observation is needed if a holistic vision is to be achieved. One should add, perhaps, that these two traits are norms or ideals to be striven for; and of the two, the first is especially difficult to realize.

In practice the monographs which anthropologists write seldom preserve this kind of balance. According to the predilections of the author we find that special stress is laid *either* on the structure of ideas *or* on the structure of society, *or* on the mode of gaining a livelihood, and the principle that we are all the time dealing with "a single interacting whole" is easily forgotten.

It is also easy to forget that contrasted predilections of individual authors are themselves part of a single interacting whole. (Leach, 1976, p. 3)

This "forgetfulness" is helped by the fact that the "natives" are unwilling to supply the researcher with a coherent vision of an integrated whole (Tyler, 1986). As I shall be repeatedly trying to make a case for the holistic approach, it is important to stress that the "picture of a whole" is both an important contribution and an obvious invention of the researcher. We glue together a picture of "a single interacting whole" in a belief that its vision will help actors and spectators alike to understand the complexity of collective action. But in doing so, we do not re-present something that is "out there" waiting to be photographed; we create a work of art, understood as the accomplished making of useful artifacts (Clifford, 1986, p. 6). Leach's criticism, then, can be eased by admitting that all ethnographies are partial, and all representations fragmentary, while still held important as a warning against reductionism. A whole is a patchwork, but a patchwork is better than one deceivingly coherent fragment.

But it was not the fact that anthropology was somewhat short on its own ideals that prevented organizational studies from putting it to greater use. What, then, is the worm in the apple?

The Original Sin: Ethnocentrism

The answer to this question lies in the history of the discipline. In order to make my way through it, I will turn to another guide who will join Leach from across the ocean, the U.S. anthropologist Rosalie Wax. The reason is that history is strongly influenced by the historian's position vis-à-vis the Atlantic. A blunt outsider could actually say that anthropology came to the United States from Great Britain—and remained there—but there are also suggestions to the reverse (see Sanday, 1979). But let us go to the beginning. As Leach (1982) presented it:

> Taken all together this band of amateurs who formed themselves into the
> first societies of Anthropology and Ethnology were a quarrelsome crew
> and, as individuals, they were clearly heading in several different direc-
> tions but, in one respect at least, they shared common ground. They were
> all concerned . . . with man in the wild, natural man, primitive man, the
> benighted savage. In practice this bias has remained the delimiting hall-
> mark of academic anthropology. Anthropology has turned out to be not
> the study of man but the study of primitive man. (p. 16)

The consequence of this, although somewhat convoluted, was the
differentiation between "primitive mind"—childlike, irrational, with
kinship structure as the main type of social organization—and "civilized mind"—adult, rational, with bureaucracy as the main type of social organization. Of course this "crude oversimplification," as Leach
called it, was seen through and criticized very early on. Nevertheless,
it continued to influence anthropological thought. The spirit of colo-
nialism, for better and for worse, permeated the beginnings of the discipline. On the one hand, Rosalie Wax (1974) pointed out that
especially in the 19th century, many of the early anthropologists had
been motivated by high goals of improving human institutions and
human society. They helped and contacted the missionaries and administrators who carried on their work in areas inhabited by tribal or
unsophisticated peoples. On the other hand, this positive and humanistic attitude was always marked by paternalism and distance from the
"primitive mind," as witnessed in the attitudes of two dedicated and
enlightened anthropologists, Boas and Malinowski. Regarding Boas,
Wax (1974) wrote:

> An occasional remark suggests that he found conversation with Indians a
> waste of time—except insofar as it related to the collection of textual
> materials—and one sometimes wonders why a man who was so inter-
> ested in gathering data so that future generations might understand the
> old cultures "from within" had so little interest in understanding the peo-
> ple who were serving as his informants. (p. 33)

And, of course, there is the story about William James asking Frazer
about natives he knew and Frazer answering, "God forbid!"

Malinowski, on the other hand, lived, ate, talked, and slept with the
natives and, judging from various indications, hated every moment of it:

> In terms of health, temperament, and intellectual background, Malinow-
> ski seems to have been particularly unsuited to undertake the kind of ex-
> peditions he lived through and recommended so highly to others. . . .
> That he managed to endure what he did is a marvel. (Wax, 1974, p. 32)

Indeed, considering his intellectual start in Cracow's bohemia at the
fin de siècle (Malinowski was a close friend of Witkacy, the Polish
painter and playwright and one of the gurus of the epoch), the contrast must have been startling.

Wax also commented on the fact that Malinowski's "radically new
procedure" would not have seemed radical or new to Marco Polo.
Marco Polo, from what we know of him, went to see the world in the
belief that there were worlds more civilized than his own. Such a
thought has rarely, if ever, been nurtured by contemporary anthropologists. For them, outside the Western world lived the primitive man
with a primitive mind, ultimately renamed "exotic." Leach regrets
this deplorable state of affairs, calling it a "hangover from history"
(1982, p. 55), and explains that when anthropologists say "primitive,"
they mean "not-us, other people." But, at the risk of being old-fashioned
(Leach, 1985), Leach is against anthropologists studying their own
cultures:

> [F]ieldwork in a cultural context of which you already have intimate
> first-hand experience seems to be much more difficult than fieldwork
> which is approached from the naive viewpoint of a total stranger. When
> anthropologists study facets of their own society their vision seems to
> become distorted by prejudices which derive from private rather than
> public experience. (1982, p. 124)

However, even "total strangers" carry within themselves a complete
inscription of their own acculturation processes. In light of this, the
last part of the above statement is especially puzzling; if anything, it
is the experience of our own culture that is processed as a public experience (via schooling, mass media, and so on), whereas encounters
with alien cultures tend to be analyzed in individual, experiential
terms. Innocence of one's own cultural bias seems to be the basis of
what I call "original sin": imposing one's own culture on exotic ones.

Also, for most organization researchers, complex organizations (other than their own) are almost as exotic as Triobranders's community. Peggy Reeves Sanday sends her students to restaurants or fire stations, and says: "My experience with these students has been that it is possible to train those who are highly motivated to see the world from another's point of view without sending them to exotic foreign lands" (1979, p. 528). Nigel Barley exercised his vocation of a "professional alien" on his native land (1989), commenting that "the problem of native informants and native ethnographers is that a world view is invisible when you are in it" (p. 48). But it is just that willingness to suspend it, or to bracket it, that marks the passage from an informer to an ethnographer. In addition, the blindness of a native ethnographer must be weighted against an outsider's clumsy ignorance, which is removed only after a complete acculturation—if this is at all possible.

> Much nonsense has been written, by people who should know better, about the anthropologist "being accepted." It is sometimes suggested that an alien people will somehow come to view the visitor of distinct race and culture as in every way similar to the locals. This is, alas, unlikely. The best one can probably hope for is to be viewed as a harmless idiot who brings certain advantages to this village. (N. Barley, 1983, p. 56)

When it is not a village but a corporation, the natives sometimes share an illusion of a common culture for a brief moment ("You, coming from a business school, would surely see that . . ."). But even Nigel Barley's Dowayos thought that he was a reincarnated spirit of a sorcerer, who took off his white skin when he went to sleep. These tender illusions do not remove the basic sense of alienation that is obvious in a prolonged contact. With luck, one can be seen as "this uninformed but well-willing researcher," a euphemism for "harmless idiot." (Barley presents the reader with a very frank and self-ironic account of his exotic experiences in two other books, 1986 and 1988.)

A naive ethnocentrism on the part of anthropologists is a thing of the past. As Leach put it, "[t]he contemporary social anthropologist is all too aware that he knows much less than Frazer imagined that he knew for certain" (1961, p. v). Geertz says that contemporary anthropologists are virtually paralyzed by the awareness of all the traps involved in the unreflective practice of the profession (1988). All this, however, does not prove that one has to stay in exotic countries; rather, it indicates that one should go there inoculated against original sin. Excursions to other cultures should be extremely instructive for organization students in the sense that they challenge the taken-for-grantedness of one's own culture. For example, to understand the social and symbolic character of accounting, it should be studied in socialist economies, where political authorities change the rules and values of the audit daily. Such experiences, however, should only enhance the character of the anthropological method that, albeit often unconscious, lies at its core: The realities to be studied are never taken for granted. If one wanted to generalize, one might say that a *problematizing* attitude should typify all research. For whatever reason, this is not the common case in other social science disciplines, and it has to be purposefully reintroduced (see Chapter 5 on ethnomethodology).

It was not "original sin" or any other sin that caused the split between disciplines. The division of labor was decided a long time ago. "Anthropologists" went to study other peoples, "sociologists" stayed at home. Or, as Tilly puts it, somewhat maliciously: "Sociology investigated the internal structure of rich, powerful societies. Anthropology, for its part, received a double duty: to account for large variations among societies and to analyze the internal structures of societies outside the charmed circle of power and wealth" (1984, p. 21). At any rate, sociologists stayed at home and revolutionized their own field.

> The disciples of the new survey sample research, with their emphasis upon statistical techniques, formal experimental designs and mechanical data processing, argued that theirs was the scientific sociology. (Wax, 1974, p. 40)

When organization research came visibly to the surface (1930s-1950s), those were their first models, and everyone else's. Ruth Benedict, in her address as the retiring president of the American Anthropological Association in 1947, made a plea for turning to the humanities for inspiration, a plea that she herself called "heretical" (Benedict, 1948). Contrary to her beliefs in the impending and inevitable reunion of influences from the natural sciences and the humanities with anthropology, the scientistic tradition in anthropology was only beginning, and it survived very well until today (see Melischek, Rosengren, & Stappers's *Cultural Indicators, 1984*).

In Great Britain in the 1940s, structural functionalism a la Radcliffe-Brown dominated, and this group proclaimed their lack of interest in economics and in economic organizations. They buried themselves in a great theoretical endeavor: an ideal typology of societies based on the role of formal and informal rules relating to social identity and marriage in generating a sense of political solidarity.

A group of Chicagoans (Howard S. Becker, Anselm Strauss, and Erving Goffman) who thought differently from both the above-mentioned groups went underground and practiced their fieldwork methods until they became useful again. They carried the ethnographic tradition through almost 50 years, until it came into fashion again. I am not going to analyze the reasons for this because it is outside the scope of my discussion here. But, the fact is that not only were fieldwork and qualitative analysis exhumed with loud fanfare, but also anthropologists had been called home.

The New Sin: Exoticism

Anthropologists did not come home empty-handed. They knew what primitive societies were like—homogenous, segmented, and mythopoetic (as opposed to legal-rationalist). However, says Leach, this is hardly true of most "primitive" societies, not to mention any others. And yet many social anthropologists, and their disciples in other fields, proceeded as if it were true of all their subjects (see "Organizational Culture," Chapter 7). Another way of holding these axioms true was to avoid complex organizations and study simple (primitive) organizations, or only parts of complex ones. This is very clear in the ethnomethodological tradition which, because of its microscopic orientation, cannot really afford to consider any larger units (see Chapter 5).

Anthropologists brought back home not only a definition of their objects, but also a research agenda. The "classical" topics were moral economy, kinship, politics, law, religion, magic, myth, and ritual (see Eric R. Wolf's "Kinship, Friendship and Patron-Client Relations in Complex Societies," 1966). Leach says that these "classical" topic lists are misleading for two reasons. First, they sound as if they were technical (objective) terms, whereas there is no consensus as to their meaning and usage. Second, they suggest a corresponding differentiation of reality, which simply cannot be found. They become alienated from their original field studies, then reified and brought back into a wrong context, and this is what I call "the new sin." If economics, politics, law, and religion have a concrete and objective (commonly accepted) meaning in our culture, this is not the case with kinship, magic, myth, and ritual. Yet they are used in relation to all cultural contexts as concepts of equal status. As a result, the concept of "religion" is freely used in societies that do not have a religion, only a cosmology; whereas "kinship," which may be central to anthropology, is surely not central to modern societies.

An interesting example[5] of such a "double ethnocentrism" can be found in a neighboring area, that of structural functionalist anthropology. When Margaret Mead went to Arapesh, she took with her, according to her own admission, Freud's and Erikson's "psychoanalytic schemata" (Mead, 1949). As Betty Friedan noted, "Instead of translating, sifting, the cultural bias *out* of Freudian theories, Margaret Mead, and the others who pioneered in the fields of culture and personality, compounded the error by fitting their own anthropological observations into Freudian rubrics" (Friedan, 1963, p. 117). Moreover, Margaret Mead had come back, said Friedan, with an imported good—a feminine mystique straight from Arapesh and Samoa—to haunt American women ever since. The reasoning, crudely represented, went somewhat along these lines: According to Freudian criteria, Arapesh and Samoan women are liberated from fears and happy. Ergo, their life should become a model for American women if they are to avoid frustration. The Viennese ladies should feel avenged.

No matter how heavy its sins were in the past, contemporary anthropology has much more to offer than just a collection of exotic pictures. Especially in its interpretive version, it promotes valuable insights and models of analysis.

The Interpretation of Cultures

Clifford Geertz calls himself a cultural anthropologist, which necessitates yet another excursion into anthropological kinship under the guidance of Edmund Leach. Roughly speaking, one can speak of *social anthropology,* akin to Durkheim and Weber, which produced mostly functionalists and, in terms of methodology, empiricists (only observable facts count). Its contrast is *cultural anthropology,* whose forebears were ethnographer-travelers, which aims at a conjectured history of humankind. Its most typical methodology is rational idealism, a linguistic philosophy in search of the "universal human mind." Malinowski can be seen as the typical representative of the first tradition, Lévi-Strauss of the latter. Leach affiliates himself with social anthropology, but rejects its value-laden functionalism together with the conjectural historicism of cultural anthropology, yet espouses the search for ideas from the latter. It is not easy to be an anthropologist.

What Is Culture?

Geertz's affiliation gave to him, in the first place, a duty to define *culture,* his legitimate object of study. (Leach, who studied *ways of life,* had no such obligation; indeed, he mockingly warned all his readers about "an anthropologist who writes about cultures in the plural" [1982, p. 43] and less mockingly protested against reification of the notion.) Geertz (1973) avoided the problem by adopting a soft definition:

> Believing, with Max Weber, that man is an animal suspended in webs of significance he himself has spun, I take culture to be those webs, and the analysis of it to be therefore not an experimental science in search of law but an interpretive one in search of meaning. (p. 5)

This is a striking metaphor and a definition that is easy to accept (perhaps with a gloss saying that woman is an animal suspended in webs of significance she herself has *not* spun). And it is a research aim that I am ready to embrace.

The method for reaching this aim is ethnography, an ethnography based on thick description.[6] What in a final form will appear as a "thin description"—let us say, a presentation of an event, a fact—is at the "data" level "our own construction of other people's constructions of what they and their compatriots are up to" (Geertz, 1973, p. 9). Culture is a text (or "acted document") difficult to decipher, faded out in places, incoherent, but containing a serial control program for the governing of behavior. Here is the realist metaphor: Webs become represented in a static imprint left for us by earlier generations, in accordance with the historicist spirit.

Geertz would oppose the reification criticism. In his view, "culture-as-manuscript" was an antidote against cognitive anthropology (that is, the view that culture is composed of psychical structures used by individuals and groups as guidance for their behavior). And the critique of the solipsistic type of construction is, in his thinking, very sound indeed. Furthermore, Geertz's approach to the study of ideas can become a rich source of inspiration for researchers interested in symbolist approaches to organizations. His argument for noting the material aspect of ideas is very convincing:

> Ideas are not, and have not been for some time, unobservable mental stuff. They are envehicled meanings, the vehicles being symbols (or in some usages, signs), a symbol being anything that denotes, describes, represents, exemplifies, labels, indicates, evokes, depicts, expresses—anything that somehow or other signifies. And anything that somehow or other signifies is intersubjective, thus public, thus accessible to overt and corrigible *plein air* explication. Arguments, melodies, formulas, maps, and pictures are not idealities to be stared at but texts to be read; so are rituals, palaces, technologies and social formations. (Geertz, 1980, p. 135)

Geertz remained, however, on the idealist side, overlooking the material side of human action. A student of organizations cannot afford this. Organizations are filled with things that cut, puncture, print, mold, ride, and drill at the same time that they denote, describe, represent, and signify. Our ambition should therefore be to grasp both aspects of their simultaneity: the materialization of ideas and the symbolic and practical aspects of things (Czarniawska-Joerges & Joerges, 1990).

The culture as text metaphor favored by Geertz does not seem to offer the analytic potential needed to grasp this dynamic duality. As

useful as it might be for other purposes, it represents the ongoing activity of social construction as its static result, a text. Similarly, it
leans toward meaning that already exists and is waiting to be found,
rather than toward a construction process that does not always end
with accomplishment. Finally, it suggests a unity of culture, "one culture, one text,"[7] an assumption readily embraced by proponents of
"corporate culture," but which proves increasingly untenable in light
of the many cultures that each organization obviously hosts.

Another metaphor repeatedly used in organization analysis is that
of the game (Geertz, 1983). It is based, however, on the metaphor of
social life as antagonistic (despite all the *nonzero-sum* games that are
promised), which for me is as equally hard to accept as the harmony:
Social life is neither or both. The theater metaphor (Geertz, 1980)
presents, to my eyes, the most promising opportunity for rendering
the crux of organizational reality.

The Practice of Interpreting

Geertz saw the practice of anthropology as an ongoing interpretation
of the symbol systems of the people being studied. For him, it was these
systems that were of ultimate interest in accordance with the semiotic
tradition. An organization researcher, however, needs to return to the
collective action that has been created by these symbol systems and connect the two. Not that Geertz ignored social action—indeed, he proposed
to study it carefully, but only because it was the road to culture. After
Parsons, he constructed a three-part system of factors: culture, social
structure, and personality, which jointly determine social action.

Geertz's interest lies in culture, and this is the greatest difference
between the anthropological and organizational uses of anthropology.
It is the social action that organization students want to understand.
To quote Geertz himself, "A good interpretation of anything . . . takes
us into the heart of that of which it is the interpretation" (1973, p. 18).
One can say that in our own culture, it is not the culture that puzzles
us, but the concrete social action and its relationship to culture. In
studies of alien communities, specific actions are clues to the culture
puzzle; in organization studies, culture is more often a source of clues
to puzzling actions (see Crozier's analysis in Chapter 4).

What kind of results can be expected from an ongoing interpretation? Geertz specified three characteristics of ethnographic description: It is interpretive, in that it interprets the flow of social discourse; it saves the discourse from perishing by "inscribing it"; and it is microscopic. I see the desired description of complex organization as *interpretive,* that is, as interpreting social action, of which social discourse is a part. Discourse is also the main tool for approaching social action (as in a discourse between researchers and their interlocutors). The resulting inscription should turn the social action studied into a topic of social (among others, academic) discourse, and cannot afford to be microscopic.

In other words, I would add to Geertz's definition of the topic of ethnographic description (and of the ongoing interpretation, of course) the physical action (although it is true that we derive its meaning through discourse, if at all), and lift the inscription to the level I consider appropriate, that is, life-size and not microscopic. In more concrete terms, the inscriptions must be readable in a variety of contexts. The problems of microscopic approaches are exemplified by the Silverman and Jones study (1976; see also "Organizational Careers" in Chapter 5), which, in my opinion, because of its microscopic character, remains virtually unknown although it deserves much attention as a unique organizational study.

Sinful or Innocent?

What is Geertz's opinion on the controversial topic of whom to study? On the one hand, he was very much against "cultural universals" (the search for these was led by Clyde Kluckholm) which he called, after Adolf Kroeber, "fake universals." He also rejected the universal functionalism approach to social institutions. Interestingly enough, he assumed a social-constructivist approach to material production, but not to the production of symbols: Culture still exists out there, like a set of costumes lying on the stage to be put on during one's childhood. If culture is shaping us, who is shaping culture? History, most likely.

This may explain the fact that Geertz, too, assumed that the anthropologist's profession was to study other cultures and the "savage mind." The focus on historical explanations and the approach to cultures as entities able to be grasped as homogenous wholes almost demands that "primitive" societies be the object of study. But this is just a guess. Explicitly, Geertz holds as a virtue what Leach considered an old-fashioned vice of his—that anthropologists are to study other cultures and, if possible, exotic cultures, in order to leave behind their own cultures and acquire a different insight:

> [I]t is from the far more difficult achievement of seeing ourselves amongst others, as a local example of the forms human life has locally taken, a case among cases, a world among worlds, that the largeness of mind, without which objectivity is self-congratulation and tolerance a sham, comes. (Geertz, 1983, p. 16)

Clifford Geertz aimed at a theory of culture(s), not a type of social action, or a way of life that can be called "living in complex organizations." He aimed at building a body of knowledge concerning the various aspects of culture ("ideology," "common sense," and "art" as cultural systems). That body of knowledge can be of great use when acquiring knowledge about complex organizations, but the elements of the two will not be the same.

How Institutions Think, If They Think at All

One of the few anthropologists who finds modern industrial societies interesting is Mary Douglas. A British anthropologist, she lives in the United States and uses models of primitive societies that she studied in Africa as lenses through which she looks at modern societies and their institutions. Her book *How Institutions Think* (1986) is, in the words of Hofstede (1988), a complement to Berger and Luckmann. If I may continue his thought, both Douglas and Berger and Luckmann try to reconcile macro- and micro-level approaches to human knowledge and cognition, but if the latter achieve it at an interactional, almost micro-level, Mary Douglas stays at an institutional, almost macro-level.

Thought Worlds

This seemingly slight shift in orientation has deeper roots: Douglas claimed that an unwillingness to accept such concepts as *thought collective* (which came from a Polish-Jewish bacteriologist, Ludwik Fleck, who continued Durkheim's ideas on social group and collective representations) is due to the inherent individualism of Western rationalist culture embodied in rational choice theory. In other words, she interpreted what might be just a rejection of anthropomorphism (after all, organizations do not think) as "outright individualism" (p. 16), and she failed to notice that the theorists of choice are among the first to claim that "institutions think" (although, it is true, in a different way than that considered by Douglas).

Douglas took as a starting point the existence of a thought collective that she renamed a *thought world,* which denoted a social group that unintentionally generates its own view of the world, developing a thought style that sustains the existing pattern of interaction (p. 32). Belonging to the structural functionalists, Douglas questioned its functionality and its rational basis, which could transcend the limits of rational choice theory. What she offered as an answer was a two-thread theory of social behavior. One thread was transaction-cost theory, and another, chosen by Douglas herself, was the role of cognition in forming the social band, a personal demand for order and coherence, and control of uncertainty. When these issues become clear, the mystery of collective action will stand revealed, she claimed.

On her way, Douglas attempted to crash the myth of a small scale: She challenged the picture of an anarchist utopian community where social order grew spontaneously from mutual trust. In order to bolster her challenge, she relied substantially on anthropological research of small societies. In that sense, she made the vice into a virtue: The exotic observations served to demythologize complex societies, not mythologize them. Douglas proposed to use the acquired knowledge without the conceptual schemata, remembering nevertheless that conceptual schemata are always hidden in the former. Her ambition was to find a new, sophisticated, functionalist argument that would avoid the pitfalls of naive functionalism a la Malinowski and Radcliffe-Brown.

Douglas was bitter about the fact that anthropology, as represented by its ancient founders and their antics, is used "only as a stalking horse for more serious quarry" (p. 43). Anyway, "without a functionalist form of argument, we cannot begin to explain how a thought world constructs the thought style that controls its experience" (p. 43). How do we go about it?

> To acquire legitimacy, every kind of institution needs a formula that founds its rightness in reason and in nature. Half of our task is to demonstrate this cognitive process at the foundation of the social order. The other half of our task is to demonstrate that the individual's most elementary cognitive process depends on social constitutions. (Douglas, 1986, p. 45)

I might add that the second half of the task was successfully accomplished by Berger and Luckmann (although, as Hofstede pointed out in his review, Mary Douglas seemed to be unaware of it). Let us focus, then, on the first half.

Before we do this, I would like to point out two elements of Douglas's reasoning that I find to be common—and puzzling—in most Western writing. One is that a need for legitimacy is taken for granted and never explained, becoming an axiom. Another, close to it, is the assumption that social institutions are legitimate (although their legitimacy is constantly questioned). These two axiomatic assertions render the institutionalist-functionalist argument unproductive in the analysis of the former socialist societies, for example, which could be regarded as illegitimate (that is, introduced against and despite the wishes of the citizens). In light of this paradigm, coercion is either a legitimate institution itself (prison, or even a concentration camp from the point of view of Nazi-ruled society) or an unintended consequence: "In most forms of society hidden sequences catch individuals in unforeseen traps and hurl them down paths they never chose" (Douglas, 1986, p. 42).

The functionalist argument, however sophisticated, cannot—due to its implicit assumption of harmony—come to grips with the hurdle of illegitimate social order and intended manipulation (actually, Douglas's remarks on the Soviet system directly confirm this impression). Just as radical theorists cannot eschew the idea of a social control that is positive (which Mary Douglas perceptively criticized), neither can a functionalist think of social control as negative (unless it is called dysfunctional and then released from this constraint).

Institutions

But let us accept these axioms and look at the analysis of the legitimation process. An institution is understood as a legitimate social grouping (a family, a game, an organization), which has acquired its legitimacy from some authority (personal or diffused) on the basis of its conformity to the nature of the universe as it is commonly perceived.[8] According to Douglas (1986), "The favorite analogy generalizes everyone's preferred convention" (p. 51). And so a convention becomes a basis for an institution. Which analogies, then, are "favorite" and "preferred?" Those that allow intervention are favored. (Truth is in experience fit, see also Chapter 8.)

Functionalism of a Pragmatic Variety

The above argument encompasses many stages that must be looked at more closely. How do people agree about an analogy? How does one analogy win over another?

> The intellectual requirements that must be met for social institutions to be stable are matched by social requirements for classification. Both are necessary for the foundations of a sociological epistemology; neither one is sufficient. The institution works as such when it acquires a third support from the harnessed moral energy of its members. . . . All three processes are simultaneously at work. Individuals, as they pick and choose among the analogies from nature those they will give credence to, are also picking and choosing at the same time their allies and opponents and the pattern of their future relations. Constituting their version of nature, they are maintaining the constitution of their society. In short, they are constructing a machine for thinking and decision-making on their own behalf. (Douglas, 1986, p. 63)

This institutional classification saves energy and channels values and emotions. (This is my addition; Douglas, obviously influenced by cognitive psychology, did not give emotions any specific place. They float between the poles of irrationality and rationality, between the social and the intellectual.)

There are many analogies—the preferred ones are those that match the already existing structure of authority and precedence. But how, then, can a change or revolution occur? Here the idea of practical use, or a pragmatic effectiveness, comes in.

> A theory about how the world should be run will survive competition if it is more than a theory, for example, if it can intervene to support individual strategies to create a collective good. . . . The successful formula is predatory. Sheer consistency of use endows it with might, and it will swallow up competition. (p.73)

Institutions will be forgotten as soon as they cannot be put to practical uses. In the examples used by Douglas, this change was due to ongoing social events and accessible techniques of validation. For a new discovery to emerge, it must be compatible with the political, philosophical, and, I would add, technological realities of the time.

Mary Douglas tried to reconcile the theory of rational choice with the theory of public choice, the theory of social structure with the theory of individual cognition, and a theory of simple societies with a theory of complex societies. The result is, surprisingly, not an overcomplicated theory of everything, but a very convincing account of the origins and dynamics of social institutions. Her functionalism and tendency to join the consensus paradigm did not prevent her from formulating a radical proposition:

> Institutions systematically direct individual memory and channel our perceptions into forms compatible with the relations they authorize. They fix processes that are essentially dynamic, they hide their influence, and they rouse our emotions to a standardized pitch on standardized issues. Add to all this that they endow themselves with rightness and send their mutual corroboration cascading through all the levels of our information system. No wonder they easily recruit us into joining their narcissistic self-contemplation. Any problems we try to think about are automatically transformed into their own organizational problems. The solutions they proffer only come from the limited range of their experience. Institutions have the pathetic megalomania of the computer whose whole

vision of the world is its own program. For us, the hope of intellectual independence is to resist, and the necessary first step in resistance is to discover how the institutional grip is laid upon our mind. (Douglas, 1986, p. 92)

Institutional classification is a frantic social and intellectual activity that, for the most part, goes on unobserved. Here, Douglas joined the appeal of ethnomethodologists and symbolic realists (see Chapters 5 and 8): The task of social sciences lies in unmasking.

Does this mean that there exists an anthropologist whose work directly fits the task of studying complex organizations? The answer is somewhat complicated. In the first place, Mary Douglas is interested in society as such, and not just complex organizations. However, whatever we know of a society as such, or its institutions, should help us understand the phenomenon of complex organizations. What should we take, then? Concepts of corporate culture and corporate identity attempt to convey the idea that large organizations are thought worlds. I doubt that very much. Nevertheless, they can be seen as products or consequences of a certain combination of thought worlds, or simply, of a larger thought world called "Western democracies," for lack of a better word. Organizational nets of collective action unfold against the background of thought worlds of various kinds, some more central, some marginal to their existence. The notions of thought world and thought style, on the one hand, and institution and organization on the other, and especially the relations between them (like those embodied in the concept of an instituted community), are general enough not to stifle a theory from emerging from the empirical grounds and specific enough to avoid drowning in an all-encompassing "culture."

Second, the method Mary Douglas employed is just the opposite of the one propagated in this book, which makes it unusable directly, but nevertheless interesting. Hers was the "aerial," deductive perspective with an all-encompassing theory of collective action in view. We cannot join her in this endeavor if we remain at the level of a substantial, grounded theory. But we can use her insights to understand the reality we observe. There are certain matters that are not open to direct, empirical scrutiny, and there are others that are only accessible by the speculative route.

Third, her speculations on the birth and death of institutions (even if they must be conceived as practices rather than groupings) might be very helpful in understanding organizational life, if their functionalism is given a pragmatist (functional, as in serving the purpose at hand), rather than a rationalist (functional, as in fulfilling a designed function) interpretation.

Finally, one has to emphasize that neither Leach, Geertz, nor Douglas has ever proposed to study complex organizations. Therefore, it is hardly practical to look to them for detailed prescriptions. What can be directly learned from anthropology is, on the one hand, new and rich metaphors and, on the other, fieldwork methods and interpretive analysis. The following sections examine these two possibilities, taking examples from concrete studies.

Reading Castaneda Together With Silverman

The famous book *The Teachings of Don Juan: A Yaqui Way of Knowledge* was written by a young American anthropologist as a doctoral dissertation.[9] It dealt with excursions to a nonordinary reality guided by a Yaqui Indian with the help of herbal drugs. According to one, perhaps most literal interpretation, it was an account of the effects of peyote and other hallucinogens. Such an interpretation, albeit quite possible, runs against the explicit statement by the author himself (Castaneda, 1968/ 1986), who claimed that, according to don Juan, drugs were only training aids needed during initial excursions into the other world, that which lies beyond the twilight, "the crack between two worlds."[10]

Castaneda's book can be seen as a parable of anthropological experience. This was how David Silverman, an organizational sociologist, proposed to read it. I shall follow him through those points that are of use in our endeavor, and add some points of my own. In doing this, as has been my habit throughout the book, I choose to interpret Silverman from the point of view of my own interest (for example, avoiding all issues related to social construction of reality, because this topic has been discussed already). I can repeat what Silverman told his readers: "What I write for you cannot possibly be 'about' *his* book, it must, at all times be 'about' *my* book" (1975, p. 27).

Let us start with the point that is directly relevant to studies of complex organizations: The meeting between don Juan and Castaneda was a meeting of two different rationalities. (There is no doubt about the formal rationality of don Juan's actions; he always chose the best ways to reach a desired result.) This is, indeed, a situation in which all field researchers will find themselves sooner or later. Because organizations, especially complex ones, host multiple rationalities, sooner or later we shall find somebody whose action is "strange" or "incomprehensible." One desirable outcome of such an encounter is a distancing from one's own rationality, a better understanding of it (this is, indeed, the necessary if not sufficient first step). A defensive defining of somebody else's rationality as "irrational" closes the way to knowledge.

Castaneda was therefore forced to look for a method: How does one find out? And even more important: What does one find out? When he was writing his book, he discovered that the old methods were useless:

> Reflecting upon the phenomena I had experienced, I realized that my attempt at classification had produced nothing more than an inventory of categories; any attempt to refine my scheme would therefore yield only a more complex inventory. That was not what I wanted. During the months following my withdrawal from the apprenticeship, I needed to understand what I had experienced. . . . I was forced to the conclusion that any attempt to classify my field data in my own terms would be futile.
>
> Thus it became obvious to me that don Juan's knowledge had to be examined in terms of how he himself understood it. (1968/1986, pp. 19-20)

He soon discovered, however, that don Juan did not use language for the purpose of transferring knowledge, but for the interpretation of (past) experience.

> [F]or don Juan the interpretation and application of a rule is always an entirely *practical* matter, related to concrete occasions at which we try to make sense of an activity for the purposes of which are relevant at the time. (Silverman, 1975, p. 39)

Talking helps to understand an experience and to live it through (experience is understanding). But it cannot substitute for experience, and this is why our research is always handicapped, in the name of economy, time, and reason. This is why, I may add, Geertz's postulate that discourse alone should be studied is not fully satisfactory. All of us who have spent some time in organizations know that organizational actors know more than they say. Polanyi's (1958) concept of tacit knowledge attempts to capture this phenomenon. Sometimes, when time or luck permits, a researcher can even learn this knowledge through experience—with no guarantee that the verbal account that follows would be any better than the original experience.

Of course, it is partly a matter of shared meanings (or rather those that are not shared). Don Juan could not teach Castaneda through generalized concepts because he did not use them, and even if he had, he and Castaneda did not share the same system of cognition. One is, after all, only able to understand what one already knows (on understanding in the hermeneutical tradition, see Palmer, 1969).

Castaneda and don Juan were, to use a metaphor coined by Donald M. MacKay (1964), two alien systems who tried to communicate. And Castaneda showed us very convincingly how much courage, pain, goodwill, and patience such necessary negotiation of meaning must require. An interesting point was that don Juan did not use metaphors. He refused to speak in terms of "as if," or "like." He looked for a proper language of uniqueness, something that is typical of action-oriented persons. A conversation with a shop-floor worker would be like this, but not with a manager.

So, Castaneda let himself be dragged into the "other dimension," or nonordinary reality, in order to learn about it. And what did he learn? The second part of the book is dedicated to a "structural analysis," in which he painstakingly translates his new knowledge into a set of "context-free" concepts; in other words, into a language proper for a dissertation. Why? Because the community of social scientists, to which he ultimately belongs, claims to have the method (or "rather, the method and the rule *is* the community," Silverman, 1975, p. 41). Castaneda legitimized his undertaking by reducing the nonordinary reality to an "ordinary reality of social sciences."

Claims that Castaneda's book was ultimately a joke that kept up "scientific pretenses" in order to authenticate what was finally an apocrypha, imply that it was a strategy that helped the author to market all the remaining books: The book, in other words, was not the startling confession of a scientist, but a clever marketing trick. That may be so, but I describe it anyway because we shall see the very same operation repeated again—a brilliant anthropological study cramped into irrelevant "theoretical" concepts in an attempt to gain legitimacy. Strangely enough, the social science community is—maybe only recently—much more tolerant of pluralistic methods than doctoral students sometimes seem to think. The next study is a good example.

The Laboratory Savage

> Since the turn of the century, scores of men, and women have penetrated deer forests, lived in hostile climates, and weathered hostility, boredom and disease in order to gather the remnants of so-called primitive societies. In contrast to the frequency of these anthropological excursions, relatively few attempts have been made to penetrate the intimacy of life among tribes which are much nearer at hand. (Latour & Woolgar, 1979/1986, p. 17)

I have chosen Latour's study of Roger Guillemin's laboratory at the Salk Institute for two reasons. First, it is an interesting anthropological study of a Western organization. Bruno Latour came straight from the Ivory Coast to the Salk Institute and for two years tried to make sense of what was happening around him. Second, it is a clear-cut example of the first part of "the new sin" as described before, that is, introducing an exotic frame of reference to analyze a phenomenon in the native culture. Recall the first quote and read on:

> We envisaged a research procedure analogous with that of an intrepid explorer of the Ivory Coast who, having studied the belief system or material production of "savage minds" by living with tribesmen sharing their hardships and almost becoming one of them, eventually returns with a body of observations which he can present as a preliminary research report. (p. 28)

The reasoning seems to be based on a kind of mechanistic chronology: A primitive society was studied first, and we are now looking for functional equivalents. Management information systems become functionally equivalent to a priest's inspection of animal entrails, not to mention the overexploited rain dance. That may well be, but in order to sensibly use these metaphors, we must either treat them with the utmost care and control their analytical consequences, or else treat them as literal equivalents and show their correspondent function, or their place in a given system of meaning (the former can be much easier than the latter, due to the familiar elasticity of the concept of utility). Latour and Woolgar plunged head on into the sea of anthropological metaphors, but the laboratory fellows were not amused. They felt ill at ease being described as sorcerers, as Salk's introduction to the book plainly indicated. (The problem with modern savages is that they are usually literate and can read English. Luckily for Castaneda, don Juan never read his books.)

The study led to the most interesting results—the scientists' main occupation was to talk (both directly and via letters and publications). Talk established facts (or rather, what can be considered a "fact"), built science, and constructed the rules of scientific conduct, supporting professional and social hierarchies. The endocrinologists (awarded a Nobel Prize in their field) very rarely performed any material actions—technicians did. Researchers talked.

This fascinating ethnography entails yet another kind of sin, a final ethnocentrism. The culture studied becomes unified with the culture of the student in an ultimate act of understanding. It turns out that the natural scientists did exactly the same things that social scientists do. (We spend our lives communicating, orally or in writing.) It seems that no matter what you study, you will always end up with your own reflection as the result. Revolutionary attempts to reform organization theory finish up by theorizing about organization theory. There is no objection to this, but I would still insist on learning something about social reality that is beyond social science. Otherwise the following sarcastic comment will find its full application: "[T]he language of science became the object of science and what had begun as perception unmediated by concepts became conception unmediated by percepts" (Tyler, 1986, p. 124).

If everything is just social science, then indeed there is not much to study. Similarities can be found in all human activities: We are all sense makers but that does not make us all into social scientists. It is the differences that are interesting, not the similarities.

Selling Hot Rituals or How to Go Too Far

Although I am fastidious about real or imagined faults or imperfections in masterpieces such as Latour and Woolgar's, more pragmatically oriented writers have noticed that anthropological metaphors sell like hotcakes. Here are some titles of books on management: *The Folklore of Management, Magic in Business and Industry, Managers and Magic,* and *The Company Savage.* I have chosen one, *The Corporate Tribe* (Wilcock, 1984), for closer scrutiny.

Wilcock, the author, is an industrial psychologist, a practicing consultant, and although his book clearly has a practical goal (how ancient tribal structures and roles are mirrored in the corporation of today—and how these striking similarities can profit *you*), it was "based on research," which gives me a legitimate reason for including it in this discussion. I also share at least two basic assumptions with Wilcock: that corporations are a very important element in the present stage in the development of humankind; and that they solve problems, formulate policies, and resolve employee controversies without paying much attention to organization theory.

It would be easy to ridicule the far-reaching promises of the book. ("I am hopeful that the corporate employees and executives who read *The Corporate Tribe* will start to see their companies in a new, more healthy, more optimistic way" [p. 8].) But this is not the point: This book belongs to a certain genre (the popularizing, how-to type), and it follows its rules. I do not propose that the author write an academic dissertation in its place. What I want to discuss is the message brought to the fore with the help of anthropological metaphors.

The message is that "all human groups abide by ancient laws of nature and that what we call corporations are, in fact, modern-day tribes" (p. 10). Hierarchies have probably existed for millions of years, and tribes are archetypal social structures, as are the tribal roles: chief, hunter, elder, gatherer, and shaman. In different cultures, consultants are called "*brujos,* fetishers, medicine men, witch doctors, high priests, wizards, and magicians . . . [who] have special knowledge which can help the tribe survive and prosper" (p. 12).[11] Corporate management groups "provide clear examples of male bonding" (p. 13), which has had a survival value for centuries. Female bonding follows a separate, gatherer-like pattern. Pecking order determines behavior in the male group, prescribing the way food, property, possessions, and wealth are distributed. Metaphors become more and more biological: "Deep within the womb of the corporation, new capitalists are nurtured" (p. 34).

An anthropological metaphor, used charmingly if misleadingly by Latour and Woolgar to enrich their interpretation of everyday life in a laboratory, turns here into a heavy club, reducing the social reality to its biological core. The joy to be achieved by this kind of organizational Darwinism lies, evidently, in a newly found argument for maintaining the status quo. Anthropology teaches us, presumably, that hierarchies dominated by the male are the best forms of social survival, acquired and perfected over the millennia. Cast in archetypes buried in our subconscious, nature leads our lives through corporate expression.

> Perhaps my own personality, abilities, interests and talents somehow led me to an ancient shaman career path. Perhaps those around me in corporate life, by responding to some behaviors and discouraging others, screened me out of some roles and led me into others. Perhaps we are all guided by half-buried understandings of tribal life that help us define our places in the tribe, our most effective ways to contribute. (p. 126)

The book continues, naturally enough, with a list of recommendations meant to help the reader use "tribality" for profit, and culminates in tackling some basic issues, such as confronting Darwin and Marx, and provides a decisive commentary on Allende and developing countries. The argument halts somewhat on the issue of war, which is, on the one hand, a typical part of the "man's eternal nature" argument, but, on the other, seems to be disliked by the author. This obstacle negotiated, we arrive at a dazzling finale:

> Studies of the relatively advanced agricultural civilization of the Aztecs and Mayans reveal that human sacrifice, as well as cannibalism, was

widespread. These revelations underline how far industrialized nations have evolved toward more humane and compassionate values. (p. 195)

In terms of benevolent ideas, corporations are clearly a refinement over earlier tribal forms. There is very little violence within corporations. No corporations apply torture or physical punishment to employees who break the rules. Corporations may fire workers, disappoint them, use them and abuse them, but no blood is shed. (p. 196)

Those who attack corporations, who complain about the boredom, fear or lack of challenge within them, should study the full multimillion-year range of tribal evolution. Only when the real anthropological perspective is understood can we begin to recognize the emergence of new, more humane, less violent tribes. (p. 187)

Of course, there is nothing in anthropology, as such, that makes it particularly useful for conservative or chauvinist arguments. This is not the only, nor necessary, understanding of the "real anthropological perspective." Nevertheless, I would like to argue that such interpretations are facilitated by equating metaphors with definitions or labels. ("Of course, I see it as much more than a metaphor. Because I see my clients as tribes, and can speak directly to their tribal souls, I can create a powerful new awareness," p. 160.) We shall see this once more in some organizational culture studies that tend to specialize in a different fallacy: identifying methods with the phenomena under study.

Socialization Under the Cherry Blossom

Thomas P. Rohlen (1973, 1974) steered well away from these problems: He studied a socialization process, "spiritual education," in a complex organization (a bank of 3,000 employees), with the help of an inductively derived set of categories. However, the organization was situated in Japan, and its context was a peculiar blending of Western and Japanese, Zen Buddhism and business logic, modernity and tradition, which is presented to the Western reader as typifying this faraway country. The author concluded by shyly proposing some cross-cultural research, but his final recommendations were of a more general character—to consider the psychology of individuals in the design of education programs.

The study is impressive. *For Harmony and Strength: Japanese White-Collar Organization in Anthropological Perspective* (1974) was a participant observation study conducted by the author (who speaks Japanese and was helped by a local anthropologist) over a period of 11 months. Rohlen's aim was to prove the applicability of the anthropological perspective to organization research, and he succeeded.

The organization was seen as hosting multiple perspectives, ideologies, and world views. Pluralistic as they were, they nevertheless differed from Western ideas, not by virtue of one all-encompassing "cultural difference," but due to their many various differences. The study sought to explicate the meanings held by the author and the people in the organization. Extensive exploration of traditions and philosophies contributed to the richness of context presentation. Rohlen did not shy away from presenting statistical data and formal organization. But this did not prevent him from presenting concrete actions against a background of systems, symbols, and rituals.

This is perhaps the most comprehensive study of an organization in existence done by one person. In many senses then, it is an example to be followed. It proves that anthropological studies of complex organizations are possible (as Latour and Woolgar's study shows that anthropological studies of Western organizations are possible). In addition, it ends on a very optimistic note:

> By attempting to study the complexities of organization, anthropologists will not only be adapting their methodology and insight to a realm of vast importance and possibility, they will also be opening their discipline to the exciting prospect of dealing with modern societies at a crucial and dynamic level, one where the nature and meaning of modern life is being forged. Nothing better characterizes modern societies than their work organizations and these are still very much in the early stage of a process aimed at discovering internal explanations and social forms that will be of lasting significance. (Rohlen, 1974, p. 270)

If a criticism can be made, it might involve the tendency to over-interpret in cultural terms. As my student from China observed during a group discussion of Rohlen's book, China has the same philosophy, but not the same economic system. A Swedish student commented that Rohlen omitted a whole chapter of Japan's industrial history—how the development of unions was prevented.

Anthropology of complex organizations should treat what is happening in organizations as a way of life to be studied using anthropological methods. It must not, however, reduce the context to that of national culture. We may speak about *cultural context* if we mean the history, politics, economy, and ways of nonorganizational life, and not folk dances or "national character." Cherry trees should not hide steel and glass, and certainly not the fact that organizations grow out of their context and not parallel to it.

Another Anthropology of Organizations

As if to confirm Robert K. Merton's (1965) thesis that every idea exists already, I came across a compendium while writing this book, titled *Hierarchy and Society: Anthropological Perspectives on Bureaucracy,* edited by Gerald M. Britan and Ronald Cohen (1980). The authors' aim was, to put it briefly, the opposite of mine: They wanted to introduce organization theory into anthropology. There are no primitive societies any more; all societies are complex. Anthropology must come to grips with this complexity, of which bureaucracies are perhaps the most important sign.

> Today, the context of human social life has changed drastically. As local communities have become incorporated into large systems, lineages, clans, age-sets, chiefs, and big men have all declined in importance. Simultaneously, classes, ethnic groups, and formal organizations have emerged with increasing significance throughout the world. (p. 9)

Following this program, contributors offered a bureaucracy-oriented analysis of such traditional anthropological subjects as exotic societies and processes that had been informal in their own society until recent innovations such as child-rearing and mental health care.

I shall not enter into a long presentation of this book because it is addressed to anthropologists and lectures them on the basics of organization theory. However, it is clear that Britan and Cohen's "an-thropology of formal organizations" is not so much an alternative as a complement. If anthropologists extend their subject matter, and orga-nization theorists their repertoire of methods and analyses, we might come to approach something that could be called "the anthropology of complex organizations."

Lessons to Be Learned, Sins to Be Avoided

At the present moment, anthropology both attracts and repels those caught by the spirit of experimentation in a diversity of fields. It is eth-nography that primarily attracts. We find philosophers, literary critics, historians, and political economists reading ethnographies of the Balin-ese and Azande, not out of intrinsic interest in the subject matter, but for their distinctive textual devices and modes of exploring theoretical issues in the process of ethnographic representation itself. It is the traditional subject matter of anthropology—the primitive or alien other—that pri-marily repels, or, rather, undercuts the full potential of anthropology's relevance in a widespread intellectual trend, which it has long antici-pated. (Marcus, 1986, pp. 167-168)

Whatever their sins, anthropologists accumulated a wealth of wis-dom and experience that can be called on in the construction of mod-els and interpretations involving large, complex organizations in modern and postmodern societies.

In the first place, organization students can adopt the humanistic message of the discipline: looking for, or creating, unity and solidar-ity by making the experience of those "who do not speak our lan-guage" accessible, be they female workers or managing directors. Second, the historical or, more generally speaking, contextual ap-proach should be adopted rather than context-free comparisons. Third, and in accordance with what has been said above, a holistic type of research requiring protracted and intense contacts with orga-nizations should replace reductionist analyses. Fourth, the aim of re-search should be an interpretation of collective action as interpreted (or noninterpreted) by actors and spectators alike. Fifth, the under-standing of the experienced world (Vickers, 1972) might be enriched by the inclusion of such speculative concepts as thought worlds and institutions. This understanding should be balanced by a similar extension in the opposite direction—inclusion of the practical aspects that can be verbalized only with significant difficulty. Anthropology-inspired organization theory would then be both more idealist and more materialist than it is at present.

The final and perhaps most important postulate to learn is what can be called an *anthropological frame of mind,* expressed by not taking social realities for granted. This means, on the one hand, modesty and openness toward new worlds and new meanings, and on the other, a constant urge to problematize, to turn what seems familiar and understandable upside down and inside out. "A sound rule of thumb seems to be that when the alien culture you are studying begins to look normal, it is time to go home" (Barley, 1986, p. 153).

Notes

1. Recall the protests and corrections caused by Burrell and Morgan's (1979) classification of major paradigms.

2. An ironist is a person who: "(a). . . has radical and continuous doubts about the final vocabulary she currently uses, because she has been impressed by other vocabularies, vocabularies taken as final by people or books she has encountered; (b) . . . realizes that the argument phrased in her present vocabulary can neither underwrite nor dissolve their doubts; (c) insofar as she philosophizes about her situation, she does not think that her vocabulary is closer to reality than others, that it is in touch with power not herself" (Rorty, 1989, p. 73).

3. On Malinowski's "fantastic functionalism," see also Asplund (1971).

4. This difficulty, noticed more often by anthropologists than by sociologists (Tilly, 1984), has been taken up recently by the sociology of knowledge. Among others, Tilly (1984) and Latour (1986) protest against treating society "as a thing apart."

5. This example may seem somewhat dated considering that it illustrates the "new" sin. However, in order to be able to come home, the anthropologists had to travel away first, and that orders the chronology of sins. So far, the new sin is more visible, partly because conscious attempts were made to eradicate the old sin, and partly because the homecoming intensified with recent political developments.

6. I shall come back to this concept in Chapter 8, discussing the forms of writing ethnographies.

7. Geertz's book, *Works and Lives: The Anthropologist as Author* (1988), would suggest an interpretation more along the lines "one author, one culture."

8. Note that this definition is different from Berger and Luckmann's (1966/1971), which I espouse, that institutions are repeated practices transferred through generations. In Douglas's definition, organizations are institutions and social groupings. In Berger and Luckmann's, organizations are institutions but not social groupings.

9. Although there have been (and are) many authoritative utterances on the topic of whether it was a dissertation or just a literary *pastiche* of one, the matter remains far from clear. The most recent version of events is to be found in de Mille (1990).

10. Another interpretation would run along the same lines as the analysis of Robert Musil's film, *The Man Without Qualities,* performed by Peter Berger with the aid of the concepts of Alfred Schütz (Berger, 1970). Travels with don Juan were travels to the "other condition," something that perhaps belongs with basic existential longings. Listen to this Schützian definition:

> The other condition, however, is not experiencing the world. As such, it is located 'tangentially' with reference attainable by means of theoretical propositions. It is a different mode of the reality of everyday life, which it 'touches' at unexpected places. It can only be entered from the domain of everyday reality by going off at a 'tangent.'
>
> There is a dissolution of differentiations, particularly of the differentiation between subjective consciousness and the objective, external world. There is a feeling of openness with the 'heart of the world,' of being carried by being as such, a cessation of movement, an overwhelming lucidity. (Berger, 1970, p. 355)

11. Note that this is another social group that is compared to witch doctors. Maybe, after all, the metaphor is actually more apt for consultants than for endocrinologists.

4

Organization Theory:
Why Has It Parted Ways With Anthropology?

At the Crossroads

Organizations-as-machines and organizations-as-organisms notwith-standing, the truly favorite metaphor of organizational theorists is that of the elephant—that is, at least, when researchers describe their own attitude toward their study object. The story of blind men describing the elephant has been told and retold ad infinitum: Charles Perrow spoke about beasts in a zoo, and, in 1961, Dwight Waldo wrote a review essay entitled "Organization Theory: An Elephantine Problem." Indeed, it seems to be an elephantine problem all the way. Waldo's article is important, however, not only because of its chief metaphor, but also because it witnesses the moment when anthropology and organization theory parted ways—the latter tempted by other voices.

Waldo's review encompasses six books, as different as *Human Organization Research: Field Relations and Techniques,* edited by Richard N. Adams and Jack J. Preiss, published for the Society of Applied Anthropology in 1960; *Understanding Organizational Behavior,* by Chris

Argyris, 1960; *Modern Organization Theory,* edited by Mason Haire, 1959; *General Systems: Yearbook of the Society for General Systems Research,* Vol. IV, Part II; *Contributions to Organization Theory,* edited by Ludwig Von Bertalanffy and Anatol Rappaport, 1960; *Comparative Studies in Administration,* edited by the staff of the Administrative Science Center, University of Pittsburgh, 1959; and *Some Theories of Organization,* edited by Albert H. Rubenstein and Chadwick J. Haberstroh, 1960. Among the most frequent contributors were Herbert Simon, James G. March, Richard Cyert, Chris Argyris, Mason Haire, Anatol Rappaport, Jacob Marschak, Rensis Likert, Peter Blau, William Foote Whyte, James Thompson, and Kurt Lewin. For someone who reads Waldo's essay in the 1990s, it is like a *roman à clef:* We know who will go and who will remain; anthropology will not stay and systems theory will.

Dwight Waldo was not a clairvoyant but an insightful observer. He was well aware of the importance of that particular period in time:

> [N]early all of the pieces printed or reprinted are the product of the past ten years; and . . . a high proportion of the authors are in their early professional years. In short, . . . there is no doubt that organization theory and research are in a boom period. . . . (1961, p. 212)

Waldo discussed the main trends in this boom as he saw it. One was a transition from administrative theory to organization theory (indeed, if Waldo were to publish his essay today, he would never have thought the *Public Administration Review* an appropriate journal). This shift was due to the triumph of an aspiration in social science methodology—behavioralism—that required following the lead of the natural sciences. This "behavioralism," as Waldo called it, was taking the lead:

> The behavioralists want above all else . . . to be Scientific in the study of social phenomena, taking as their model what they conceive to be the outlook and methods of physical science. The general goal is a value-free generalization about how the subject phenomena behave, given specified conditions. "Values" are proper data for scientific generalizations, but the social scientist, as scientist, has no concern for their "intrinsic validity" (if I may be forgiven the term). (1961, p. 217)

This approach did not go along with the notion of administration, which was "an applied science—if it is not indeed a profession, an art, or something less. 'Administrative theory' suggests an engagement with the world, a striving after values" (Waldo, 1961, p. 217). Organization theory was, on the other hand, a theory not of action, but of a unit existing "out there." The researcher, sitting "in here" (presumably, at a university desk) "can become an anthropologist, so to speak, completely detached from the society he observes" (p. 217). And here Waldo adds a footnote: "I am aware that many anthropologists argue that they must become a part of a society they observe in order to understand it. But some of the students of organization are more anthropological than the anthropologists!" (footnote 7, pp. 217-218).

The other way around, perhaps, is that some anthropologists used the qualifier "applied anthropology," and under this name conducted studies of organizations in a more positivistic spirit than could be claimed by any sociologist (for a good example, see Leonard Sayles, 1962). Nevertheless, anthropology was not usually associated with this research orientation. Thus we learn from Waldo that organization theory was on its way to becoming pure, value-free science, and, in passing, that the involvement of the analyst, an issue that constantly crops up, was bothering anthropologists and nonanthropologists alike.

Let us, however, concentrate on the requirements posited by the dominant paradigm. One of the most important requirements was the departure from holism and the adoption of reductionism. The organizational phenomena were to be explained by analyzing their constituent parts. This turn of events can be explained by organization theory's ideological commitment to the newly espoused positivist paradigm, but also by a quite pragmatic concern that will haunt us throughout these pages: How do you grasp the whole of an elephant? Yet this used to be an ambition of a true anthropologist: "to see the particular problem with which he is concerned as part of a larger functioning configuration of organizational and behavioral patterns, rather than in isolation" (Waldo, 1961, p. 213).

Waldo did not hide his sympathy for what was now out of fashion: holistic, comparative, value-sensitive, and well written. Nevertheless, his duty was to report the triumphant entry of the "scientific study of the American business organization." Yet when all respect due to the young geniuses was paid, he could not prevent himself from noticing in the end that the beginnings of organization theory could be found in Plato and Aristotle, and could be traced through Machiavelli and Hobbes to Fayol and Urwick. In other words, we have seen many elephant drivers already and there are more to come!

This chapter is dedicated to an examination of a few of the most famous depictions of the beast, produced as outcomes of the break. Although each of them contains some nostalgic bows to the old-fashioned "nonapplied anthropologist's" view, all but one are primarily dedicated to attaining the new ideal. The result is not only the empirical ground of today's mainstream organizational theory, but also the feeling of dissatisfaction that prompts us to search further.

The sample begins with Selznick's famous Tennessee Valley Authority (TVA) study, followed by Rice's study of textile mills in Ahmedabad, studies of a tobacco factory and a public agency by Michel Crozier, and Rosabeth Kanter's *Men and Women of the Corporation*. It closes with a reader edited by Etzioni and Lehman, presenting empirical studies on various aspects of complex organizations. The chronological and methodological consistency is broken by the last study—by Melville Dalton—the only one that is anthropological in character. It became famous but was not imitated.

Although the theoreticians introduced so far focused on complex organizations in the United States, there were also studies of non-U.S. organizations and their related theories. However, the spirit of the times was common to all of them. Indeed, it is ever more surprising to see that such seminal works, which left an imprint on organization theory for decades to come, were subsumed under a common, universalist denomination, which after some scratching reveals the sign, "Made in U.S.A."

Partly Abandoned, Partly Surviving: The Tennessee Valley Authority

Philip Selznick's study of the TVA, originally published in 1949, was intended as a "scholarly study of complex organization"; it remains a classic in the field. Conducted and written more than a decade before Waldo's essay, it is of double interest to us. On the one hand, it represents all that the science-oriented researchers tried to cut themselves free from: a value-laden theory of administration and an inductive methodology. On the other hand, it announces all the major trends to come: structural functionalism, behavioralism, and objectivization. One could claim that, in fact, Selznick initiated two research traditions that took separate routes: public policy studies (especially visible in studies of regional resource development, see e.g., Hirschman, 1967; and Joerges, 1975) and organization theory research. This was possible due to the fact that his work contained two messages: moral-pragmatic and structural-functionalist. The strength of Selznick's argument lay in the combination of the two.

A Scientific Inquiry With No Strings Attached

The Tennessee Valley Authority was, in the words of President Franklin D. Roosevelt, "a corporation with the power of government but possessed of the flexibility and initiative of private enterprise. It should be charged with the broadest duty of planning for the proper use, conservation and development of the natural resources of the Tennessee River drainage basin and its adjoining territory for the general social and economic welfare of the Nation" (Selznick, 1949/ 1966, p. 5).

For many, the TVA is still a symbol of successful state intervention—a project that, in tragic post-Depression times, gave meaningful employment to a great number of people in an environmentally conscious and democratically run project. For others, the TVA is an example of the corruption, waste, and ideological hypocrisy that typifies state intervention. For Selznick, it was an organization in the years 1942-1943, "which opened its door to scientific inquiry 'with no strings attached'" (1949/1966, p. xv). Using documents and interviews with TVA personnel, official and unofficial records, and interviews with Washington and Tennessee Valley state officials, Selznick studied "the recurrent dilemmas of power, ideology, and organization" (p. xiii).

His main concern was to establish whether the TVA had succeeded in becoming "a technique of democratic planning," that is, a local authority capable of using local citizens' contributions in local resource planning. His object of study was a technology of creation, defense, and reintegration of values, which is "of primary importance for whatever we may wish to do about that vague but demanding reality which we call our 'way of life' " (pp. 6-7). This technology, said Selznick, might be rendered invisible, intentionally or not, by an official ideology of an organization, that is, an image of the organization's goals and methods as presented by its leaders.

The official ideology or doctrine of the TVA was that of political centralization combined with administrative decentralization. This ideology was put to both internal and external uses, educating people within and outside the Authority. Did it, however, accurately describe reality? Selznick noted the vagueness and abstractness of the doctrine: How, exactly, was local influence to bear upon the agency's proceedings? How was the quality of "being close to the people" to be achieved? What did "working through established agencies" mean? And how were terms such as "coordination," "unity," or "participation of the people" to be made operable? Nevertheless,

> The grass-roots theory is not a mockery or fraud simply because it has served a function tangential to democratic values. A living organization must use tools which are at hand, with due regard to consequences for its own existence, accepting compromise as a normal state of affairs. (p. 62)

An anthropomorphic metaphor of organization ("Organizations, like individuals, strive for a unified pattern of response," Selznick, 1949/1966, p. 181) introduced a pragmatic way out of a moral dilemma. The ideology turned out to be a mechanism of legitimation, that is, "a mechanism by which the agency achieved an adjustment to institutional forces within its area of operation" (p. 85). I would like to emphasize this because the dilemma of humanistic values in conflict with organizational practices torments many field researchers of organizations. Selznick's own solution was rarely followed literally, but it became a source of inspiration for several different approaches to this question. This was possible because, as already stated, there were two types of messages to be found in his conclusions.

Selznick as a Moral Pragmatist

> To my mind, the proper perspective of the social critic is that of the moral pragmatist. The latter does not shrink from symbolism, nor does he reject the rhetoric of hope and aspiration. He knows that a steady diet of cynicism and self-doubt can be spiritually corrosive and politically enervating. Therefore he cannot forego ideology. Yet as a pragmatist he seeks never to lose his critical sensibility, never to stop asking whether the end he has in view or the means he uses are governed by truly operative criteria of moral worth. (1949/1966, p. xii)

As a moral pragmatist, Selznick allowed his inquiry to be led by values—humanistic and actor-oriented—and did not hide behind a false neutrality.

This stance encouraged the use of an inductive method in his inquiry. It was not, however, the approach that we know as grounded theory, in the sense that the reader, in this case, cannot follow the theory's emergence. Instead, the author presented it full-fledged in conceptual terms, with some closer-to-the-ground illustrations of general categories.[1]

In this abode, Selznick can also be seen as a precursor of symbolism in organization theory. What had been abandoned for years to come, now comes back quite visibly. First, there is the general idea of symbolic aspects of organization: "In its capacity as symbol, the organization derives meaning and significance from the interpretations which others place upon it" (pp. 19-20). Second, there is the idea of leaders as providers of meaning (*Weltanschauung*), which was carried on by Pfeffer (1977) and later by Smircich and Morgan (1982). Selznick also analyzed the role of organizational language, among other things, organizational labels. What distinguishes him from contemporary symbolists is the fact that he perceived the symbolic and concrete realms as separate, and in fact, contrasting: "Yet however significant its symbolic feature may be, TVA is and must be more than idea. It is a living organization in a concrete social environment" (Selznick, 1949/1966, p. 20). In other words, Selznick was also, perhaps primarily, a structural functionalist.[2]

Selznick as a Structural Functionalist

Reading Selznick's theory should be very instructive to young organization students, who often read antipositivist critiques and probably wonder what the basis was of the alleged "value-hiding." Selznick was still at a prescientific stage, so to speak, and thus stated openly that his functionalism was value-laden—namely, that it is morally good if an organization fulfills its societal function through a successful adaptation to its constituents and its institutional environment. He did not see any inconsistency in combining moral pragmatism with structural functionalism.

The structural functionalist type of research that followed purified itself from this moral aspect. Functionality replaced morality and was no longer justified by it. In this light, an important tenet of Selznick's theory was his rhetoric, his tendency to objectify.[3] His search for meaning was not directed toward the subjective awareness of the participants, which he felt would be "a serious error" (p. 255). The meaning of the act was in its consequences, as spelled out by Selznick, even if coaxed out of stories by the TVA participants.

> [W]e may distinguish the random search for meanings—which can be, at one extreme, an aesthetic interest—from the inquiry of the organizational analyst. The latter likewise selects consequences, but his frame of reference constrains his view: it is his task to trace such consequences as redound upon the organization in question; that is, such effects as have an internal relevance. . . . There is an obvious and familiar sense in which consequences are related to action: the articulation of means and ends demands that we weigh the consequences of alternative courses of action. (pp. 253-254)

And so on, and so forth: rationalistic criteria, applied by an outside observer, involved (in a sense of general moral orientation) but free from biases in what he notices, as there is an objectively rational route to be followed as a standard for evaluation.

But Selznick's most important contribution was the firm establishment of a biological metaphor: organization as a living organism, dependent on and shaped by the institutional environment to which it is trying to adapt in order to reach an equilibrium that will guarantee survival. Both the consequent open-system theory of organization and the current neoinstitutionalism have firm roots in the TVA story.

In 1954 Alvin W. Gouldner attacked Selznick, on the basis of his TVA study, for embracing a "pathos of pessimism" and focusing on social constraints that thwart democratic aspirations while neglecting those that might help them be realized (Selznick, 1949/1966, p. x). In 1986 Charles Perrow, who was Selznick's pupil, attacked John W. Meyer and Brian Rowan (1977/1980) for their cynicism of the functionalistic acceptance of organizational adaptation. And yet their analyses have basically the same tone—pessimistic, cynical, or are they simply realistic?

Setting the Style

Selznick's account of the TVA story was not an ethnography of a complex organization, because it chose an aerial view of the organization. We do not acquire an understanding of daily life in the Authority, or the Authority as a way of life—an expectation that is perhaps unrealistic, considering TVA's size and complexity, which might well have rendered such an ambition impossible. The presentation took place against a macro, political background. It might also be seen as a study of a large project, or a social change, rather than a study of an organization.

The importance of Selznick's work for a theory of complex organization is, nevertheless, quite obvious. His early treatment of the symbolic aspects of organizational life reverberated at full volume in the 1980s as a new analytical perspective. In the 1950s, however, it was Selznick's structural functionalism that was to become a leitmotif for works to come. In that sense, Selznick as moral pragmatist is closer to our anthropological outlook than is Selznick as structural functionalist. But it was the latter that set the style for elephant watching for the next two decades.

Sociotechnical Systems and Their Doctors

The next elephant story is appropriately located in the country where elephants originated. Albert Kenneth Rice's *Productivity and*

Social Organization (1958/1987) tells the story of an organizational experiment conducted in an Indian textile mill in Ahmedabad. The experiment and the study were closely linked to the activity of the Tavistock Institute of Human Relations in Great Britain, where Eric Trist, a close collaborator of Rice, introduced the concept of a sociotechnical system, as a result of a study on the longwall method of coal mining in Great Britain. Two things may be added at this point: First, Eric Trist's education was as an anthropologist, but he found traditional methods wanting and opted for a systemic approach; and second, Indian industry at that time was still very much under the influence of the British industrial system.

The Site

In 1953 Ahmedabad Manufacturing and Calico Printing Company Ltd., popularly called "Calico Mills," was a company employing 8,000 people located mostly in the city of Ahmedabad, the capital of Gujarat, a northwestern state in India. Ahmedabad was the city where Gandhi started his march in 1933, and he was frequently involved in the fate of the mills. In 1953 Ahmedabad had about 1 million inhabitants.

The Calico Mills manufactured finished cloth from raw cotton and had a chemical division, with two plants, that manufactured bulk chemicals. The chairman of the company visited the Tavistock Institute in London in 1952, and presented his problems concerning the inevitable clash between the modern technology that his company had introduced and the traditional work organization. The latter was founded on the belief that, modern technology notwithstanding, the tropical climate, physical conditions, and standards of nutrition would always lead to a lower productivity rate in India than in highly industrialized countries with a temperate climate. So the Tavistock Institute, personified by Albert K. Rice, was given the broadly formulated consulting task "to collaborate with management and workers in an attempt to solve the social and psychological problems which faced them through changes in methods of work or of management" (Rice, 1958/1987, p. 6).

The Tavistock Remedy

The concept of sociotechnical systems assumed that every production system contained a technological organization (equipment and process layout) and a work organization (people and their tasks). The two must fit together to fulfill their function, as judged by the economic viability of the production system.

The Tavistock Institute took up the Elton Mayo tradition (the human relations school) in order to combine it with an open system theory as represented by Von Bertalanffy.

> Each system or sub-system has . . . at any given time, one task which may be defined as its primary task—the task which it is created to perform. Thus the primary task of private enterprise in a Western economy is to make profits, while that of a public utility is to give services. (Rice, 1958/1987, p. 32)

However, systems can also fulfill many other tasks, for example:

> At both conscious and unconscious levels production systems provide mechanisms for the satisfaction of social and psychological needs and for defense against anxiety. (p. 32)

This is one side of the fit between people and systems. The other side was well explained by Wilfred R. Bion (1961), the influential therapist of the Institute, who claimed that insofar as the employees' behavior is adult-like and reality-based, they contribute to the performance of the system's primary task. However, they might also be prone to "the hatred of learning by experience," that is, "the hatred of having to behave as adult human beings in a sophisticated and reality-based manner" (Rice, 1958/1987, p. 33). In this way, the knowledge coming from small, group laboratory experience was inserted into complex organizations on the assumption that complex organizations are, after all, composed of individuals with universal, psychological properties.

This was very typical reasoning for the period. Objectively existing social structures are filled with psychologically determined individuals, who together form a social system. The fit between these two "elements" guarantees the smooth functioning of a system. It is like saying that good theater consists of actors fitting the costumes and the stage, and vice versa. The play has been forgotten. But the latter is my metaphor, not that of the proponents of sociotechnical systems. Theirs is the organism, where organs should perform functions ascribed to them in the process of exchange with the environment.

A Doctor's Visit to Calico Mills

In Calico Mills, certain subsystems did not function as desired. One was the subsystem of automatic weaving. The new (British and American) technology was not supported by a change in work organization, and therefore failed to achieve the productivity increase envisaged. Rice analyzed the systems in terms of roles, tasks, and incentive schemes, and redesigned it for a better fit. (It should be noted, in passing, that he did not change the meal breaks routine nor did he introduce the third shift, even if both steps could be recommended for an increase in productivity. He was aware, though, that such changes would run too dramatically against current beliefs and attitudes.) The experiment was enthusiastically accepted, and other workers asked to be permitted to join. After a time, even changes in the meal break routines and a third shift were introduced without much trouble. However, "because of language difficulties and of the speed at which the reorganization was implemented, it was not possible to discover from the workers themselves just why they accepted the new organization with such spontaneity and with so little question" (p. 81). Rice tried to speculate as to what their feelings and attitudes might have been. Those speculations proved necessary when a fall in productivity occurred. But in time that was dealt with, too.

Rice acted as a "company doctor." He came to help an organism that was functioning poorly. He could not be "understood": One cannot talk to Tamil workers but neither can one talk to a liver. The only way to proceed was to manipulate the variables according to a certain medical theory, wait for results, and adapt the treatment when and if necessary. The understanding would come post factum, if at all. ("The surprising thing is not that efficiency fell at the end of October, but that it did not fall much sooner" [p. 95].) The interpretation ("what has really happened?") was purely speculative. It utilized, although marginally so (compared, for example, to Rohlen, see Chapter 3), the author's knowledge and understanding of the local context.

One could have formed an impression that the good doctor did not rely on science as much as he wanted us to believe, and that he relied on many things that he did not quite tell us and maybe did not even know himself: his intuition and his understanding of the ongoing events from the point of view of at least some of the actors. He was not merely an external consultant. It seems to me that the description of the second experiment, the reorganization of nonautomatic weaving, contains many more examples of real life events at Calico than the first. However, the sources of interpretation remain unclear:

> The second incident is concerned with the issue of permanent passes to those who had previously been "badli" workers in other sheds and who by new management policy were entitled to permanent passes in the experimental shed. . . . The new permanent passes were distinguished by the overprint of a letter 'R,' and the passes were known as 'R' passes. It was found that the 'R' stood for my name. While this distinction was intended as a compliment, it also represented a lingering disbelief among middle management, who had to issue the passes, in either the seriousness or the rectitude of higher management in making them permanent. (p. 150)

Rice, who devoted great effort into proving that productivity increased or that absenteeism decreased, did not tell us *how* he knew the above event was meant as a compliment, nor how he had arrived at his conclusion concerning middle management attitudes. I do not doubt the correctness of his interpretations. I only want to point out that he treated real life events as tiny anecdotes, irrelevant for the true substance of the experiment. If the "tissue of life" appeared in the description, it was to make colorful vignettes. The conclusions from the second case show, nevertheless, a struggle to keep the unruly life apart from the elegant explanation, which had been built on psychological dispositions combined with organizational structures. The phenomenology of the actors involved must be reduced to those two "factors," because the author's knowledge and understanding of local conditions grew more extensive as the difficulties became greater. This is even more striking in the third case, the reorganization of management, where the contacts were more direct, the time span longer, and the fight even fiercer. The final conclusion reads: "Results could not be adequately related to their causes, but the new management was able to exploit changing conditions more ably than had the old" (p. 224).

Sociotechnical Systems as Stylization

This is a purely hypothetical assertion, but I am deeply convinced that Albert K. Rice could have presented us with an amazing anthropological description of Calico Mills were that his aim. It is quite clear that, despite his inability to speak native languages (but then even the locals could not speak to Tamil workers), his contacts with the employees at all levels were frequent and intensive; that he was very interested in the history, customs, and traditions of the place; and that his knowledge grew as he continued his project. He acted as an unwilling anthropologist because the paradigm to which he aspired did not foresee a possible inclusion of this type of knowledge.

The credibility of a scientific report comes from a rhetoric that, following a tradition of a given time, is considered credible. The rhetoric used by Rice can be called "the style of scientism" (after McCloskey, 1985). The building stones of this tradition were scientific method, (context-free) universalism, and functionalism. And Rice's report is interesting not only as a classic and monumental work in its own right, but also because it shows how difficult it was to fit the fieldwork into a set of rules the authors themselves were creating.

Beginning with its method, the presentation is one long apology. The only quantitative data are data of "normal industrial practice"; these comprise the events Rice managed to record, either directly or through members of the company. It was impossible to keep variables unrelated, and also to conduct truly controlled experiments. Those who would tend to think that Rice's method must have been particularly faulty should be comforted by knowing that it could only be worse, never better. The field is not a laboratory, and no organization will do as researchers want. The question is, rather, why one would set up untenable standards.

Universalism was achieved by generalization and separation from the context. It is clear that the organization under study was situated in the cultural setting of an old and Eastern civilization, into which Western technology had been only recently introduced, and with limited impact. Nevertheless, "In our era, the majority of cultures are endeavouring to exploit the same possibility—the increased productivity arising from the application of technological advance to human effort" (Rice, 1958/1987, p. 5). In this sense, India could be seen as Great Britain in the early stages of industrialization. Culture became a matter of history.

It is probably the universal value of technological progress that explains the surprising fact that nowhere in the book does Rice analyze the possible impact made by himself, not as an external consultant, but as an English excolonialist. I believe he did not think it important; the technology came not only from Great Britain but also from the United States, and he felt himself to be its messenger, not its master.

Universalism is easy to understand as a result of functionalism. Functionalism, of the British make, becomes especially visible in contrast with Indian working culture. For the author it was obvious that all "adult, reality-based behavior" should be oriented toward the realization of the organization's "primary task," and it was painfully clear that Indian workers failed to understand this. This seemed to be due to lack of opportunity, however. The patience of the messengers from the world of technology would bear fruit by making everyone understand the objective laws of production systems: Bad work leads to dissatisfaction, and as such is unprofitable for everyone in the long run. This value system was both the reason for the study's scientific stylization and its result. It was not a matter of form as a tribute to fashion; it was a matter of form as a carrier of values.

Ultimately, and ironically enough, we learn much more about technological systems than about social systems from Rice's book. The book is an impressive work on the textile mill industry—with tales from India, Ahmedabad, and Calico Mills coming in through the side windows of the principal story.

Discovering the Continent: The Bureaucratic France

Michel Crozier troubled the quiet waters of Anglo-Saxon research by a powerful introduction to French bureaucracy in his book *The Bureaucratic Phenomenon* (1964), which contains two empirical studies and a theoretical essay on the subject. It should be added, though, that the first idea of his theory of bureaucracy came out of his discussion at the Center for Advanced Study in the Behavioral Sciences at Palo Alto, California, in the academic year 1959-1960, and that the first draft of the book was written in English, even if the University of Chicago Press only published it in 1964, a year after *Editions du Seuil,* Paris, France. The study was conducted inside two organizations—one in public administration ("Clerical Agency") and the other in industry ("Industrial Monopoly").

Clerical Agency

Clerical Agency was a simple organization in terms of work tasks and organizational structure. However, it was complex due to its size, the work load, conflicting requirements, and a mixture of efficiency and inefficiency. One could say that an insistence on keeping things simple made it into a delayed bomb of complexity. Traditional solutions, such as routine, discipline, pressure, and direct supervision in times of crisis, ensured efficient customer service, while eroding the base of the organization itself. This was an organization where traditional and bureaucratic aspects were in conflict.

Initially, Crozier spoke about "the Agency," which did or did not do something, "was caught in a vicious circle," and so on. The picture is clear and succinct, although we are not sure who hid behind "the Agency." Surely it was not female line clerks, nor even their male supervisors, who were responsible for this state of affairs.

Later, we reach concrete people through a work satisfaction survey, whose results were compared with similar surveys in other workplaces. There were no startling differences, we are told (although there was no analysis of significance, and the numbers do look different; at any rate, what we shall never know is how similar concepts of work satisfaction are among young French women in the Agency and the employees of an American insurance company in Chicago). But Crozier went further by interviewing the employees and presenting us with the contents of those interviews against the social background of the respondents. This led to the conclusion that it was impossible to understand the way the women saw their workplace without understanding the women themselves. And that, in turn, would be impossible without knowing the history, economy, politics, and public opinion encircling the Agency.

This, however, was only one part of the analysis, which concentrated on relations between the Agency's clerks and the cultural context of the Agency's operations. Crozier undertook another analysis in order to understand not only why the employees saw the Agency as they did, but also why things were as they were. That meant going up-the-line, toward the Ministry, and although the author apologized for lack of systematic surveys, the reader hardly notices this deficiency. The line of reasoning follows smoothly and with convincing examples. The result is a functionalist conclusion, but of a peculiar kind:

> Our argument finally relies . . . on the widespread reluctance of all members of the organization to accept situations where they must depend on and be controlled by the conventional hierarchy. Rules and routine, in that sense, may have a protective value. They ensure that no one can interfere in the internal affairs of the immediately inferior category. They give, therefore, a certain kind of independence. People do not participate, they remain isolated and they suffer as a result. But freedom with respect to personal involvement can be viewed also as an advantage. . . . They complain bitterly about the price they have to pay for it, but they are, in the last analysis, ready to pay that price. They adjust to it in a grumbling way but, one way or another, they adjust. (1964, p. 55)

How common might such adjustment be? Another study can help answer this question.

Industrial Monopoly

Crozier's second study encompassed intensive analyses of three plants and an extensive survey conducted in 20 out of Monopoly's 30 plants. Free interviewing was followed by observation, structured interviews, and group discussions. The research revealed a coherent set of reactions and attitudes on the part of one group of employees: the workers. Crozier speaks, therefore, about the workers' subculture:

> The content of this subculture is in opposition to the goals of the organization and the aims of management. It implies an idealization of the past, some pessimism about the present, devaluation of the future, and distrust of management. The group's demand for autonomy, and its affirmation of independence, are directed primarily against the organization to which it belongs. (p. 80)

One interesting methodological aspect worth observing is the way the "facts" support the "opinions":

> Generally speaking, workers have an image of their director as cold and distant and having no consideration for the status aspirations of his workers. . . . In fact the results show a rather low degree of interaction with the production workers. (p. 82)

The "facts" consisted of answers—by the same people—to questions, such as "How many times have you had a chance to exchange a few words with your director?" One cannot help but notice that "opinions" could have influenced the "facts," or rather the memory of facts, just as much as the other way around. Michel Crozier used a screen of statistics with great moderation, but it is nevertheless possible to trace this desire to support arguments with "facts," which are, of course, represented by numbers. This runs strongly against the interpretive tradition, which looks for interpretations of facts, and not the other way around.

The gender of the employees was lost as an issue, as Joan Acker and Donald Van Houten (1974) noted later. However, in discussing the workers' subculture, it returned as part of an issue that has since become standard in studies of large organizations: the power of the maintenance men. Their power replaced the power of the official line of command, which acted in accordance with an impersonal bureaucratic ideal.

Having noted various adjustment strategies—the hostile subculture of the workers, the illegitimate power of the maintenance crews (the topic that subsequently earned great attention from the Aston school, see the classic article by Hickson, Hinnings, Less, Schneck & Pennings, 1971), and the apathy of supervisors—as before, Crozier went deeper into the organization. The management group turned out to be a seat of eternal conflict, a conflict that was rooted in different occupational backgrounds. And these backgrounds also led to different patterns of adjustment.

Interpretations

From this book's perspective, Crozier's study provides an almost ethnographic description of two organizations and a very powerful nonfunctionalist message. Large organizations are not good places for human beings who, in order to survive (and, presumably, to earn their life and status in the society), make contorting adjustments where they resign some aspect of their own integrity in order to be able to safeguard more important aspects. Studying such patterns of (mal)adjustment could be a full-time task for an anthropologist of complex organizations. But let us return to Michel Crozier's own conclusions.

> The paralyzing structures and virtually irresistible mechanisms of routine that we have described seem closely associated with the fears, hesitations and conduct of all the participants in the matters of power and of relations of dependency. (p. 145)

These "empirical evidences" had to be interpreted. A missing link between threatening social structures and frightened individuals was searched for, and was found in two theoretical concepts: a combination of the sociological concept, *power,* with the psychological concept, *anxiety.*

Crozier's study is much richer in thick description than Rice's and more relaxed in its ambition to be "scientific." Nevertheless, when the final task, interpretation, is approached, the author leaves natives on their empirical ground to enter the realm of an external theory. This jump is justified by the fact that Crozier's method of collecting data, faithful to the tradition in which it originated, leaves a serious gap between social structures and individual actions and attitudes that must somehow be closed. How can we discover how they relate? The most obvious way, one would think, would be to ask the actors themselves. But this could not be done because of two methodological grounds.

First, natives' theories were not to be trusted. They probably did not know (if they knew, what is the role of the researcher?) or, if they knew, they might have had motives for misleading the researcher. Therefore, the most obvious and probably most interesting area of study—people's accounts of their actions—was ignored in this paradigm. Yet the natives' accounts do not have to be taken literally. It is the way they are presented that is the most promising source of interpretation. Such an interpretation might consist of confirming, challenging, confronting, or simply collecting native interpretations. The ways in which people lie are as informative as the researcher's observations from the outside, perhaps even more informative. Furthermore, if there is a unitary lie behind all organizational action, it tells us more about this action than some deeply hidden individual truths that are never revealed. The most common level of our experience is intersubjective—we act upon those subjective grounds whose reality is confirmed by other people.

The second, and perhaps more basic reason, was an assumption of general, objective causal laws behind the social action. However, if we exchange causes for reasons, it becomes obvious that the natives must be asked. (People allow themselves to be mistreated by social structures probably because they do not believe they can influence them.) Speaking the language of causes,[4] though, Crozier said that social structures caused anxiety that, in turn, paralyzed the actors.

The two arguments coincide: Actors could not possibly know the *causes* of their action (if they knew, they would have changed them), and therefore, it did not make sense to ask them. The opposite stance would claim that actors obviously do know their *reasons* and, confronted with a different reasoning, might change their actions. This, however, requires a mutual understanding on the part of the researcher and the actors. *Explanation,* in terms of objectified causes, will scarcely provide a platform for such a dialogue.

Interestingly enough, Crozier's main contribution, presenting organizational actors as "free agents who can discuss their own problems and bargain about them" (p. 150), prevented him from seeing them as social actors. Even if he noticed that they "not only submit to a power structure but also participate in that structure," he still considered it an individual behavior by actors in a game, actors who, though separated from each other, rationally calculate their losses and gains. Groups were seen as aggregates of similar individuals (production workers, maintenance workers, supervisors, and so on), as long as Crozier kept to the empirical ground. However, his speculations (intuitive interpretations, based on neither the theory nor the data) went precisely toward the social construction of organizational reality: the awareness that all groups have to coexist, the awareness of the interconnectedness of privileges, a general consensus concerning a minimum of efficiency, and the symbolic—and therefore not literally threatening—character of the power struggle.

Bureaucracy as a Cultural Phenomenon

Speculations about the empirical evidence were elevated by introducing purely theoretical arguments to the height of an essay that attempted to analyze the bureaucratic phenomenon against the cultural background of France. The task was somewhat opposite to that formulated in this book, although based on the same assumption about the crucial role of organizations in contemporary cultures. I want to understand organizations within their cultural contexts; Crozier claimed that the best way to compare and understand different cultures was to study organizations.

> It is through the medium of complex organizations that modern man can express himself realistically, and it is through this same medium that a society can learn by being confronted with the problems of action. (p. 211)

Crozier's final goal was thus more ambitious and far-reaching. It was also more risky because it concerned itself with "basic national traits" and the like. By the same token, the methods had to be different—Crozier's empirical studies become only a pretext for speculative reasoning on a macro-anthropological level. As such, Crozier's final essay is beyond our direct field of interest. One might say, however, that considering how daring the enterprise was (especially where he embarked on a comparison of French, Russian, and American bureaucracies), Crozier emerged from it far more triumphant than most who had attempted such a comparative *salto mortale*. The eloquence of the essay and its historical and literary richness indicate clearly that no matter how modest the anthropological ambitions may be, this approach requires a much broader knowledge than what is provided by standard courses in business administration.

Even so, the conclusions show how dangerous attempts at summarizing "national cultures" are. A Swedish reader will be very surprised to learn that "face-to-face dependence relationships are, indeed, perceived as difficult to bear in the French cultural setting" (p. 222), and that both the main strength and the dilemma of French people lie in "preserving the independence of the individual and ensuring the rationality of collective action" (p. 222)—both statements could have been taken directly from a description of the "Swedish mentality" (Daun, 1989). A malicious reader could go through the multitude of comparative studies and find exactly the same statements applied to many different cultures as culture specific. One must not forget Leach's warning against "comparing cultures," be they Balinese or French. The promising way out, it seems, is to treat "national cultures" as another type of social construction, influencing social action by virtue of their shared traits. (The French people who believe that "French culture" consists of given traits and accept it will probably be influenced by their belief; the same applies to those Swedes who believe that "Swedish culture" consists of certain traits, even if these traits may be identical.) Cultures are not so much what they *are* as what they *are believed to be*. . . .

A Double Message

Crozier's book is immensely rich, ambitious, and complicated. In this sense, it is not an easy model to imitate; the genius of its author makes it idiosyncratic. It offers us many important insights into the nature of modern complex organizations; it reasserts the importance of power relationships; and it conveys a very humanistic portrait of people coping ingeniously with life inside bureaucratic prison-shelters.

From a methodological perspective, the book is strangely dualistic. On the one hand, the author was extremely iconoclastic: We get enormous chunks of organizational reality, through legitimate or illegitimate channels (Crozier seemed to be very impressed by Melville Dalton's *Men Who Manage,* although he thought it exaggerated), and many intuitive speculations and subjective insights. On the other hand, the author was greatly indebted to the rationalist-positivist tradition: He wanted to be empirical, scientific, and functionalist. Crozier's attitude toward functionalism was perhaps the most telling feature. Functionalism is both bad and good, immoral and scientific, dangerous and unavoidable. Indeed, probably every organization researcher recognizes this dilemma and struggles for a way out.

The result is as dualistic as the way it was achieved—the recommendations are convincing, but the actual research practice less so. Social action, judged the most important of all, is studied only as a conjuncture of social structures and individuals; cultures become described not through the organizations studied, but as separate entities, comparable in their reified existence. Nevertheless, this duality, in itself, is proof of the inadequacy of older methods and the announcement of new, unorthodox searches to come.

Disclosure of a New Species: Women in Organizations

Organization theory, especially in its heroic, scientific versions, vests itself in a robe of objective impersonality. Discoveries build on previous discoveries (Smith, 1950; Brown, 1960; Karlsson, 1970; Czarniawska-Joerges, 1980). Science develops like a long red carpet, no matter whose shoes trample on it. And yet a biographical piece such as Perrow's (1980) reveals an amazing world hidden behind it. As in the movies, we learn who was married to whom, who left London for Chicago, and who was red and who was pink, and it becomes clear that this personal and institutional history has an enormous bearing on what science itself offers us. This sort of analysis, quite acceptable in philosophy or the history of science, is absent from organization theory so far, perhaps because the field is still young. Yet, I believe that it is essential to the discipline itself, and as such should be brought to life.

A book such as this can use this type of analysis, too. Therefore, I began to read the one part of books that I used to jump over—prefaces (for the most sarcastic and witty, I recommend Alvin Gouldner). It turns out that all this complementary knowledge—schools of thought and affiliations—is within our reach, even if it is unused. This applies to Kanter's *Men and Women of the Corporation* (1977). Her preface explains a great deal about her book, and why it is the way it is.

Corporations: The Most Typical Complex Organizations

Originally, the author set out to write "a rather theoretical account of how consciousness and behavior are formed by positions in organizations" (p. xi). At the same time, the consulting work in a large corporation was bringing in data that were interesting enough to make the author consider writing an ethnography of a corporation. Next, "the two streams came together" (p. xii), and a book emerged that can be counted as an anthropological description of a complex organization. The main difference between it and the approach emerging in this book is that *Men and Women of the Corporation* is a deductive piece of work, where ethnographical material serves to test and illustrate sociological, a priori categories. Otherwise, the goals and basic assumptions are identical.

Kanter also stressed the fact—trite by now—that the assumption that social action was a result of social structures and individual personalities was not enough. The very way in which they interlink had to be studied. Kanter unerringly located the rationale behind studies of complex organizations:

> [T]he corporation is the quintessential contemporary people-producer. It employs a large population of the labor force, and its practices often serve as models for the organization of other systems (p. 3);

and their obvious usefulness:

> Large corporations are often formidable and mysterious to people outside them, like giants that populate the earth but can only be seen through

their shadows. Yet informed participation in civic culture requires knowing more about how corporations operate or what people in them do than is contained in stereotypes of ambitious organization men or insensitive bureaucrats. Corporations are often equally mysterious to the people inside, whose views can be limited and parochial because they rarely get a sense of a whole. With the interest of villagers who have never seen the rest of the world, insiders often ask an outsider who has just travelled to another part of the organization, "Is it all like it is in my little corner? Is it the same other places?" Insiders, too, need the larger view in order to manage their situations, to understand the forces acting on them, to see options, and to consider alternatives. (p. 4)

When Kanter entered the corporation, she saw not so much that the emperor was naked, but that he was married.

Corporate Women

In most Western countries, women approach 50% of the working population. Due to gender segregation, clerical jobs tend to be allocated to them, and as complex organizations are characterized by disproportionately large overheads, the increasing proportion of women employed accompanies the growth of complex organizations. Nevertheless, organization theory needed Kanter to point this out. Previous studies, as Joan Acker and Donald Van Houten (1974) showed, dealt with "workers" or "employees," who, upon closer scrutiny, turned out to be men.

One possible explanation is that they might actually have been mostly men, at least at the beginning of the century, or in places such as the Ahmedabad Calico Mills. Alternatively, one can suspect that even if researchers did notice the gender of organizational actors, they were not sure what to do about it. The point is, it was not their place to be there. Within the societal structure, women's function was clear:

> The woman's fundamental status is that of her husband's wife, the mother of his children . . . (Parsons, 1949, p. 223). Where married women are employed outside the home, it is, for the great majority, in occupations which are not in direct competition for status with those of men of their own class. Women's interests, and the standard of judgment applied to them, run, in our society, far more in the direction of personal

adornment. . . . It is suggested that this difference is functionally related
to maintaining family solidarity in our class structure. (p. 174)

It would be very courageous, however, to analyze women's presence in organizations as a "societal dysfunction." A Solomonic solution has been reached—not to see. Michel Crozier could be a good
example: He noticed that all the clerks in Clerical Agency and nearly
all the workers in Industrial Monopoly were women, but he dropped
the subject like a hot potato, comforting himself that "[t]he sex difference, of course, is probably an important element in shaping the situation. But this influence should not be exaggerated. No comments
were ever made about it . . ." (Crozier, 1964, p. 97).

One important thing about organization theory before Kanter is
that, with the exception of Mary Parker Follet (who was dismissed in
the 1950s as unscientific and commonsensical), it was written by
men. Perhaps it took a woman to notice not only that a large proportion of corporate employees are women, but also that their gender
plays a significant role for them and their male counterparts. And so,
on the stage set by Kanter, we saw a gallery of roles: managers, secretaries (playing vicarious wives or mothers), and, outside but inside,
managerial wives. It is her analysis of the cycles of powerlessness in
which women tend to end up, and their minority position (tokenism),
that made Kanter's book famous.

The book culminates in a three-variable explanatory model: the
structure of opportunity, the structure of power, and the social composition of peer groups. The ethnography gives rise to a hypothetical
theory that is meant to be tested later on.

The Daughter of Her Times

In the preface mentioned above, Kanter recalled two books that
were of great importance for her work: Michel Crozier's *The Bureaucratic Phenomenon* and James D. Thompson's *Organizations in Action*. We have discussed the first, and most readers probably know the
second. It is sufficient to say that Thompson's book is the epitome of
a scientific formulation of organization theory: a set of law-like propositions, formulated and presented in a highly formalized way.

Kanter's is a dual book, where these two influences—"ethnographic" à la Crozier, and "scientistic" à la Thompson—coexist in the voices of both a "moral pragmatist" and a "structural functionalist." Listen to one of the final formulations:

> This study represents primarily a search for explanation and theory rather than just a report of empirical research. I was interested in understanding a complex social reality and its impact on the people who experienced it. I wanted to develop concepts that would make sense out of the actions of people located in different parts of organizational worlds. With Michael Crozier, I wanted to demonstrate that everyone is rational, that everyone within organization, no matter how silly or irrational their behavior seemed, was reacting to what their situation made available, in such a way as to preserve dignity, control, and recognition from others. (p. 201)

In other words, to have one's cake and to eat it, too—an explanation, but also an understanding; a sense, but a rational sense. How easy to understand and how familiar these strivings are.

Kanter stated initially: "Here people of the corporation begin to speak for themselves, as they do through the rest of the book" (p. 5). But they do not. The book is constructed like a television program with Kanter as a hostess, giving air now to the "people of the corporation," then to the researchers. There is nothing wrong with this kind of formula; in fact, it is very popular and highly legitimate. Still, it goes against the feeling of "how the life is over there" produced by the thick description; it is a projection of slides rather than a film.

Interestingly enough, it produces different effects depending on the topic. When Kanter speaks about well-studied phenomena, such as career opportunities or power in general, the use of sociological categories trivializes her report. Uncertainty, social conformity—we know all that. However, when she speaks about new things, such as women's roles, or the cycles of powerlessness or tokenism, the conceptual categories magnify the message and make it more penetrating. True, it can be said that there are fewer ready-made categories for these phenomena, metaphors rather than labels, and therefore, the theory emerges more powerfully from the ground of reality. But, after McCloskey (1985), one must also point out the legitimating role of the rhetoric. Unlike many feminists before and after her, Kanter introduced the gender problem through the main doors of organization theory, coating it in a proper language.

The Attractions of Reality

The dilemma presented here becomes almost paradigmatic: the wish to be scientifically detached combined with the lively interest in reality as it is, the language "as they speak" and "as we speak."

Kanter's study is probably the most anthropologically oriented among those introduced so far. Only Dalton went further, and she used his example, although she preferred Crozier's safer "rationality" paradigm. But Kanter's study announced what was to come in great numbers—ethnomethodological and organizational culture studies.

The greatest lesson for us who are potential students of complex organizations is this: There are still great discoveries to be made, despite those wishing to close their theories. There are emperors to be denounced, tribes to be located, and perspectives to be conquered. The elephant continues to change and to show unexpected aspects.

To see all these things properly requires effort, however. Kanter lists 10 different methods she used. Even if she counts them rather like Central European Catholics reckon their 14 dishes for Christmas Eve (that is, including salt, pepper, and bread), in both cases the net result is still impressive. Surveys, interviews, content analysis of documents, group discussions, participant observation, and free conversations are all quite natural tools in an attempt to understand a complex organization.

A Composite Portrait of Complex Organization

By now, a careful reader can be overwhelmed by doubt. Where are the scientific, positivistic, reductionist, value-free studies of organizations announced by Waldo? Even if we discount Selznick as preceding the mainstream proper, the impression remains the same. First of all, each of the scholars mentioned appears to be a moralist. It does not matter that they saw moral value in rationality: The fact remains that they all believed that organizations should be humane places, where people can maintain their dignity and develop themselves.

Inefficiency in itself was immoral, degrading to all concerned. Second, virtually none made a proper use of the positivistic method, even if they tried, and they all profusely apologized for deficiencies and inadequacies in their methods (with the possible exception of Kanter, whose conscience was clear both because of her industriousness and because standards had become looser by then). The point is that an attempt to study the whole of an organization (or even a big chunk of it) is a holistic enterprise by definition and, as such, does not fit properly into the positivistic framework. Studies of chosen aspects of organizational life that rendered themselves operable in terms of measurable variables best typified the period between 1950 and 1970.

In 1980 a third edition of *A Sociological Reader on Complex Organizations* appeared, edited by Amitai Etzioni and Edward W. Lehman. The two earlier editions were collected by Etzioni. The first edition (1961) begins: "Complex organizations constitute one of the most important elements which make up the social web of modern societies." The second edition (1969) starts: "Finding a balance between the rational and nonrational elements of human behavior is a cardinal issue of modern life and thought." Research in the 1960s made the issue of rationality versus nonrationality the central preoccupation in and about complex organizations.

The third edition is very comprehensive. It is a tribute to continuity. It reviews the most representative studies of the positivist period and it completes them with glimpses of what is to come: mavericks (in this context) such as Marxists, ethnomethodologists, and critics of the positivist method.

What Has Been and What Is to Come: Classical and Modern

Etzioni and Lehman's third edition (1980) commences with a reprint of Max Weber's "The Three Types of Legitimate Rule," (1922/1980). The reader who opens the book in the 1990s cannot help but reflect that at the time the book was edited, it was still assumed that traditional and charismatic authority were phenomena of the past, whereas legal authority was here to stay. The conservative 1980s, however, witnessed a triumphant comeback of both types of authority, even if through the side door.

Chester I. Barnard's "Organizations as Systems of Cooperation" (1938/1980), is another classic brought to our attention, in part to show continuity by documenting his relationship to Herbert Simon. Barnard's definition of organizations, "system[s] of consciously coordinated activities or forces of two or more persons," was later criticized for its unreflective harmoniousness. What is perhaps more interesting is Barnard's negation of reifying metaphors. Organizations are neither people nor buildings, neither machines nor organisms: They are systems of action.

James G. March and Herbert A. Simon, however, reformulated this definition: "An organization is a system of interrelated social behaviors of a number of persons whom we shall call the *participants* in the organization" (March & Simon, "The Theory of Organizational Equilibrium," 1958/1980). Coordination became interrelatedness, action became behavior—the intentionality was taken away. The harmonious aspect became more visible—persons became participants.

Dualism, the concept of social structures versus individual actors, became firmly established under the umbrella of functionalism (Robert K. Merton, "Bureaucratic Structure and Personality," 1957/1980). Organizations are social structures created to fulfill certain goals. Insofar as they damage the personalities of "participants," they can be seen as dysfunctional (for example, overconformity, trained incapacity, or erosion of organic solidarity).

These difficulties give us a pretext to evoke the ghost of human relations (H. Roy Kaplan & Curt Tausky, "Humanism in organizations: A critical appraisal," 1977/1980). Are self-actualization or other humanistic ideals at all possible in organizations? The authors conclude that researchers' ideological affiliations systematically distorted the image of reality: "Clinging to a belief in the desire for men to be creative and autonomous, they label as pathological the preoccupation of large segments of the contemporary labor force with material rewards" (Kaplan & Tausky, 1977/1980, p. 52). Human motivation is manifold. What should really be studied is the inherent conflict between individuals' egoistic interests and organizational purposes, be they profit or collective happiness.[5]

For an outside observer, the tendency of organizational theory to go to extremes and then to rediscover its equilibrium may seem very astonishing. The final result is usually a kind of contingency theory ("it all depends"). In his article "Closed-System, Open-System, and Contingency-Choice Perspectives," Richard H. Hall (1977/1980) comes to such a conclusion: "Rationality is still a key factor in the contingency-choice perspective. Organizations attempt to make their structure and operations rational by their strategic choices in regard to the environment" (p. 41).

The attempts to reintroduce and reestablish rationality as *the* basic rule of organizations will continue and intensify, together with various attacks on rationality. In this light, even the traditional opposition—Marxists—came closer and closer to the mainstream, especially those Marxists who were also positivists and structuralists.

Nevertheless, Marxists initiated a stream of critical theories, and their inclusion in the third edition proves the increasing importance of their critical thought (Wolf Heydebrand, "Organizational Contradictions in Public Bureaucracies: Toward a Marxian Theory of Organizations," 1980; and J. Kenneth Benson, "The Interorganizational Network as a Political Economy," 1980). Two other mavericks were Erving Goffman's "The Characteristics of Total Institutions" (1957/1980), which firmly documents that studies of different organizations permitted the survival of a different methodology, and John W. Meyer and Brian Rowan's "Institutionalized Organizations: Formal Structure as Myth and Ceremony" (1977/1980), the article that earned the authors a classification as cynics (see Perrow, 1972/1986) and portends both symbolism and neoinstitutionalism.

Had the book been edited, say, five years later, the number and kind of alternative theories would have multiplied dramatically. Theories that Etzioni called "modern" would now be called "modernist" to differentiate them from "postmodernist" theories—which teaches us that "contemporary" is a much safer adjective to use.

What Have We Learned About Organizations?

In between the tributes to the classics and glimpses at the "sidestreams," lies what can be seen as the most representative course for the mainstream of 1970s organization theory. Etzioni and Lehman's compendium addressed most of its attention to problems of structure.

Processes, the main focus of study today, were limited to a short section on organizational change. Instead, we have all the possible variations of relationships between structure and other elements, for example James D. Thompson and William J. McEwen's "Organizational Goals and Environment," (1980) which spoke about the relationship between structure and goals.[6]

But it is the section on "Structure and Technology" that contains the most impressive aspects of that period of organization studies: the findings of the Aston group (David J. Hickson, D. S. Pugh & Diana C. Pheysey, "Operations Technology and Organizational Structure: An Empirical Reappraisal," 1980; and Howard E. Aldrich, "Technology and Organizational Structure: A Reexamination of the Findings of the Aston Group," 1980). The Aston group was perhaps alone in managing to truly study complex organizations within the dominant paradigm. They succeeded in doing so by reducing organizations to a series of variables (for example, centralization, hierarchy, and technology), which, once made operable and measured, could then be confronted and composed into theories.

Leadership was studied in a similar vein. Stanley Lieberson and James F. O'Connor's "Leadership and Organizational Performance: A Study of Large Corporations" (1980) is a breathtaking demonstration of operationalizing macro-variables in such a way that the individual level is considered along with the organizational and environmental levels.

Etzioni and Lehman's *A Sociological Reader on Complex Organizations* (1980) also lists the problems of an organizational society: women's tokenism, by Rosabeth Moss Kanter; contents of grand ideologies, by Charles E. Lindblom; disappointment of codetermination, by Herbert R. Nothrup; and ends with a section on methods. This section is headed by an article coauthored by Paul L. Lazarsfeld, who, together with Talcott Parsons, can be seen as primarily responsible for this period and paradigm. Lazarsfeld, the methodologist of modernism, wrote with Herbert Menzel: "On the Relation Between Individual and Collective Properties" (1980). But later in the same section Morris Zelditch (1980) already wondered, "Can you really study an army in the laboratory?" The new, rebellious times begin to show their true face. Or so it seems to me.

In all fairness one must admit that Neil J. Smelser, the editor of the *Handbook of Sociology* (1988), identifies "social structure" as the central organizing concept in sociology. Structure is still a very relevant concept in organizational theory:[7] The new rebels coexist with old rebels. Or maybe it is just the rhetoric that changes: We speak about "processes," "phenomena," and "cultures," rather than about "structures," "variables," and "strategies." But the way we speak about things reflects the way we think about them; so it is not *just,* but *even* rhetoric that changes.

A Fragmented Picture

It is easy to wisecrack 10 years later at someone else's expense. But the fact is that what we oppose today is also the thing that brought us to where we are. A rebellion against the church of one's childhood is indirect proof of that church's influence. And, I do not propose to start organization studies from scratch. After all, we all stand on the shoulders of giants, as Merton (1965) put it, or, as McCloskey (1985) corrects him, at least on a pyramid of midgets.

Nevertheless, the compendium as a whole does not present a convincing picture of complex organizations. In the 1960s, when computers were on their way into people's private lives, the magazines were fond of presenting various types of composite pictures produced by computer. I remember an attempt to produce an image of the ideal woman. The computer took Ava Gardner's eyebrows, Sophia Loren's mouth, Grace Kelly's forehead, and so on. Well, the result was far from satisfactory. The journalist who wrote about it commented that the spirit of the whole beauty was lacking, even if the parts were all very correct.

That is also, in a sense, the impression left by the composite picture of complex organization. We have accumulated knowledge of its various aspects, but our understanding of the phenomenon is still rudimentary at best. With an ethnography of a given organization, such as Kanter's or, even more so, Dalton's (from which I will draw below), we may not have a feeling that we understand all complex organizations and certainly not the whole of the phenomenon, but at least we have glimpsed concrete organizations, and we seem to understand what makes them tick. This is not to say that single case studies are the only or the best method of studying organizations. It is rather to say that we need a variety of approaches to get at this particularly awkward elephant.

Men Who Manage and the Man Who Studied Them

What happens if a representative of the "true" sciences, a chemist for example, joins the social sciences? One result is caustic remarks such as the following: "Influenced by the dogmatism of nineteenth century science, research methodology in the social and psychological sciences is now more cocksure than in the increasingly humble physical sciences" (Dalton, 1959, p. 273). The natural sciences can afford intuition and "sympathetic understanding," but not the social sciences:

> The dominant attitude in the social sciences today is that science implies a method, a procedure characterized by the invariant steps of hypothesis, observation, testing and confirmation. It is presumed that (1) following these steps is a simple matter confirmed, and agreed to, by all scientists; (2) personal feelings must not and do not enter into the pure inquiry—except to check such feelings; [and] (3) this is the only route to valid knowledge. . . . (Dalton, 1964, p. 51)

Another result is a study conducted in accordance with the sarcastic spirit of these remarks and therefore in disaccord with the dominant paradigm, a study called *Men Who Manage: Fusions of Feeling and Theory in Administration,* by Melville Dalton (1959). Everybody quotes Dalton's study, but nobody is advised to imitate it. Written by a "marginal researcher" (as Dalton described himself, alluding to his double role as a practitioner and a researcher, and under the guidance of Herbert Blumer), this work helped to preserve the spirit of an insightful, qualitative study throughout the scientistic paradigm's years of dominance.

How and What Do They Manage?

Dalton studied the actions of managers in four companies: Milo (where he himself was employed, and was therefore a focus of his study), Fruhling, Attica, and Rambeau. His was not, however, a comparative study in the traditional sense of the word. He did not do four separate studies that were then compared. Located at Milo, he encountered many puzzling phenomena that he attempted to understand. Comparison was a natural imperative to him: He first looked back at his old company, Fruhling, and then moved, more purposefully, to Attica and Rambeau, while still working at Milo and studying it. A grounded theory in a nutshell: Constant comparison is an imperative in the sense that, in order to call something red, one must first see something that is not red.

Dalton studied managerial actions, not in the inventory-like way Mintzberg (1973) did, but as a system of meaning. In order to do this, particular actions had to be connected to a wider context of time, other people, the company, other companies, the community, and other organizations. The search started with his own puzzle:

> A participant at Milo and Fruhling, I was repeatedly puzzled by the gap between official and unofficial ways of doing things, and by the emotional splits and name-calling among associates devoted to one general approach or the other. (Dalton, 1959, p. 3)

As he went on, he discovered and described power struggles: official versus unofficial authority, operation versus maintenance, and actual versus formal practices of control. Soon, he was digging at least one level under the surface. He discovered that cliques (groups with shared interests) were fountainheads of action, that union-management relations were "a blur of conflict, cooperation, and compromise initiated and guided by cross-cliques" (p. 146), that managerial careers followed political and religious, and not merit and seniority ladders, and that many cues to what was happening in a company were to be found outside.

A Naive Chemist in the Jungle of Social Science

Dalton's picture of management was horribly clear and penetrating. What is more, it was not condemnatory. Even if practices such as theft and nepotism were openly discussed, and although the author made it clear that he did not accept them, he did not deliver the final sentence. Worse, he went even further: "All the firms we have described were normal. All were economically sound, and none have been involved in public scandals or have been the target of whispering campaigns" (1959, p. 262).

He continued, in the same balanced tone, that conflict was typical, and although some of its outcomes were positive there were many that were negative. Each company had a right to confidentiality, but that right was extended to acts that were illegal and dishonorable. Rationality was compromised by social demands. Organizations as entities were legal fictions—in reality they were sets of actions embedded in larger sets of actions. One result of this embedment was, among others, that many actions that were harmful to organizations realized and conserved "human nature," and many actions that were beneficial to organizations harmed and disrupted that nature. Conformity kills individuality, but it also preserves individuals by providing them with a protective mimicry. What is more, the battle between impersonal organization and the personal individual is old: "At least as early as the fifth century B.C., Athenians were yearning to escape urban conflicts" (p. 271).

Dalton's managers were caught in an existential struggle, and that is why functionalism was an irrelevant criterion for evaluating their actions. For each functionalist, there is another, either somebody else or a different order, which makes dysfunctional what was functional, rational what was irrational, and so on.

Dalton's study is a deeply humane and penetrating study of organizations. No wonder it made its all too human audience uneasy. If Dalton used the protective covering of an ideology, those who espoused it would acclaim him as a great denouncer, and those against it would denounce him as a great demagogue, and all would be safe. I see him as a victim of the scientism of his time: He took matters seriously and presented his results as he found them.

Preconceptions and Methods

Prompted probably by comments on his "unscientific approach," Dalton wrote a separate account of his method, more detailed than the one contained in the Appendix to his book (Dalton, 1964). In this account, he made a clear breast of his biases—"preconceptions"—that ruled his research method. Because they seem to be quite universal, I will repeat the most important of them here.

Dalton admitted to having been led in his work by hunches, which he then consciously refused to treat as hypotheses. Any hypothesis—even a private one—is a kind of commitment that could then prove obligatory. Hunches may be dropped, or abandoned for better hunches; hypotheses must be tested, binding time and intellectual resources to defend what can turn out to be not much more than personal vanity. Besides, "Probably all is hypothesis save the one absolute, that we must continue to hypothesize ourselves to new positions from which to make more helpful hypotheses" (Dalton, 1964, p. 55).

Even in the absence of hypotheses, the general expectation of the time was to present quantitative data. Dalton did this to a certain degree, but not much, noting, however, that with some ingenuity probably all the data could be fitted into tables, provided he did not mind cutting them out of the context that made them meaningful. This he refused to do, on the assumption that meaning is the final target of research, not the form that it takes.

> My preference for idea over number has probably been buttressed by my unsystematic observation, in and out of the academic world, that idea is usually supreme over number as an influence in thought and behavior. Idea also dominates those with the idea that number is more important than idea. (Dalton, 1964, p. 56)

Finally, there are ethical questions naturally raised by an undercover study, a study without official permission but with unorthodox techniques. I remember that I was fascinated when I read in Glaser and Strauss (1974) that Dalton had bribed a secretary in order to get access to confidential personnel files. If we believe Dalton, he did not bribe the secretary. She used him as a marriage consultant in exchange for access to files, and eventually won the bitter prize and married her chosen man against sound counsel.

But the matter is more serious and more general. Dalton classified himself as an ethical pluralist (in contrast with dogmatic idealists and ethical nihilists). Between absolute values and "everything goes," there is a field where the individual continuously has to make moral choices. In the case of social research, this means that "the social investigator must sort his values and obligations and weigh them repeatedly throughout the research process" (p. 61).

This does not imply that ethical pluralism is the only attitude that permits good social research. But it does mean that all researchers are obliged to admit their ethical stands before, during, and after they embark on any research project. "Scientific impersonality" is not an escape from moral dilemmas.

Dilemmas are embedded in any study of complex organizations. To begin with, as every experienced researcher knows, there are basically two kinds of organizations—those with problems and those with access. (A third category, giving access because of its problems, expects help, which creates an even more complicated moral situation for the researcher.) Company loyalty, as we know, can also lead to corporate crime. In any case, loyalties, disclosure, and openness are all personal questions. The only route that should be absolutely forbidden is the escape route—pretending these questions do not exist. By conducting one formal interview, we are already meddling with the social tissue of an organization, and we must take this into account.

This brings us to the question of the techniques used. Unlike Kanter, Dalton diminished his merits by reducing them to formal interviews, work diaries, and participant observation. Despite this short list, Dalton was actually an extraordinarily rich source of ingenious, unobtrusive techniques (besides, he simply forgot the document analysis in his list). Not all of these techniques are universal—the choice must be personalized.[8] But I would like to emphasize the importance of work journals or diaries, which are usually mentioned in passing by authors and not taken seriously by students. Dalton gives a very convincing account of how and why they are important.

Values and Methods

There is no doubt, I imagine, in the mind of readers, that I personally consider Dalton's study one of the most important models to follow. And yet, I understand that the reason he is not recommended to young students has to do not only with his "unscientific" method (which is becoming increasingly legitimate again), but also with the generally idiosyncratic character of his study. Who could plan to become employed at Milo, and, if one could, who would be able to conduct such a study successfully? After all, Dalton himself has not repeated his success. (Maybe he was banned access to any organization for years after.)

We cannot plan such things. But we can be prepared to take any opportunity of that sort when it arrives, and in the meantime, do our best in approximating it. As Rosalie Wax's touchingly honest account of her anthropological work over the decades shows, chance and luck are coauthors of every study. She and her husband devoted years and enormous effort to starting a study that never took off. And, at the very beginning of her career, she was placed in a very unclear role in a Japanese detention camp, the study of which made her famous (Wax, 1974).

The moral is to hold tightly to your (research) values and to make your methods flexible. Each situation and each organization requires adaptation and specific understanding. It is a pathetic enterprise to confront them with stiff research principles, laboriously elaborated in one's office. To quote Dalton for the last time: "Only a godlike student may align himself with the *one* god in research conduct" (1964, p. 61).

Rhetorics, Rationalities, and Morals

Concurrent with organization theory's rapid development, structural functionalism and positivist empiricism had the lead in the social sciences. Organization theory, unburdened by any long tradition, swiftly followed suit. Because of its heritage, anthropology was much slower, which resulted in its often being perceived as staying "an episteme behind" (Geertz, 1988, p. 7), even if this same "backwardness" helped to preserve methods and perspectives that are now coming into focus. Janowitz observed:

Because of the heritage of anthropology, the typical monograph is by its very substantive character likely to avoid the extensive trivialization and mediocre character which characterize much research in psychology and

sociology generated under pressure of "theorizing" or of immediate social problems. But, by contrast, the heavy hand of competence prevents
these anthropological materials from being relevant for any broader comparative and theoretical analysis. (1963, p. 151)

In other words, the strength of anthropology—a fieldwork search for
meaning and holistic perspective—did not fit the spirit of the times
and was not an inspiration for organization theory. Of course, anthropology itself followed the spirit of the times—in structural functionalism, empiricism, and the reductionist perspective—but organization
theory was far ahead, ever so agile, and following the sociological
avant-garde more closely.

In all fairness, one must say that the scientistic orientation was more
often an ambition than a result. Indeed, it seems more helpful to speak of
a rhetoric of scientism than a methodology of positivism, as an actual
way of proceeding while conducting an inquiry (with the possible exception of experimental studies, for instance in psychology).

Positivism was kept alive more in the minds of opponents than in the
daily practice of scientists, becoming in the end more epithet than signi-
fier, more the ghost of horrified imaginations than a coherent body of
thought. (McGee & Lyne, 1987, p. 383)

Under the cloak of scientism, researchers seemed to be deeply involved
in pondering the uneasy junction of rationality and morals. Organizations, seemingly the epitome of rationality, produced results damaging to
humans. Was this due to rationality or to a lack of it? Was "more rationality" or "different rationality" a functional solution?

Selznick and Dalton adopted the perspective of moral pragmatism,
where judgments, if they were to be made, must be based on existential grounds. Practical solutions work, if they fulfill other functions
than those for which they were created. Such an interpretation would
be difficult to maintain, however, if organizational practice is to be
understood against the background ideal of instrumental rationality.
This ideal assumes absolute dimensions within the scientistic approach. Constant, direct contacts with organizational realities, as in
anthropologically oriented studies, would prove threatening to this
ideal, as Crozier's and Kanter's experience indicates. Rice's work

was, in that sense, closest to the core of the paradigm. Avoidance of ethnographic knowledge helped avoid the rationality-morality dilemma.

It is only recently that pragmatism has returned as an interesting perspective (Rorty, 1982), opening old and new possibilities of redefining the dilemma. This, however, does not mean that its previous formulation did not teach us much. As Waldo said:

> A study of stock phrases and postures in the opening and concluding portions of social science writings is interesting and, if one is so inclined, amusing: predecessors generally have been stupid, confused, and bemused. Now, however, there are Momentous New Developments, we are beginning to Get the Subject Organized, and the present essay hopefully is a Modest Contribution to that end. (Waldo, 1961, p. 216, footnote 6)

Let us then conclude on a different note: Our predecessors have been giants, on whose shoulders we all stand. The issues they formulated and tried to illuminate remain with us, and if we are able to try new perspectives, it is partly because the old ones have been tried. Further research is informed equally by dissatisfaction with the results already achieved as by the increased understanding that these results brought. And this search, in several instances, aims at returning to the crossroads where anthropology and organization theory parted many years ago.

Notes

1. Although barred from scrutiny, the approach was doubtlessly an inductive and a qualitative one. The quantitative data served as a background presentation of relevant facts.

2. It is interesting to notice that his spiritual guide into the domain of pragmatism was John Dewey, maybe the only pragmatist whose ideas could be reconciled with Talcott Parsons's, Selznick's guide into structural functionalism.

3. This tendency to objectify was, of course, also present in the anthropological version of structural functionalism. However, as I try to argue, the constant and prolonged contact with actual people in concrete situations inevitably brings moral issues back into the picture, and thus into research itself.

4. On explanation by causes and explanation by reasons, see Richard H. Brown (1977) and Chapter 8.

5. I predict that in years to come we shall witness another breakthrough in organizational motivation studies. Somebody is going to discover that people would like to be creative, well rewarded, *and* autonomous. All it takes is introducing such a question into a survey (until now, respondents had to choose between various rewards). Somehow, no one thought they might want it all.

6. Surprisingly enough, the editors decided to put Michael D. Cohen, James G. March, and Johan P. Olsen's "A Garbage Can Model of Organizational Choice," (1972/1980) under the same heading, probably to record the success of the no-goal, anarchistic model of organizational structure.

7. On the other hand, the "processual [sic] analysis" seems to acquire a central position in anthropology, or at least in its interpretive branch (see Rosaldo, 1989).

8. For example, I could not resign from tape recorded interviewing because I am unable to memorize interviews as Dalton did. Taking notes, of course, is not a solution at all with open interviews, because they require the interviewer's active participation.

5

Ethnomethodology:
Taking the Cover Off Everyday Life

What Anyone Like Us Necessarily Knows

Far from the objectivity of functionalism, past the intersubjectivity of
social constructivism, on the solipsist pole, resides cognitive anthropology, which claims that culture is located in humankind's hearts
and minds, and only there. Somewhere before that, one can find
ethnomethodology as formulated by Harold Garfinkel (Garfinkel,
1967; also presented and discussed in Heritage, 1984, and Mullins,
1973).

Ethnomethodology: Revealing the Taken-for-Granted

Social life consists of accounting for what one does in the presence
of other people, imagined or real, who serve as auditors. The point of
such accounting is to prove the (situational) rationality of our actions,
and therefore our social competence. Only children and the insane are
not under such obligation, but children's socialization is actually a

training in such accounting. Accountability is a sign of social competence. Where there is no actual accounting (one does not have an audience, either during or after the action), the action is nonetheless tentatively accounted for, for oneself or for potential audiences. (Why am I doing it at all? or If my boss questions what I did, I shall tell him that . . .)

The process of accounting (which for some people, for instance physicians or social scientists, constitutes their work) is characterized by three traits.

First, there is an unattainable wish for a tenable distinction between context-bound and objective (context-free) expressions. The professionals (for example social scientists) tend, when faced with the inevitable failure of fulfilling this wish, to exempt themselves from their self-imposed demand, presenting elaborate grounds for their exemption.

Second, the accounts are usually not the focus for the accountants themselves. (One could say that they are not interested in doing sociological studies of their own actions, although they could if they wanted to.)

Third, thanks to this lack of interest in meta-accounts, what is taken for granted can thus continue to be taken for granted—an accounting of the accounting would break down the "taken-for-grantedness." Accountability, then, is an aim in itself that when achieved becomes an accomplishment. Hence, everyday life is an accomplishment for its participants, whom Garfinkel calls "members." To put it in Berger and Luckmann's terms, the end of a day is a success to the degree that the social reality did not collapse, which it sometimes does in times of personal or social crises.

Ethnomethodology, then, is "the investigation of the rational properties of indexical expressions and other practical actions as contingent ongoing accomplishments of organized artful practices of everyday life" (Garfinkel, 1967, p. 11). The three traits mentioned above apply to the lay members of society and to social scientists alike. "Lay accountants" want their accounts "objective"; and researchers avoid analyzing their own accounts.

Garfinkel's studies of lay and professional accounts led him to conclude that, basically, the *how* and the *what* of talking are indistinguishable. Therefore, the how is the only way of approaching the what. Any interpretation of talk (what they really talk about is . . .) is an instruction "in how to use what the parties said as a method for seeing what the conversationalists said" (Garfinkel, 1967, p. 29). Thus even when we arrive at the deepest level of interpretation, all we know is *supposedly,* even if we continually aim at an *actually:* "To recognize what is said means to recognize how a person is speaking, e.g. . . . narratively, or metaphorically, or euphemistically, or double-talking" (Garfinkel, 1967, p. 30). Shared meaning or, as Garfinkel calls it, a "shared agreement," is not an agreement on substance but on method; "rationality" is a method that is acceptable without discussion (that is, a Schützian concept of rationality, Schütz, 1964b). Hence, ethnomethodology looks at the method and logic of accounting for practical, everyday actions, with the assumption that this method and logic are intelligible only within the context that they took place. Social contexts are self-organizing, that is, they have a drive toward accountability. In other words, social contexts are *sets of methods and the logic of accounting.* (We know that we are out of "our" context when the accounts of persons who seem perfectly competent socially, are unintelligible or seem irrational to us.)

> Every kind of inquiry without exception consists of organized artful practices whereby the rational properties of proverbs, partially formulated advice, partial description, ecliptical expressions, passing remarks, fables, cautionary tales, and the like are made evident, are demonstrated. (Garfinkel, 1967, p. 34)

Life is incomplete sentences (Rotter, Rafferty, & Schachtitz, 1949), and our social competence is judged on the basis of how well society accepts the endings we give them.

Garfinkel's ethnomethodology is a significant contribution to the theory of action. Heritage (1984) summarizes this contribution in the following terms:

> [W]hat is self-evident is that the actors treat their own and one another's actions as the intelligible products of knowledgeable subjects whose talk and conduct is more than a conditioned babble. It is self-evident too that these same actors believe themselves to be, and treat one another as, confronted by real choices in conduct for which, unless "excused," the chooser will be held accountable as the agent of his or her actions. (p. 130)

How can such a theory of action be used in studies of complex organizations?

Ethnomethodology and Complex Organizations

Ethnomethodology can be seen as a kind of basic social research; an anthropology of complex organization is, by comparison, an almost applied type of study. Leadership as management of meaning (Smircich & Morgan, 1982) assumes the management of ordinary descriptions (Heritage, 1984), but puts it to a specific use. Organizations are built on the foundation of everyday life, but organization-specific life differs substantially from everyday life.

One major difference is that it is taken for granted to a much lesser degree. In a sense, complex organizations are always more problematic than other everyday life social settings, such as families or communities. Our involvement in organizations, if increasing, is still of limited duration; the socialization process, if expanding, is still of limited scope.

An obvious illustration of this is the presence of many explicit (and therefore, open to discussion and negotiation) rules. Compare, for example, the fact that a statement such as "your line was busy" almost without exception solicits the explanation,[1] whereas an unwritten rule stating that one should give one's name or position while answering the phone in the office is continually challenged, debated, and defended. Most people never even notice that saying "your line was busy" produces apologies and explanations, whether they were to say it or to respond to it. People who are rude (that is, who do their private Garfinkeling) sometimes say at the end of these explanations: "It's none of my business who you talked to." Both sides know it is rude, but it is hard to say why, unless one is aware of the hidden rule.

In offices, however, some people think that one should answer with the name of their unit and not their name, whereas others defend the opposite point of view, believing that giving the name accentuates willingness to take responsibility. All of this is openly discussed. In Sweden, people respond with their names or telephone numbers even at home, which many foreigners consider impolite ("bureaucratic") or misleading. In the work place, rules are usually much more on the surface of the actor's awareness, even if the socialization processes try to hide them. But organizational acculturation is neither as deep nor as enduring as societal acculturation, and those who live happily for years in complex organizations are often put out by deviants, mavericks, uncouth youth, or innovations. "What do they really mean by that?" is a common question, and accounts of the accounts (which meet with hostility in a marriage) are a common activity in an office. Practical interest leads organizational actors to a reflection similar to that fed by the theoretical interest of self-reflective researchers. Rationality is not a taken-for-granted, inherent trait of all acceptable accounts. It is an openly formulated request and a separate subject of investigation (accounting is, after all, a profession exercised in economic organizations).

In addition, the social competence of "members" is, comparatively speaking, very local. In other words, social contexts are narrow. There is a core of things that are taken for granted, but they can be very alien to a newcomer. In that sense, studies of complex organizations need to be anthropologically oriented—organizations are alien settings, and even within them there are very few fully competent natives. In formal organizations, members are not expected to be fully competent, except in the usually narrow area of their competence. We have a much wider repertoire of commonly understood actions in everyday nonorganizational life than in the organizational world (compare, for example, going to different shops with going to a meeting in another department).

One could point out at this junction that all of Garfinkel's studies were conducted in organizations: the Los Angeles Suicide Prevention Center and the UCLA Outpatient Clinic. However, these studies did not focus on organizational life, but on an intellectual activity of inquiry and classification that happened to be an important element of work in those organizations. (This is also relevant for the analogy Garfinkel makes between lay inquirers and sociologists: His "lay sociologists" are also professional inquirers.) The point is, in a great many organizational positions, the job itself is taken much more for granted than the organizational life. (As long as I sit and type my stuff, I can account almost automatically for what I do, but just think about the most incomprehensible behavior of the director at the last meeting! And do we really have the right to discuss and analyze it in the coffee room afterwards?)

Garfinkel proposed challenging (disrupting) the structure of everyday life if we want to see how it is built. But in complex organizations, there are many challenges already in place. (This is, by the way, another strong point for making anthropological studies, that is, a direct and long lasting type of inquiry.) It is relatively easy to present a rational account of taken-for-granted organizational life to an outsider in a single encounter, but it is almost impossible to maintain this façade when, for instance, the researcher has to wait an hour for an interview in the secretary's office. (This is why clever secretaries put the visitors alone in a waiting room, with the most boring public relations brochures around.) In that sense, organizational actors accomplish much more in comparison to other "members." Every completed organizational day is a wonderful achievement. Also, we are Garfinkeling a great deal in our research, quite instinctively. We interview organizational actors, and when they say, "You know how it goes," we truthfully say, "Not really. Could you explain what you mean?" Is it not common sense that the one who governs in a specific complex organization can be challenged and it is not perceived as an insult as it would be in a family?

But the most important point in Garfinkel's work is his most convincing plea for a search for meaning. He told his students to make a "behaviorized" account of their home life. Here is an example:

> A short, stout man entered the house, kissed me on the cheek and asked, "How was school?" I answered politely. He walked into the kitchen, kissed the younger of the two women, and said hello to the other. The younger woman asked me, "What do you want for dinner, honey?" I answered, "Nothing." She shrugged her shoulders and said no more. The older woman shuffled around the kitchen muttering. The man washed his hands, sat down at the table, and picked up the paper. He read until the two women had finished putting the food on the table. The three sat down. (Garfinkel, 1967, p. 45)

Garfinkel's main point is that the student's impersonal "objectivity" broke the social tissue and made other people angry and offended. I would like to emphasize the absurdity of this "objectified account," which looks like a perfect sociological account, according to the "observer from Mars" ideal. Joining the social context, in life and in the story, would reveal in no time that the people were a "family" and that they were having dinner. But think of the effort needed to discover the *meaning* of this event if we did not know it already and were forbidden (as were the students, or the researchers trained to "objectivize") to communicate with the people we observed.

But let us return to the main difficulty with Garfinkel's perspective: his extreme social constructivism, which verges on solipsism. It is easy to agree that texts are part of reality; but it is more difficult to accept his thesis that they are *all* of it. Organizations are not texts, but a text is a common form of interpretation that we deal with. (The text can also be a visual image, but the same reasoning applies.) I claim that we can get at *what* the actors are talking about through *how* they speak. The structure of account is operational, but it does not mean that I, as a researcher, have to stop at that; intersubjectivity gives me an additional opportunity.

When Garfinkel instructed his students to play onlookers in their families, this break with convention—objectivity—brought forth different accounts of different families, as Garfinkel himself said. Some were loving and happy, and some were bickering and hateful. Similarly, we use, as laypersons and as researchers, different accounts concerning one and the same reality in order to learn about this reality. If a complainer tells us the resort we planned to go to for a holiday is windy and has bad food, we listen to a "positive thinker" next; we might even include a travel agent's account (assuming that it is not an expensive trip and he would not be overly interested in selling it to us). But, even if we take into account their specific methods and logic, our final conclusion concerns the beach in Fuerte Ventura and not the peculiarities of these accounts, even if we might throw them in only to discount them later in an attempt to account for our own rationality.

Hence, let us break and doubt the rules, in order to see how they work—to see the substance of which they are an inseparable part. The fact that their duality cannot be proved by anything but hypothetical and artificial separation does not mean that this duality does not exist. There is no soul without a body and no substance without a form—if I am allowed to run the old list—but a solution that recommends only the study of the body and the form does not solve much.

In summary: To understand people's actions, one has to look for the meaning attributed to those actions by the actors themselves, and by the observers. This does not mean that there are some meanings that are "better" than others; as long as they make sense to some people (even to researchers), the meanings are acceptable (therefore extreme naturalist and extreme positivist perspectives are rejected). However, this does not exclude moral judgments. As a researcher, I can register various meanings that are moral judgments; as a person, I can accept some of these judgments (provided that I do not use my researcher's authority to support these). Ultimately, learning the *techniques* of making sense, of looking for meaning, is very important, even necessary, but this is not the end of the pursuit, at least not for a student of complex organizations.

Life Is a Linguist's Tale

There are several differing interpretations of the various aspects of ethnomethodology as professed by Harold Garfinkel, ascribing to him a more or less solipsistic epistemology, a more psychological, or a more sociological perspective, and the like. He is said to be misinterpreted often (see Heritage, 1984), and his studies differ very much in character (compare "Agnes, The Case of Gender Change," Garfinkel, 1967; and "The Discovery of Pulsar," Garfinkel, Lynch, & Livingston, 1981). But there is one person among his associates—Aaron Cicourel—whose work most clearly illustrates the two traits commonly attributed to cognitive anthropology, or ethnoscience: the subjective character of social reality and a microscopic approach to it, through analysis of social interaction, accomplished by the use of language.

Refreshing the Old Concepts: Social Roles and Social Norms

Language and meaning, says Cicourel (1974), are at the core of all social interactions. Thus any analysis of social phenomena must be performed in these terms.

> Social structure remains an accountable illusion of the sociologist's commonsense knowledge unless we can reveal a connection between the

cognitive processes that contribute to the emergence of contextual activities, and the normative accounting schemes we use for claiming knowledge as laymen and researchers. (1974, p. 7)

It is quite possible that traditional sociological categories, such as social roles (including institutionalized roles; also called "status" or "formal positions") and social norms (including "internalized social norms"), can continue to be useful for meaningful analysis, but they must prove relevant to the understanding of the social interactions they propose to interpret. This is not to say that these terms must be identical with those used by the actors themselves, but they must relate to recognizable social reality. (Indeed, it would be very hard to imagine a "lay" social actor using ethnomethodological terminology.)

This can be achieved if we treat social roles as processes of role taking or role making. Cicourel reiterates (after Ralph H. Turner [1962], a pupil of George H. Mead):

The actor is not the occupant of a position for which there is a neat set of rules—a culture or set of norms—but a person who must act in the perspective supplied in part by his relationship to others whose actions reflect roles that he must identify. (p. 22)

No matter how well specified a role as a "wife" or a "professor" is supposed to be, every person who undertakes to play one of these roles plays it anew, tentatively. As Milan Kundera put it mockingly in the *Unbearable Lightness of Being,* "What can life be worth if the first rehearsal for life is life itself?" And the performances and expectations of others—husbands, students—are among the most important factors shaping this tentative performance. The concept of social norms must be revised accordingly.

Provided there are some norms, how do actors recognize those that are relevant for them or for the situation?

The actor must be endowed with mechanisms or basic procedures that permit him to identify settings which would lead to "appropriate" invocation of norms, where the *norms would be surface rules and not basic to how the actor makes inferences about taking or making roles.* The basic or interpretive procedures are like deep structure grammatical rules;

they enable the actors to generate appropriate (usually innovative) responses in changing situated settings. The interpretive procedures enable
the actor to sustain *a sense of social structure* over the course of changing social settings, while surface rules or norms provide a more general
institutional or historical validity to the meaning of the action as it
passes, in a reflective sense. (Cicourel, 1974, p. 27)

Notice the all-pervasive linguistic metaphor, which comes to domi-
nate the whole analysis. This metaphor leads to focusing on *social
cognition* as the only process of significance.

Interpretive procedures are to replace the notion of "internalized
social norms." They allow the actor to assign meaning to (find sense
in) the environment. Normative, surface, rules—social norms—allow
actors to concert their behavior into a collective action. Normative
rules constitute the shared meaning—not necessarily in the sense of
acceptance, but of recognition. ("This person blows his nose into a
handkerchief. Even if I think it is horribly unhygienic, and would
never do that myself, I recognize his action. I know he has a cold.")

As in the above example, the interpretive procedures ("I know he
has a cold") provide a sense of social order that is crucial if the normative order ("one blows one's nose when one has a cold") is to be
negotiated ("handkerchief or paper tissue?") or constructed ("let's
stay away from each other while you have a cold"). Interpretive procedures are necessary to make sense of social norms; the social order
and the normative order are inseparable. Cicourel proceeds to explain
the analogy between these two and the linguistic surface structure and
deep structure; he then moves toward his main interest: the study of
acquisition of social structure—the way in which children acquire a
socially approved sense of meaning.

Is Communication All That There Is to Social Action?

We enter a big factory hall with an assembly line at its center. A
woman passes by on an electric truck; she arrives at the head of the
line, unloads her truck, and leaves. A young man is loading a similar
truck at the end of the line. Thirty men and women are sitting on both
sides of the line, busy with what they are doing. They do not speak to

each other. Some of them follow us with their eyes when we pass by on our way to the director's office.

What we observed was, undoubtedly, collective action. All these people were collectively assembling a product, with a form of technology—the line—coordinating and controlling their actions. It was also an interaction, in the sense that the collective action was not parallel, but required cooperation and created dependence. And, finally, the action was undoubtedly social in the sense that all the actors participated in a situation that was common and known to them all. It would be impossible to work on an assembly line without knowing what an assembly line was and that everyone's work depends on his or her neighbor and that every neighbor is similarly dependent on their neighbors, and so on. The point is that the interaction is accomplished without the use of language.[2]

It is possible to portray technology, in this case an assembly line, as a materialized piece of one-way communication: a nonhuman autocrat that gives orders and does not allow discussion. It is, however, doubtful whether such a metaphor would be fruitful, especially as Cicourel himself strongly opposes reification of social constructs (Cicourel, 1974). But it is clear that ethnomethodology, as professed by Cicourel, ignores all practical action, which is crucial for social life in general and complex organizations in particular. Otherwise, life is indeed nothing but a tale.

Cicourel's ethnomethodology, however, is very successful in doing just what it proposes to do:

> [to study] . . . the general problem of how persons in different social or cultural groups have sought to develop, represent, and evaluate their communicational strategies . . . how social or cultural groups create something we have called "language," the way the representational form captures and truncates our experiences, and the way we use language to make claims about knowledge. (1974, p. 9)

In other words, cognitive anthropology can contribute a great deal to the study of communication processes in complex organizations, mostly because it never loses sight of the social aspect, unlike cognitive psychology. Assuming that people carry social structures in their heads is partly a matter of ontology and partly of perspective. Seeing social life as purely a material for the cognitive processes of an individual (who may, for all we know, just be imagining the whole thing), which most cognitive psychologists do, misses the social character of our lives. Cognition is a social process, says Cicourel, and it is hard not to agree with him.

Elephants Under the Microscope: Organization Studies

Conversation analysis almost inevitably invites a micro-perspective. This is especially visible in ethnomethodological studies of complex organizations.

Organizational Careers

David Silverman and Jill Jones conducted a study of organizational careers: how people get into and through an organization (1976). The study was an ethnomethodological account of rules of events as collected in conversations with and among selectors, trainers, administrators, and appraisers.

What is striking in their account is that it hangs suspended in nowhere—or rather, in an organization, which itself hangs suspended in nowhere. Yet the reader notices some clues: the English class system here, the public sector there, but they only lurk behind the conversation. The threads are never picked up to form a complete picture, probably in order to avoid reification of concepts such as social structure, culture, or the like. Even if big chunks of the socialization process are presented in detail, we still do not know whether this is the whole story, parts of the story, or just special exhibits. And career paths are never presented as streams of events or acts, we only witness some conversations related to some careers.

This is not a methodological criticism. Indeed, Silverman and Jones's study is one of few that do not "exempt themselves from self-imposed demands on good grounds," to paraphrase Garfinkel. Besides, it does not make sense to criticize a biologist studying a cell under a microscope for having failed to describe the whole of the elephant from whose skin the cell was taken. The biologist knows that the elephant exists, but he cannot conduct analysis on more than one level.

Nevertheless, for those interested in elephants, studies like Silverman and Jones's will be disappointing. Their final conclusions are as follows: In their organizational actions, people follow a complicated set of implicit and explicit rules, which they try and are able to account for, both before and after the action, and spontaneously or upon request, therefore reproducing and clarifying those sets of rules. Accounts, themselves, are also submitted to some sets of rules, because the rules exist only when applied (or broken).

But we already knew that after reading Garfinkel. What we do not know, and what does not interest the authors, is just what rules are constructed and applied in this public administration organization, which elements of context are relevant for their understanding, which people are promoted, and whether they are happy with their promotion.

On the other hand, ethnomethodological approaches can be highly suitable in certain political contexts. In his study, Krzysztof Konecki (1990) presented a shocking and richly detailed picture of ridicule and flirtation in a Polish factory. The study was like a window through which a Western voyeur could peep through the Iron Curtain. But the window was of limited size, and it was only possible to connect this picture to macro-descriptions of the political and economic system only through guesswork, even if it was painfully clear to the reader that there was such a relationship. I doubt that there were any conscious political decisions involved, but if Konecki had tried to relate his micro-observations to the wider Polish reality, we would probably have had to wait a long time to see his results in print. (The study was done in Poland during the period of martial law.)

It is worth stressing that Silverman and Jones deserted the extreme subjectivist, solipsist stance. They sought "to analyze the practices through which talk and written reports *come to stand* as depictions of an external social structure" (1976, p. 140). This is very important because it stresses that people feel that social structures are something external, which must be taken into account if we want to understand their actions. Alas, this is where Silverman and Jones stop. As a reader, I would like to know the contents of these "depictions of the external social structure," because I believe them to be maps that guide the actions of organizational actors. But this is not the same as taking them for "representations of a world unproblematically available to participants and researchers alike" (Silverman & Jones, 1976, p. 140). These representations are constructed by social practices, then enacted in consecutive actions, and accounted for in socially acceptable terms; all three stages are part of the circular social construction process.

Ethnomethodology aims at a general theory of meaning (Cicourel, 1974). An anthropology of complex organizations should be interested in *forms and contents* of repetitive processes in the social construction of organizations.

Organizational Work

Insofar as ethnomethodology can be derived from anthropology, one can ascribe to it one of the anthropological sins: ethnocentrism. Most (although not all) ethnomethodologists assume that the world is populated with "lay sociologists" and that life is a "nonscientific inquiry." In other words, people do for free what social scientists do for money. Like any other metaphor, this one should be judged in terms of the increased understanding produced.

The point is—understanding of what? In their final chapter, Silverman and Jones state emphatically that they are interested in how meaning is constructed and represented *in general:* The organization studied was only a pretext for analyzing meanings constructed, for example, in scientific communities. Latour and Woolgar's study (1979/1986) ended up with a similar "convergence theory" conclusion; that is, natural scientists do the same thing as social scientists (the natural scientists were not amused).

These studies were an answer to an appeal by Garfinkel, formulated at the 9th World Congress of Sociology at Uppsala in 1978:

[T]he studies-of-work programme is directed to analyzing the specific, concrete material practices which compose the moment-to-moment, day-by-day work of occupational life. These practices are treated as endogenous to the work domains in which they occur and which they constitute.

Access to these practices is gained through the fact that in a variety of ways—some tacit, some partially formulated—they are produced and recognized by the parties to work environments as locally accountable competencies in working activities. (Heritage, 1984, p. 293)

This is important because there is a gap in the social science literature: Systematic descriptions of occupational activities are rare. It is easy to agree and to applaud Garfinkel's program, especially as he did not espouse Cicourel's linguistic subjectivism, but instead proposed to study "concrete material practices" and, generally, took

... a theoretical stance which lies beyond not only traditional determinisms which imply unrealistic levels of predictability in the social world, but also the Pirandello-esque worlds of "anything goes" interpretivism which end up threatening the very possibility of a stable social world. (Heritage, 1984, p. 307)

Although it is not necessary that the result of studies of work will remain the "all is social science" statement, especially if the participants in the program move to occupations that do not have inquiry as their central objective, we can for a moment assume that this is its main result. At least, this applies to the existing studies. The question is then, how studies of work can help us understand complex organizations—no doubt to a great extent, but they cannot be truly exhaustive. As a social scientist, I can see clearly that my work and my organizational action are very different. My work is guided by professional and societal rules that I consider appropriate for an intellectual in my time and area. My organizational action is guided by rules created by my school and the group I belong to, which sometimes includes the professional rules, but which, more often than not, I see as an impediment in complying with the latter. My work takes place within professional paradigms, and I went through three different ones in the same period of time—20 years—through seven organizations, with only loose couplings between paradigms and organizations (pluralistically-minded organizations tolerate many different paradigms). My work is far from unproblematic for me, for my colleagues, and especially for "external spectators." I tend to reflect upon it, to disrupt it, account for it, and so on. But all these activities do not help me much in understanding my organizational life, which is only loosely coupled to my work, and much more problematic. There are also some obvious connections between organizational life and general everyday life; the latter being, I suggest, the basis for the former (how to greet each other, how to dress, how to be angry, etc.). Nevertheless, neither studies of work nor studies of everyday life can replace studies of organizations. But they might contribute.

Organizational Talk

Silverman and Jones's book, methodologically impeccable, permits what many other studies promise but fail to deliver: a reinterpretation of their results. For me, the study reveals talk as an important organizational action, leading to results as concrete as any technical production process (Czarniawska-Joerges, 1988b). What appears to be a series of conversations, in fact shapes human lives, making people into organizational members or refusing them access, channelling their feelings and shaping their aspirations, promoting or degrading them—in other words, shaping their organizational career. What was traditionally presented as "decision-making," turns out to be a group sense-making process, wherein following a legitimate technology is more important than the inputs and outputs of the process. Or, rather, what are considered "inputs" must be drastically redefined. It is not inherent attributes of people or objective rules for the career path in a given organization that are revealed and reconfirmed in interactions between candidates and recruits, young officers and training personnel, or members of selection and promotion committees, but various interactional properties attributed to both people and rules. The organization is constituted by these interactions that are seemingly "just talk," but are actually a complicated social action, crucial in any complex organization.

A study of work was very close to a study of organization in Latour and Woolgar's study (1979/1986), both because the organization as such was not very complex (it is the work that imposes complexity on organization) and because it was situated in the center of the workplace (a Nobel prize-winning laboratory).

Here, again, organizational talk was shown as action that produced important results. Discussions led to decisions about what is a fact and what is not, which led to papers, which eventually led to the Nobel prize. Latour and Woolgar reconstructed the rules of scientific conduct and professional reputations (by affirming some and challenging others), and enacted interpersonal relations between organizational members. Talk is not the whole of a complex organization, but it is a great deal of it.

Organization-Related Concepts as Experiential Constructs

The following is an illustration of the possible uses of ethnomethodology as professed by Egon Bittner (1965) and applied to my own study of the concept of power (Czarniawska-Joerges, 1988b, 1990b). Bittner (1965) differed from many other ethnomethodologists[3] in that he claimed that investigations by lay actors are not the same as those in social science inquiry:

> Insofar as the procedures and considerations actors invoke in relating terms of rational commonsense construction to things in the world exhibit some stable properties, they may be called a method. It is, of course, not proper to assume that this method is identical with, or even similar to, the method of scientific inquiry. (p. 247-248)

But the most attractive feature of Bittner's work was the fact that he was interested in complex organizations, which he called "formal organizations."

We were speaking, at the outset, of ethnomethodology as "basic" research on social life, as for example, in the analysis of greetings (Heritage, 1984). Greetings take place in organizations as elsewhere; but organization-specific greetings are practices that are constructed with the "basic stuff of everyday life" as the foundation and with organization-related specificity added, which creates an action that is both like and unlike everyday life. The question is, how to use ethnomethodology to do research on this specific aspect of organizational life. Bittner made the first step in this direction by postulating that the "scientific" concept of formal organization was, in fact, a common-sense concept borrowed unreflectively from social reality:

> In general, there is nothing wrong with borrowing a commonsense con-cept for the purposes of sociological inquiry. Up to a certain point it is, indeed, unavoidable. The warrant for this procedure is the sociologist's interest in exploring the commonsense perspective. The point at which the use of commonsense concepts becomes a transgression is where such concepts are expected to do the analytical work of theoretical concepts. (Bittner, 1965, p. 241)

Thus Bittner proposed to study the concept of organization as a common-sense construct. Going further, one can proceed to study organization-related concepts as *experiential constructs*. I have used his prescrip-tions in a study of organizational power as a commonsense construct (Czarniawska-Joerges, 1990b).

To paraphrase Bittner's reasoning, if we isolate the concept of power from the world of everyday organizational life, it becomes empty, in the sense that we do not know how it relates to (and to which) facts: "Without knowing the structure of this relationship of reference, the meaning of the concept and its terms cannot be deter-mined" (Bittner, 1965, p. 247).

In order to tackle this difficulty, a researcher can use one of three procedures. The first consists in assuming that "the unexplicated com-monsense meanings of the terms are adequate definitions for the pur-pose of his investigation" (1965, p. 247). Thus one could think of constructing a questionnaire asking questions about power distribu-tion, power allocation, power structure, and so on, on the assumption that the respondents know what power is and that what they know is identical with what the researcher knows. (This is, of course, a fully defensible assumption if the researcher is able to prove the existence of relevant shared meanings.)

Another procedure, and a more common one, is to ascribe an opera-tional definition to the concept. For example, "power is when *A* makes *B* do what *B* otherwise would not have done." This procedure proposes that the actors reject their own perspective in favor of the researcher's.

The third procedure, and the one I adopted in my study, is to discover the meaning(s) of the concept by studying its use in real situations of action by people who are considered socially competent (in these situations). In this case:

> [I]n order to understand the meaning of the actor's thought and action . . . one must study how the terms of his discourse are assigned to real objects and events by normally competent persons in ordinary situations. (Bittner, 1965, p. 247)

The investigation starts when (and because) the researcher notices the phenomenon in question in the same way that everybody else in the social setting does. One must first check, then, whether people in organizations talk about power without being prompted. When we know that actors are using the concept, we can proceed to look for its meaning, which is located, as already stated, in relation to actions taking place in the actual social setting. We can discover and establish this relationship only through actors' accounts of their own actions. Note that observation in itself is not sufficient; it amounts to the second procedure (the researcher's definition dominates: I define what I see as "power"). Nor does it mean that we should adopt a naturalist perspective: Actors' explications of power do not establish what power is; they only explicate how actors construct their concept of power.

In other words, the concept appears as a general formula to which certain events (actions) are assigned. Our task as researchers is to find out which formula, and therefore establish how this assignation takes place. The assignation gives the events "a distinctive meaning that they would not otherwise have" (Bittner, 1965, p. 249). The fact of person *A* standing in the corridor and smoking acquires meaning by relating it to the action of a group of nonsmokers, who fought for the introduction of a ban on smoking in working areas. We know now that *A*'s smoking in the corridor is an instance of "effective power."

In my study of power, the fact that organizational actors spontaneously used the concept of power justified my subsequent questioning of people for their accounts of organizational power. I therefore asked students of business administration to describe concrete events illustrating organizational power. The results showed, in the first place, the difference between competent and incompetent actors. While most of the students had jobs, and almost all considered themselves organizational actors in their schools, some denied being organizational actors and proceeded to define organizational power according to theoretical definitions that they had read. Their *definitions* did not, as a rule, tally with the *descriptions* supplied by their colleagues.

In the second place, the study revealed a set of techniques for assigning organizational events not just to a general formula of power, but also to a multiplicity of formulas. In other words, although people use similar methods to construct their concept of power, it does not mean that the result is one and the same reality. Organizations differ; organizational power differs. The fact that we cook white and red sauce for pasta in basically the same way does not mean that they taste alike; they do not; the ingredients are not the same. To use Heritage's formulation, the actors' accounts are *indexical*—they must be interpreted by reference to where, when, and how they occur. They are *reflexive*—they maintain or alter the sense of the activities they refer to. But, unlike ethnomethodologists, I claim that they are also *representative*—not in "the mirror of nature" sense (Rorty, 1979), but in the social sense of representing. Collected intersubjectively, they represent a kind of social reality of which they themselves are a part. They do not represent "objectively," "truthfully," or "once and for all." They do represent "intersubjectively," "for all practical purposes," and "for the time being."

Ethnomethodological Possibilities

Let us study the methods of constructing complex organizations. It will allow us to understand what they are, or rather, what they mean. The main difference between a possible anthropology of organizations and ethnomethodology is not, as I see it, the basic methodological assumptions, but the goal. The substance of everyday life is known, and this is the form that must be better explicated. The substance of organizational life is not known, and must be discovered through the study of its forms. And the key to this study lies in interpretation, which is the main tool of ethnomethodology.

I am thus subscribing to this moderate version of hermeneutics, which assumes that the understanding of a text includes the reader's experience, the author's intentions, *and* the "subject-matter about which it was written, the question that called it into being, and to which it is an answer" (Palmer, 1969, p. 235).[4] All of this is embedded in two contexts: an author (or organizational actors who account for their actions) and a reader (or an observer, like myself). All of these are intertwined and inseparable, but none of them can represent singly all of the others: forms *and* content, author *and* reader, their context *and* mine.

Stewart Clegg constructed a triangle of various approaches toward defining language (1987). According to him, ethnographers treat language as transparent: It reveals a reality outside of itself to which it refers. Ethnomethodologists see language as opaque, to be regarded as a social reality. Clegg proposed to see language as material, as one of the important media for and outcomes of the accomplishment of both social structure and social action.

Within such a framework, my approach is closest to the ethnographic one, with the caveat that language reveals a "reality outside" as seen by the speakers; in other words, language is like television. Besides, this definition combines rather than chooses between the three definitions above. Television is transparent because, as an institution, it builds its meaning on the assumption that it shows some other reality than the one that is immediately accessible to us. It is opaque in the sense that we literally see what we see, a picture on our television screen. As technology, it is undoubtedly material. What better metaphor for language in its complexity: the convention, the vision, and the technique.

The television metaphor reveals further possibilities. Switching between the channels creates the sense of relativity; switching off the television gives an opportunity to examine the apparatus itself. All such operations can be subsumed under the name of interruption (Silverman & Torode, 1980). Thus language can be seen as transparent and material depending on whether the analysis concentrates on what a text *says* or what it *does*. For an organization analyst, both are clearly of relevance.

Notes

1. The example comes from Heritage (1984, p. 127ff.)

2. Our interpretation will always be couched in linguistic terms. Similarly, "tacit knowledge" does not mean that its possessors are mute, only that their vocabulary is hard to reconcile with that used in our interpretations, that is, it is difficult to understand their actions.

3. Incidentally, Bittner thought that Garfinkel shared his opinion (Bittner's article was published two years before Garfinkel's book).

4. Palmer speaks about literary criticism, and thus the term "written."

6

Political Anthropology:
Antidote or Complement?

Political anthropology, mostly with a Marxist background, and therefore with an objectivist, materialist, and structuralist slant, may seem
a straightforward opposite to subjectivist, symbolist, and process-oriented
ethnomethodology. Yet they share a critical stance, in all variations,
toward the positivist methodology, and in some, toward the taken-for-
granted aspects of complex organizations, either on humanitarian or
political grounds. Perhaps a dialectical synthesis of both would prove
fruitful.

This chapter discusses attempts of this kind. It starts with Abner
Cohen's presentation of the assumptions of political anthropology,
and its illustration: his study of the power elite in Sierra Leone. Michael
Burawoy and his Hungarian counterpart, János Lukacs, present, rather, a
political sociology with an anthropological pitch. Finally, there is an
attempt by Richard H. Brown (theoretically) and Tony Spybey (empirically) to reconcile organization study's political perspective and
interpretive method.

Political Man and Symbolist Man

The Aim and Specificity of Political Anthropology

Abner Cohen followed Edmund Leach's type of social anthropology to a significant degree, but he did not hesitate to cross the threshold between "primitive" and "complex" societies. According to Cohen (1974), a political anthropology should be "a systematic study of the dynamic interdependence between power relationships and symbolic action in complex society" (p. ix). Compared to a possible anthropology of complex organizations, such an aim is narrower in the sense that it excludes material (or physical) action that interests students of organizations. On the other hand, the aim is much wider, as it proposes to encompass all power relationships in a society: in formal and informal, contractual and normative organizations. Power is taken to be an aspect of almost all social relationships. Thus Cohen proposed to study *politics* as such and, further, chose informal organizations as a specific focus for his study. Nevertheless, the methodological question he asked was the same as that which is at the core of this book: Can theories, concepts, methods, and techniques of social anthropology be adapted for the study of complex organizations in modern societies?

Cohen contrasted two possible ways of approaching anthropology, that of Geertz and of Lévi-Strauss. Geertz's approach, he claimed, was interesting but noncumulative; it lacked systematicity. Lévi-Strauss's approach was systematic, but concentrated on the individual and cognitive at the expense of the social and political. Why are there no social *and* systematic studies? In other words, why has sociology not used anthropological inspiration to a greater extent? Because, maintained Cohen, complexity and change in large, modern societies blurred patterns of social action; a holistic approach was not feasible. On the other hand, the pressure to quantify led to a search for what was quantitatively measurable, neglecting what was relevant. Symbolic actions and formations are basically "dramatistic" and therefore not quantifiable. Paradoxically then, due to the lack of proper quantitative measures, it could still be claimed that modern society is secular, manipulative, and rational. But any study interested in social institutions had to put symbolic, unquantifiable action back in its place.[1]

The major shortcoming of anthropology, Cohen pointed out, was also its main strength. Anthropologists used to study small, primitive societies, and therefore were never paralyzed by overwhelmingly complex subjects. Nor did they worry much about breaking the social issue. These experiences, according to Cohen, should be spotlighted and used for studies of complex societies.

Symbolic and Political Orders

Even if Cohen chose to study everything that was *not* a formal organization, his approach was very instructive for the lucid treatment of symbols:

> Symbols are objects, acts, concepts, or linguistic formations that stand ambiguously for a multiplicity of meanings, evoke emotions, and impel men to action. (Cohen, 1974, p. 23)

Hence cultures, customs, norms, values, myths, and rituals could all be categorized under the generic term *symbol*. Cohen continued to emphasize the instrumental role symbols play through their connection to power relationships:

> For the individual, symbols are fundamental mechanisms for the development of selfhood and for tackling the perennial problems of human existence, like life and death, good and evil, misery and happiness, failure and misfortune. Although they can be said to be phenomena *sui generis* existing in their own right and observed for their own intrinsic values, they are nearly always manipulated, consciously or unconsciously, in the struggle for, and maintenance of power between individuals and groups. They may be said to be "expressive," but they are at the same time instrumental. (1974, pp. x-xi)

Similarly, they are concurrently subjective and objective. Cohen reconciled the idea of objectively existing social structures with Berger and Luckmann's idea of the social construction of reality. Symbols are created and interpreted by individuals. But once they have become accepted by a group,[2] they also become objective, in the sense that they confront the members as things that exist independently and will influence their action. Very often they become public and acquire the character of a collective representation coming from ("authorized by") a given group. That means, among other things, that social interpretations of symbolic action cannot be kept separate from individual interpretations, as dealt with in psychology. Collective interpretations, albeit created by individuals, in their turn influence the formation of individual interpretations.

An understanding of this spiral-like relationship is necessary in order to understand the role and meaning of symbols, not the least of which are organizational ones:

> For most of us, the major groups, the great corporations, to which we belong take care of this side of our life (problems of human existence) as well as of other sides. They provide us with explanations, sharpened by the endeavours of expert ideologists, and also offer remedies. They teach us that we die, but continue to live within our lineage, motherland, nation, the party. We are made to identify with and project ourselves into a continuing, eternal, force which is larger than ourselves, within which we should continue to live after our death. (Cohen, 1974, p. 62)

This is Wilfred Bion, or Sociotechnical Systems, *au rebour*: It is not so much that organizations have a function of anxiety removal, but that they try to tempt us into believing that they can accomplish such a feat. Cohen saw it as a conscious, political attempt undertaken by interest groups. Objectifying relationships between individuals and groups, accomplished by symbols and contributing to stability and continuity (without which social life could not exist), was one of the most important conditions for such an attempt to succeed. An interest group may not know when a time for action will come, but stable symbols will help it to be prepared:

> Through the "mystification" which they create, symbols make it possible for the social order to survive the disruptive processes created within it by the inevitable areas of conflicting values and principles. (1974, p. 31)

In this sense, symbolic order is more "conservative" or more stable than political order. It is possible to change the power order overnight, but not the symbolic order. The two are not mechanically, but dialectically related, Cohen contended. They are basically autono-mous or, as Karl Weick would have it, loosely coupled. The conserva-tism of the symbolic order is relative, because it is close to existential issues. Additionally, symbols are ambiguous (open to many interpre-tations), flexible (dynamically preserving the precarious equilibrium of social reality), and tend to be integrated into meaningful wholes ("systems of meaning"). Nevertheless, symbols are also powerful car-riers of change.

> It is this lack of mechanical "fitness" between the symbolic order and the power order that makes socio-cultural change such a significant field of study. For it presents the social scientists with situations in which old symbolic forms perform new symbolic functions. The detailed analysis of this dialectical process will shed substantial light on the processes of symbolization and institutionalization. (Cohen, 1974, p. 39)

All that remains is to see political anthropology in action.

The Dramaturgy of Power in a Modern African Society

To avoid the methodological problems of attacking the power or-ders and symbolic orders in such gigantic units as the Western nation-states, one can study smaller-scale, developing nation-states. For such a study, Cohen chose the power elite of Creoles in Sierra Leone (Cohen, 1981; the study was, however, conducted in the early 1970s, and its publication was deliberately delayed for political reasons).

A power elite is a group that seeks to validate and sustain its elite status by claiming to possess rare and exclusive qualities essential to the society at large ("excellence" of some kind). Liberal societies do not recognize such status as legitimate, and therefore power elites cannot use formal organizations to achieve their purposes. An effec-tive power elite is perceived as a social category, but it operates as a social group. It develops its organization by transforming rational, consciously thought out organizational strategies into nonrational, self-mystifying symbolic forms.

Cohen proceeded to describe Creole identity in terms of two vari-ables and their dialectical interdependence: *culture* (symbolic forms)

and *power* (positions and professions of authority). Apart from ana
lyzing these variables separately and together, Cohen also revealed
them in certain crucial dramatic performances: a ball, a university
graduation ceremony, a funeral, and a thanksgiving service. I stres
this as a technique of analytical exposition that is very typical in an
thropology yet seldom met in organization theory.

The assumed mutuality of influence between symbolic and politica
orders gave Cohen an unusual methodological tool with which to dis
cern power elites. The customary approach was to look for people ir
power and see what kind of symbols they employed. But, said Cohen
the opposite should also be possible. Look for someone who is best
described and characterized by the (then) dominating symbols and
you will know who the power elite is. (At that point, the readers can
conduct a little exercise of their own.)

The performances, called dramas ("a drama is a limited sequence of action, defined in space and time, which is set aside from the ordinary flow
of purposeful social activity," 1981, p. 156), served as pragmatic tests of
both the accurate location of the power elite (or any other group of interest)
and the plausibility of the analysis. If everyday reality is confirmed daily
by everything that we do, the ceremonies, rituals, and dramas provide an
intensive, condensed confirmation. One could say that dramas, especially
serial ones, deal with deviances accumulated since the last time—by ex-
purgating them or by incorporating them. The most successful change of a
ritual takes place during the ritual itself. (Remember Scarlett O'Hara,
dressed in mourning clothes, dancing with Rhett in *Gone with the Wind*.
The spectators know immediately that she will either be excluded from the
community, or the new custom will be accepted.)

Finally, when speaking about relationships between culture and
power, and their dynamics, Cohen presents an interesting analysis of
the dialectic between the rational and the nonrational:

> The formation of an elite is a collective endeavour embodying the cumu-
> lative efforts, rational and non-rational, creative and routine, of all the
> men and women within the group. It is a construction which is continu-
> ously questioned, continuously modified, continuously created. As the
> collectivity confronts its problems and debates them, it throws up leaders
> of various types, who contribute to its strategies in different fields. But at

any one time, the ability of a few individuals to change the collective culture is very limited. (1981, p. 230)

The rational leaves its mark and fades away, but is eventually unconsciously achieved through the nonrational (p. 231).

Abner Cohen has grasped the essence of the paradox that is constantly observed in complex organizations: The rationally evaluated effectiveness of cultural strategies lies in their nonrationality, their political success in their nonpolitical character. The rational can only be achieved, at any given time, through the nonrational.

Three-Dimensional Man and Woman

Are the above conclusions valid? Is there an analogy between a study of the power elite in Sierra Leone and a study of a complex organization, or between a study of an informal and a formal organization? Is Cohen's method applicable to research on complex organizations?

In the first place, there are several mechanical analogies. There were 41,783 Creoles in Sierra Leone, which is the size of a large company, showing that a study on such a scale is feasible. In addition, Cohen's "variables" were, indeed, highly typical phenomena and processes studied in formal organizations.

But there is more to it. Compare Dalton's study (1959) with Cohen's Sierra Leone study. Dalton studied organizations and, consequently, described a kind of power elite. Cohen studied a power elite and described many kinds of formal organizations supporting it. To wit, in both cases the Freemasons's Lodge was a very important factor in supporting the power.

In his study design, Cohen revealed certain positivist tendencies, marked already in his *Two-Dimensional Man;* for instance, looking for causality. He softened these tendencies, however, by saying that he was looking for sociocultural causality, that is, dialectical and loop-like relationships. As for reductionism, he said, holistic studies of entire societies are impossible; they must be broken down into variables, such as distinctiveness/boundaries, communication, decision-making, authority and the leadership process, ideology, and socialization (Cohen, 1974). These could not be "operationalized" in terms of measures, but they had to be "operated" in an experiment-like fashion. There was no question of controlled experiment, of course: It only meant systematic comparisons of variables and/or studies of social changes over time.

If we remove the positivist rhetoric from this prescription, the procedure seems very sound. Constant comparison (of certain processes, always embedded in a wider context), not necessarily guided by an a priori hypothesis, and the study of change as revealing hidden structures (by disrupting the everyday process) are indeed important elements of any study of social processes.

Cohen finished by proposing a paradigm of culture studies, in which

> . . . culture emerges not as a logical system that can be studied in its own right, but as a syncretic body of symbolic patterns which is heterogenous in its composition and is systematized only through interaction between individuals and groups. (1981, p. 215)

The author castigated the "19th Century" use of the concept of culture as a separate entity. The same was true, in a sense, for the term "power," which, in research as in common use, was reified and mostly treated from a distinct political stance. Cohen proposed pluralism—not as a political ideology, but as a heuristic research device.

Studies of power and large organizations can eventually complement each other very effectively. Studies of political order offer many clues concerning the context in which an organization operates. Studies of organizations offer concrete, visible examples of the political order in operation. One postulate must be added, though: Social action can be political and symbolic, but it is also practical, material, and physical. People are three-dimensional, and this third dimension is very much evidenced in another type of politically oriented study of large organizations.

Social Anthropology and Industrial Sociology: A Meeting on the Shop Floor

Manufacturing Consent

Michael Burawoy, the author of a famous study of shop-floor work that employed participant observation (Burawoy, 1979, 1981), is also an anthropologist by training. Like Cohen, he was interested in achieving a joint explanation of processes, which theories of conflict and consensus try to explain in opposite ways, and he was inspired by Antonio Gramsci and his work. However, Michael Burawoy was aiming mostly at a sociological theory (he hoped to liberate industrial sociology from the pseudouniversalism of organization theory) and was therefore willing to sacrifice the ethnographical account for the sake of the theory. Burawoy was also specifically interested in industrial organizations and labor processes; so much so that he finally abandoned Gramsci in order to return to Marx, albeit in a revised, self-reflective way. That meant three assumptions: Capitalism should be conceived as a way of appropriating unpaid labor from real producers; capitalism is not the final type of society in history; and a communist society (unlike the societies that until recently claimed this label) is possible.

In short, Cohen's approach was much closer to the one advocated here than Burawoy's. But Burawoy's object of study, an industrial organization, was closer to a potential subject of an anthropology of complex organizations.

Allied Corporation

In 1974 Michael Burawoy started to work as a miscellaneous machine operator in the engine division of Allied Corporation, a multinational company. What he saw and felt during that one year contributed to the conclusion that both conflict and consensus theory are wrong, not in their answers, but in the primary question they ask: Why do workers not work harder? The right question, as he saw it, was Why do they work as hard as they do?

In order to make sense of his experiences, Burawoy decided to

> . . . treat the activities on the shopfloor as a series of games in which [the] operator attempts to achieve levels of production that earn incentive pay, in other words, anything over 100 per cent. The precise target that each operator aims at is established on an individual basis, varying with job, machine, experience and so on. . . .
>
> This game of making out provides a framework for evaluating the productive activities and the social relations that arise out of the organization of work. We can look upon making out . . . as completing a

sequence of stages—of encounters between machine operators and the social or non-social objects that regulate the conditions of work. The rules of the game are experienced as a set of externally imposed relationships. The art of making out is to manipulate those relationships with the purpose of advancing as quickly as possible from one stage to the next. (Burawoy, 1979, p. 51)

The *making out* as a "making sense" frame of reference regulating workers' behavior allowed Burawoy to come to an alternative interpretation of the "power of the maintenance men" compared to the harmony-based explanations of Crozier (1964) or Hickson et al. (1971). The maintenance men might have been "removing uncertainty," but, in doing so, they hindered the making out game, due to the work organization imposed from above. And, indeed, if we imagine each worker backed up by one maintenance person, there would hardly be any uncertainty to remove. In other words, it was management who created unnecessary "pockets" of uncertainty that were then used for control purposes—systematically or by chance. "Uncertainty" cannot possibly be the ultimate explanation in organizational contexts. Our duty as researchers is to ask, Where did it originate?

What is more, Burawoy demonstrated that the games workers played, making out, "goldbricking," and others, were not in opposition to the interests of management, as assumed by both conflict and consensus theorists; rather, the games protected management interests. In the story of pulley balancing, Burawoy, together with a higher level manager, ruined a day's work by following the instructions, something that Burawoy's "dayman" had told him to avoid at any price. The irreverent worker became the positive hero of the story, especially in the eyes of top management: "Management, at least at the lower levels, actively participates not only in the organization of the game but in the enforcement of its rules" (Burawoy, 1979, p. 80).

Playing the game, said Burawoy, generated consent concerning the rules. It was not that consensus existed (and perhaps was only damaged, unfortunately, by faulty communication), and that therefore the game was possible; consensus was created by playing the game. The game, in turn, was created as a way of adapting to the work's deprivations, such as boredom, physical strain, or lack of influence. The game introduced a feeling of autonomy, an excitement, an arena for jokes and commonsense making. These were much more important than economic gains, although they were stylized as such, as they were couched in the idiom of economic gain. As Burawoy (1979) put it:

> It is not so much the monetary incentive that concretely coordinates the interests of management and worker but rather the play of the game itself, which generates a common interest in the outcome and in the game's continuity. Any game that provides distinctive rewards to the players establishes a common interest among the players . . . in providing for the conditions of its reproduction. (p. 85)

Thus workers played games *with* management, and not *against* it. Management regulated the game, at least at the outset. (The originally intended "piece-rate game" had turned into a "making-out game," which was a realistic version of the former.) The game formed the link between individual rationality and that of the system, that is, ". . . we do make history, but not as we please" (1979, p. 93).

Burawoy then went on to make his contribution to the analysis of labor processes through concepts such as internal labor markets, selection, recruiting, and allocation procedures that, in relative terms, isolate the company from the external labor market, allowing for more secure reproduction of its main traits: the internal state (the incorporation of political conflicts into organizational processes of grievance and bargaining), influence of markets, and workers' consciousness. He did look for connections within the wider context— but omitted the closer context, that of management (that is, of higher management, as opposed to shop management). Higher management showed its impersonal face only in a short comparison between the time study in 1945 (Donald Roy's, as quoted in Burawoy, 1979) and an industrial engineering study in 1975.

Organization studies are constantly (and rightly) criticized for their focus on management issues and their neglect of the shop floor (see, for example, a thorough critique by Zey-Ferrell, 1981). From an analysis of a "control subsystem"—if I may call it so—the researchers move to the analysis of markets, technologies, and national culture. The shop floor researchers, however, seem to be suffering from a similar tendency *au rebour:* From the shop floor they move to labor markets, technologies, and social formations. Both consider the group that is not studied (workers, managers), as an undifferentiated group moved by simple interests, as opposed to the group under study. Michael Crozier's study is one possible exception.

It may be that we can only put the control and operation subsystems together mechanically. Or, as Burawoy predicted, a renewed labor process theory would deny organization theory the right to exist as a separate discipline. For my part, I claim that the possible strength of an anthropology of complex organizations would be the joining of these two artificially severed organizational aspects.

On Comparative Studies and Luck

Michael Burawoy initiated his study with the explicit consent and knowledge of management: He was allowed to work as a machine operator, had access to managerial records and data, and was able to interview both managers and workers. A close relative, who was manager of the engineering department, helped him gain access (Burawoy & Lukacs, 1985). But he was not only lucky with access, he also discovered that a similar study had been done in the same company 30 years earlier (Roy, 1952).

Donald Roy worked in the same plant as a radial drill operator in 1944-1945 under complete cover. In spite of differences in the theoretical approach (Roy followed the closed-system perspective of the 1940s), Burawoy was able to register and analyze organizational change over a span of 30 years and place it against the background of social, political, and economic changes of that same period. This was indeed a unique opportunity.

But that was not all. It turned out that a Hungarian researcher, János Lukacs, worked for two months as a radial drill operator in a similar machine shop in Hungary, and complemented participant observation with nonparticipant observation and interviews (Burawoy & Lukacs, 1985). This led to the next development: Burawoy working first in a champagne factory, and then as a radial drill operator in a machine shop in Hungary. The last study resulted in an ethnographic account from the Hungarian shop floor, where the narration was blended most skillfully with comparison ("Allied" served as a background) and with theory (Burawoy, 1985). Theory was never protected from the facts; one of the interesting traits in Burawoy's approach was that he did not abandon his Marxist stance, yet he never hesitated to correct the theory if it did not interpret reality. He also noticed the double oppression of women, by gender and by the class system, an unusual observation coming from a male, Marxist researcher.

The series of studies led to a challenge to the *mythologies of work*—the stereotypical, nonempirical beliefs concerning the difference between "capitalist" and "socialist" systems of work.

Because of my initial specialization in socialist economies, I am well acquainted with the struggles that used to accompany the attempts of "Western" and "Eastern" economists and organization theorists to communicate. In the first place, both sides held to their own analytical categories—that is, to different languages. As to the possibility of translation, it is feasible insofar as one knows what a given notion stands for. In other words, empirically based knowledge is needed. However, the "empirical" studies made by courageous Western researchers, under the surveillance of political guardians, using inexpert interpreters, and guided by categories coming from another frame of reference, compete with "empirical" studies done on the basis of statistics that were not even considered valid and reliable in the country of origin.[3] In this light, the Burawoy-Lukacs method seems to be the most promising. Ethnographies should be the route for comparative organization studies. Precategorizing makes a study inaccessible or difficult to compare; therefore, Burawoy had to break down Roy's "closed system" frame of reference in order to achieve ethnographical description.

There is one more point to this story, as announced in the heading for this section: the role that luck plays in research, frequently stressed by Rosalie Wax (1974). What if Burawoy did not have a relative, and that relative was not employed in the same plant as Roy, or Burawoy had never heard of Lukacs's work, which would hardly have been surprising, as Lukacs writes in Hungarian? However, this is not an invitation to fatalism. On the contrary, it is an encouragement to catch opportunities instead of relying on "research as planned."

Reconciling Macro and Micro, Marxism and Phenomenology

Abner Cohen and Michael Burawoy were both attempting a synthesis between moderate Marxism and social constructivism in the first case, and between moderate social constructivism and Marxism in the second. However, Cohen's main interest was in informal organizations, whereas Burawoy considered formal organizations the pretext for studying and understanding labor processes. Therefore, we are still looking for the same combination, but as formulated by authors specifically interested in formal organizations: one, theoretically, the other, practically.

Toward a Political Phenomenology of Formal Organizations

Traditional organization theory, claimed Richard Harvey Brown (1978), basically produced two views on rationality. The first perceives rationality as an attribute of actors who have goals and try to maximize some means-end relationship. However, because actors have multiple goals, it is easy to follow this definition and produce a tautology: Any action can be seen as rational if taken from the point of view of certain goals (recall Crozier and Kanter defending the rationality of organizational actors).

This paradox was solved by attributing rationality to organizations (organization as collective actor). Actions that did not follow this rationality were labeled "unanticipated" or "deviant."

The problem with the collective actor approach is, on the one hand, that it almost inevitably leads to anthropomorphization; on the other hand, it is unclear how individual actors achieve their notion of collective rationality and where it is to be observed. A pragmatic solution to the last question was to let the researcher establish where.

Ethnomethodology, said Brown, had unmasked rationality as a social construction in itself. Social actors employ rationality as a rhetoric to account for actions that, from a rationalistic point of view, are chaotic and faulty when performed.

> Garfinkel shows us that rationality neither instructs us as to what action to take, nor is it a property inherent in conduct or in the social system as such. Instead, rationality emerges in interaction, and then is used retro-

spectively to legitimize what has already taken place or is being enacted. (R. H. Brown, 1978, p. 369)

Thus rationality is not an input, but an output; not a starting point, but a product (on rationality as an organizational product, see Czarniawska-Joerges, in press). We are busy rationalizing, in both senses of the word, and so we are busy organizing (see also Weick, 1969). Ethnomethodological studies, said Brown, had to be extended from "twilight" social situations to highly visible, formal organizations.

In challenging the "objective" character of rationality, ethnomethodology approached neo-Marxism, which also proposed to relativize the concept by seeing it as an element of class and bourgeois ideology. The "making out" came again into light as workers' search for meaning, allowing them to preserve their autonomy and dignity in the face of alienating work.

> Like "primitive man" who must patch together (*bricoler*) accounts of what goes on around him, . . . so the modern worker must make "myths" ad hoc that reconcile the actual processes of his work with the official rhetoric of the organization. (R. H. Brown, 1978, p. 372)

Therefore, proposed Brown, a possible way of reconciling Durkheim, Weber, and Marx (or rather, their present disciples) was to treat organizations as paradigms.

> By paradigm we refer to those sets of assumptions, usually implicit, about what sorts of things make up the world, how they act, how they hang together, and how they may be known. In actual practice, such paradigms function as a means of imposing control as well as a resource that dissidents may use in organizing their awareness and action. That is, we view paradigms as practical as well as cognitive, and as a resource as well as a constraint. (1978, p. 373)

This is a symbolic definition of organization, in which political man is subsumed under the symbolist, and where physical man does not exist. Again, a two-dimensional model dominates a political approach. What is more, Brown, following ethnomethodologists, plunged into the recurring metaphor: social life as social science.

Nevertheless, organizations undoubtedly use paradigms to govern action (if they are understood not only as formal rules of thought, but also as rhetoric and practices employed). In this sense, the paradigm-model, however two-dimensional, certainly allows us to study the conjuncture of symbolism and politics by using a plurality of approaches. There were studies on negotiation of reality, but fewer on imposition of reality. And yet,

> in hierarchical organizations (or in a bureaucratized society) it is not only the means of economic production that become concentrated, but also the means of theoretical reflection. (R. H. Brown, 1978, p. 376)

In large, complex organizations, one side of this process is that the power elites control more and more, but the other side is that there are fewer and fewer positions from which the critical connections between different actions can be seen. This will result in a concentration of control of the *contents* of reality ("what is") and of the *definition* of reality ("what is what").

Such control is, however, paradoxical per se; Brown called it an irony. Managers control rules of relevance, or the official paradigm, but cannot control how it is tacitly used, rules of irrelevance. And yet it is the latter on which the survival of the rules of relevance depends; the rules of irrelevance either make the rules of relevance tractable, or else break them (as Burawoy's study amply shows). Thus managers control not what they should, but what they can.

Finally, in Brown's perspective, organizational change is a change of paradigms:

> [F]ormal organizations have histories, undergo internal and external changes, and experience strains. The dominant paradigm may be confronted and even overthrown by an insurgent one, or it may be modified to absorb its challengers. (1978, p. 374)

And this perspective guided the empirical study I will turn to now.

An Example: Moving From Tradition to Professionalism

Tony Spybey (1982, 1984) did not quote R. H. Brown, yet he fulfilled all his postulates in an empirical study. "Paradigm" was called, after Giddens, a frame of meaning, and understood not as a metaphor for an organization, but as a way of seeing things. There can be many frames of meaning in any single organization.

The study examined the activities of managers in a business organization in the British wool textile industry. Spybey's basic task was theory building rather than theory verifying; no a priori hypotheses directed his fieldwork. The managers interviewed were the "first-level observers," and the researcher was the "second-level observer" who analyzed managers' accounts in terms of intersubjective, emerging categories.

Spybey was looking for an organization that (a) would be close enough to visit often (like myself, he found the participant role too trapping); (b) would be involved in a process of change (in order to reveal power structures); and (c) would employ more than 1,000 people, to assure a proper managerial representation. Of 10 organizations addressed, 9 said no, either because managers were too busy to have time to spare or else because reorganization was taking place. (A reader with fieldwork experience will, no doubt, recognize both.) The 10th said yes.

The 10th organization, a large manufacturer of wool textiles had been organized in a way that was traditional in the British textile industry, that is, as a set of small mills with relatively autonomous managers and little administration. This picture is completed by deferential, change-resistant workers, with paternalistic owners holding rigid control over strategic decision-making. This was accepted and used to advantage by a group of managers, sharing what Spybey called a "traditional" frame of meaning.

A group of younger men, however, trained as professional managers, considered the existing organization "ineffective" and proposed the introduction of corporate control. Efficiency was the keyword for professionals; creativity, for traditionals. The owners (two brothers) died almost at the same time, and their heirs listened to the professionals. Interestingly enough, the latter used a future scenario as a threat: If we do not reorganize, we shall end up in a decline! (Although there were no concrete signs of such, it was, on the whole, an era of economic decline.[4])

This victory of one "frame of meaning" over another, as witnessed by the reorganization, was studied by Spybey through the accounts of managers. At the outset of his study, when the owners were still alive, Spybey's interviews produced a description of the two frames of meaning as static and interlocked. (That probably explains why Spybey was allowed access at all—the changes at that stage were minimal, and the feeling of a deadlock might have made managers more prone to an opportunity of cathartic interviews.) Then the brothers died and a drastic change of ownership and control followed suit, which prompted Spybey to repeat his approach.

The divorce of ownership and control (the new owners were merely interested in profits) occurred in a climate of economic recession. This gave the upper hand to the professionals. The traditionals watched the changes inflicted by the reorganization in horror and predicted a sad end for the company, just as the professionals had done before. Divisionalization was to top off all the previous changes, and therefore a third round of interviews was performed. These interviews confirmed the reality of changes introduced and the stability of the frames of reference.

Tony Spybey's work is a rare example of an unplanned study of organizational change, with all the desired stages: before, during, and after; and that is why it has been reported here in such detail. Such studies were usually only carried out by researchers who were also change agents, which in itself produced many complications, as we have seen in Rice's study.

In terms of the theoretical contribution, Spybey showed how frames of reference structured action and also interpreted action and inaction. Finally, he placed all of his analyses in the context of an advanced capitalism, as opposed to the history of the British wool textile industry. To use the words of Richard H. Brown, Spybey put his analyses into political, economic, and ideational contexts (Brown, 1978), in both a static and dynamic perspective.

The Promises of Political Anthropology

As I see it, they are great. Political anthropology offers a possibility of avoiding the Scylla and Charybdis of solipsism and reification, subjectivization and objectivization, a possibility "to illustrate the persuasive features of social constructs without abandoning the fact that they have been and continue to be constructed by people" (Spybey, 1982, p. 3).

More importantly, however, political anthropology offers examples of a smoother, step-by-step passage from micro- to macro-analyses, through the study of accounts in which actors explain the reasons for their actions, using perceptions of both their immediate reality and the wider processes (see, for example, the use of economic recession by professionals in Spybey's study). Although the necessity of building such a bridge is not a particular trait of political anthropology as such, it is more often achieved here. Other approaches state the desirability of such connections; however, they often leave this for studies to follow, staying at their original micro or macro level. The ethnographic descriptions used by political anthropologists focus on the micro level; the political frame of reference necessitates making sense of micro experiences within a macro perspective; thus a meso-connection must be built.

If ethnomethodology focused mostly on the symbolic aspect of reality, here we are reminded that people are both symbolist and political. However, the neglect of their physical, or practical being is often present in the works of political anthropologists. (Burawoy's study must be exempted from this criticism.) Physical or material action is glimpsed only briefly and occasionally, for example, in the material aspect of symbols or social relationships (domination, etc). A comprehensive theory of organizations cannot neglect their practical side.

Before we can begin to sketch a study program of three-dimensional organizations, let us move to another group of studies that were inspired by anthropology as a discipline.

Notes

1. To answer Cohen: One reason why this has not been accomplished yet is revealed by ethnomethodological analysis—the taken-for-grantedness character of everyday life guarantees its smooth flow. Questioning and analyzing it (or, in Schützian terms,

bracketing it) disrupts the social tissue. Managers are usually looking for help in increasing the taken-for-grantedness of organizational action, not in diminishing it.

2. Even rejection is in that sense an acceptance, as Zinoviev shows in his *Homo Sovieticus* (1983).

3. As a result of historical irony, Western researchers are now paying back by selling to the "East" a second-hand knowledge that is no longer considered valuable in the countries of origin.

4. On economic decline as stage setting, see Czarniawska-Joerges (1989).

7

Organizational Culture

A Code of Many Colors

In 1951 Elliott Jaques of the Tavistock Institute published his dissertation entitled *The Changing Culture of a Factory,* thereby setting in motion a trend in organization theory that was to bloom in the 1980s. In 1983 the *Administrative Science Quarterly* acknowledged the trend, dedicating to it an entire issue (Barley, 1983b). The European journals *Journal of Management Studies* (Hofstede, 1986) and *Organization Studies* (Berg, 1986) followed at a dignified distance. Treated sometimes with distaste and sometimes with enthusiasm, organizational culture is still with us, growing into a jungle of subtrends, approaches, and directions. This means that not all studies use what can be called an anthropological approach, giving me a legitimate reason to cut through the jungle with the machete of relevance. Using Linda Smircich's (1983) conceptualization of culture in organizational analysis, I intend to bring into focus two perspectives on organizational culture in order to analyze them more closely. Consequently a great number of approaches will have to be omitted. I would like to emphasize that "organizational culture" serves also as an umbrella concept, where almost all studies can find a place if their authors so wish.

Organizational culture studies seem to be connected almost naturally to anthropology, yet in many cases it is just a metaphor that has been borrowed and not the approach, as such. Alternatively, one could say, as did Smircich, that because there is no consensus as to the concept of *culture* in anthropology, different organization theorists borrowed concepts originating in different anthropological traditions.

Linda Smircich distinguished five perspectives on organizational culture. Two of them treat culture as a variable: cross-cultural management (culture as an independent variable) and corporate culture (culture as an internal variable). The remaining three assume culture as a basic metaphor for organization; they are organizational cognition, organizational symbolism, and psychodynamics. The cross-cultural management approach selects cultural factors from the environment and examines their operations inside an organization. (Approaches stressing organizational cognition and psychodynamics were briefly characterized in earlier chapters.)

As I see it, the corporate culture and organizational symbolism approaches are closest to social anthropology, as it has been characterized throughout this book. The following sections draw on studies within these two approaches. Three sections deal with those applying an instrumental perspective (Wilkins & Ouchi, 1983, call it "utilitarian"); and three sections describe studies that use "culture(s)," as a metaphor for organization or a network of organizations. Research is a first step toward intervention or change; the goal (from the point of view of management) is to improve organizational performance; culture seems to be an apt instrument to achieve such a goal.

A Frontal Approach: Another Tavistock Study

Restoration in British Industry

Elliott Jaques's report on a study of a factory done by the Tavistock Institute (1951), considered one of the main predecessors of the organizational culture trend, has value not only as a historical reference, but also as an example of a very ambitious, holistic, and thorough approach to a complex organization.

The project started as a part of a larger program administered by the Medical Research Council, with support from the Human Factors Panel of the Committee on Industrial Productivity, set up in the United Kingdom in 1948. The ultimate aim of the research was to establish and analyze sources of social stress and strain in British industry. Therefore the research team was looking for a company that would be interested and willing to undertake a program of change aimed at improving social relations; and it had been decided that such a company would be easiest to find among advanced firms that already knew that superficial procedural changes and standard organizational remedies did not constitute a real change.

The fundamental idea of the project was to make it beneficial for the client; however, full acceptance and the need to be helped had to be established. The management group was approached first. When a tentative agreement was reached, the Works Council's approval was sought.

> The eventual adoption of the project by the Works Council after three months of consideration did not necessarily represent active interest on the part of the total factory, nor was it taken by the Research Team as having such a meaning. As far as the situation could be assessed, there were perhaps half a dozen members of the firm who positively and strongly wished the project to take place; there was also a larger group of thirty to fifty members who were moderately in favour, on the ground that some good might possibly result for the factory and for the country, and who were in such key positions as to allow them to decide on behalf of the total factory that a first trial period be undertaken; and finally there was the main body of members of the factory, who either had heard very little about the project, or were not particularly concerned. (Jaques, 1951, p. 12)

In other words, the first step consisted in legitimizing the project by anchoring it in politically crucial points.

After negotiating the conditions of the project, a research team of eight people moved in; its composition reflected to a degree the social composition of the factory. The team started with an historical and

"geographical" background study: Factory history and social organization were examined and the results were presented to the Works Council.
The study began in September 1948, and in October the first requests for
help arrived. (It had been agreed that the research team's work would be
guided by concrete requests for help from organizational units.)

I am reporting what can be seen as the tedious organizational de-
tails of a project in order to highlight one obvious possibility, that of
achieving a holistic picture of a complex organization through the
concerted effort of several researchers, acting in cooperation and with
the support of crucial organizational actors for a prolonged period of
time (the study lasted three years and a series of follow-ups were initiated). The research itself turns into a system of collective action, a
temporary organization. Although such opportunities are rare and cannot be procured at will, they are nevertheless the most satisfactory
source for inquiry into organizational life.

The Changing Culture of a Factory

The research team conducted five substudies at the request of various organizational units and groups, which were subsequently described in five case studies. The final, common analysis focused on
social change and was based on Kurt Lewin's field theory (1951),
which assumed that organizational events had to be understood as an
outcome of other interacting events within a larger field of forces,
and not as a simple chain of causes and effects.

The main types of forces operating in the organizational field are subsumed under three headings: social structure, culture, and personality.
Social structure is a network of roles and role relationships; personality
is the "total psychological make-up of the individual," and the culture

> . . . of the factory is its customary and traditional way of thinking and of
> doing things, which is shared to a greater or lesser degree by all its mem-
> bers, and which new members must learn, and at least partially accept, in
> order to be accepted into service in the firm. (Jaques, 1951, p. 251)

Thus the culture of the factory is not its rituals or ceremonies, but its
way of life, which Jaques characterized in quite traditional organization

theory terms: policy, sanctioning of authority, leadership, and communication. Change consisted in changing structure, culture, and "personality distribution," but was finally seen in a changed culture. The role of the consultant was to elucidate the operation of structural, cultural, and psychological factors at various stages of the change: when a problem was diagnosed, when a plan of action was decided upon, and when resistance had to be overcome.

The Company Doctors

We have discussed the clinical approach of the Tavistock Institute from Rice's study (Chapter 4). The differences worth stressing are that Jaques's study mentions technological aspects (and thus the third, physical dimension) only sporadically; the system is mostly social, and the technical aspect is not yet firmly introduced. Further, there is no mention of culture in Rice's study, only of an interaction between structure and personality. One might suspect that culture, not easily measurable, was declared irrelevant in the growing spirit of positivism. Finally, Jaques's study presents the clinical approach of a general practitioner rather than that of a specialist in a given disease and is therefore worth reporting.

The clinical approach meant that all research actions were guided by the needs of the client alone. Any action undertaken purely for research had to be seen as a breach of the professional role of the research worker. The research team had to act independently and avoid identification with the interests of any involved groups or individuals.

These principles meant that the Research Team would work with any section of the factory at its request. In so doing, the members of the group concerned could talk about whatever they wished, but the Research Team for its part would comment only on relationships within the immediate group, and would most definitely not discuss any individuals or groups not present. In order to carry out these principles, the Research Team has limited its relationships with members of the factory to strictly formal contacts which have to do with project work publicly sanctioned by the Works Council. No personal relationships with Glacier members either inside or outside working hours have been entertained. . . . By thus maintaining an independent role in the factory, it was anticipated that assistance could be given most effectively to those groups which sought help with a problem. (Jaques, 1951, p. 14-15)

Confidentiality and responsibility were the two keynotes of the researchers' attitude. This meant that Jaques's team was fully aware of their influence on the course of events not only as agents of change, but also as simple observers intruding into the system. Clients and consultants share responsibility for every step undertaken in an attempt to change; and such an awareness is, incidentally, also the best remedy against self-confirming hypotheses and irresponsible interventions.

Interventions have their unpleasant side effects, thus the medical analogy holds further: Patients usually dislike the taste of the medicine, even if they asked the doctor for help. It was foreseen that the reported problems would not be the only source of trouble experienced, that there were no simple solutions, and that even those who asked for help could be resistant to it. All of this had to be coped with under a general philosophy that proclaimed, "the simplest approach was to accept the complexity of social reality, and the most rational, to accept the irrationality of many of the unrecognized forces which contribute to social behaviour" (Jaques, 1951, p. 6).

Jaques's approach was almost heroic in its uncompromising moral attitude (to help those who need help) and ambitious methodology (to learn everything that can be learned). Although the aims of ethnographically and clinically oriented studies differ (as we shall see later on), Jaques's ideals can be embraced by all those who are interested in understanding complex organizations.

The Clinical Approach 30 Years Later

Edgar H. Schein, an organizational psychologist, dedicated his career to studies of socialization processes (in extreme forms such as brainwashing, 1961; and in normal organizations, 1969, with Van Maanen, 1979). The reintroduction of the concept of culture into organizational research must have been accepted by socialization researchers with joy; during the reign of the positivistic paradigm, it was never clear what it was that was being learned and taught in the socialization process. Now the answer was obvious—culture.

Ethnographic Versus Clinical Perspectives

In his *Organizational Culture and Leadership* (1985), Schein came much closer to anthropology than Jaques ever had, and at the same time, made explicit the difference between an ethnographic and a clinical approach to organization studies.

> The ethnographer obtains concrete data in order to understand the culture he is interested in, presumably for intellectual and scientific reasons. Though the ethnographer must be faithful to the observed and experienced data, he brings to the situation a set of concepts of models that motivated the research in the first place. The group members studied are often willing to participate but usually have no particular stake in the intellectual issues that may have motivated the study.
>
> In contrast, a "clinical perspective" is one where the group members are clients who have their own interests as the prime motivator for the involvement of the "outsider," often labeled "consultant" or "therapist" in this context. (p. 21)

If we want to be severe on ethnographers and friendly to consultants, we could say that ethnographers are motivated by their own interest (be it a career request or noble curiosity) and "clinicians" by that of their clients. If we reversed our sympathies, we might say that the client of the ethnographer is humankind, whereas that of the clinician is a particular organization, which in itself might be a boil on humanity's face. In other words, ethnographers, if they so wish, are free to declare the existence of a particular organization as a problem in itself, whereas clinicians, like doctors, must improve the performance of their clients.

This obligation has to do with the fact that in contemporary clinical approaches, it is rare that anybody but management (union leadership included) are the clients. In Jaques's case, the true client was the United Kingdom, who paid for a "cure" to whoever wanted to try. Similar situations sometimes arise in the public sector, as I have noted in my study of public sector consulting (Czarniawska-Joerges, 1990a), but even there they are not desirable. The present trend is toward self-financing, and those who call the doctor pay the bill. The times of a social health care system for organizations seem to be over, at least temporarily.

Schein, on the other hand, assumed a harmony perspective, in which conflicts were due to communication defects, and therefore management was the most obvious client by definition. Moreover, it was the managers who created culture.

The Functionalist Concept of Culture

For Jaques, culture was a customary way of thinking and acting, shared to some degree by organizational actors; Schein, however, proposed a deeper and stricter concept in which culture was

> . . . basic assumptions and beliefs that are shared by members of an or-ganization, that operate unconsciously, and that define in a basic "taken for granted" fashion an organization's view of itself and its environment. These assumptions and beliefs are learned responses to a group's prob-lems of survival in its external environment and its problems of internal integration. (1985, p. 6)

Organizations are organisms, survival oriented, in which all the parts co-operated harmoniously toward a common goal and dysfunctions are elimi-nated in the face of environmental demand. Culture is the organism's learned repertoire of survival-oriented responses. The most important issue for study, according to Schein, is the dynamics of culture: How do the indi-vidual intentions of leaders become a *shared, consensually validated set of definitions* of reality, under what conditions will they change, and when do they stop being shared and accepted? Culture is the key to external adapta-tion and to internal integration, the two main conditions for survival. It is built by negotiating a series of agreements on all important organizational issues, which, if functional, will consequently be drawn into the taken-for-grantedness of smooth, organizational life.

The contents of (any) culture revolve around basic assumptions con-cerning the relationship between humanity and nature, the nature of real-ity and truth, the nature of human nature, the nature of human activity, and the nature of human relationships. This list, more than anything else, discloses the strength of the harmony-assumption behind Schein's theory. Not even in a nuclear family do people share all these assumptions, not to mention in any larger organizations.

The process of culture formation was presented as a basically micro, sociopsychological group dynamic process. Organization is seen as a small group or rather a series of small groups (e.g., leadership group, training group, personnel department group). The pattern of their interactions constituted an organizational culture.

Schein ends his analysis with the conclusion that "the unique and essential function of leadership is the manipulation of culture" (p. 317). At the "early" stage of the organism's development, this meant culture's creation and establishment; in the "midlife" stage, an insight into the functioning of culture; and at "maturity," an ability to change, if necessary. The clinician, like a CAT scanner, helps the leader to notice the invisible culture and to manipulate it (for more on clinical perspective, see Schein, 1987).

Culture as an Umbrella

Schein's analysis of organizational culture summarized his experience as a consultant in a psychodynamic tradition, originally inspired by anthropological and sociological influences. As he put it himself:

> What makes culture an exciting concept is that its analysis forces one to take an integrative perspective toward organizational phenomena, a perspective that brings together key ideas from psychology, sociology, anthropology, social psychology, systems theory, and psychotherapy. (1985, pp. 313-314)

He did not suggest that leaders could easily and directly change organizational culture, only that they should try, in order to accomplish significant organizational change. But some authors go further still.

On the Wings of Excellence: Controlling Corporate Cultures

If Jaques and Schein borrowed the concept of culture from anthropology in order to assemble and integrate various aspects of organizational life, other consultant-oriented researchers decided to borrow the whole set of anthropological concepts and use them as metaphors, or more attractive labels, in order to replace worn-out and dry traditional concepts such as authority, incentive systems, information systems, and so on. The operation in itself was, to some extent, like the one described in Chapter 3 (the section on the corporate tribe), but this time it was less wholesale and therefore more acceptable. The author of *Corporate Tribe* proposed a new definition—organizations *are* modern tribes—whereas the approaches discussed below propose that organizations can be *seen* as tribes.

Corporate Culture as Rhetoric

Deal and Kennedy's book *Corporate Cultures* (1982) became one of the first messengers of the organizational culture theory put to consulting use, together with *In Search of Excellence,* which, although even more popular, is not so clearly couched in "cultural" rhetoric and therefore is not presented here. But Tom Peters, one of the authors of *In Search of Excellence,* was called the "intellectual and spiritual godfather" of Deal and Kennedy's book, and so the present analysis can be applied to both works.

What I want to suggest is that the organizational culture concept as applied by consultants is tapping anthropology for its source of colorful metaphors, in order to produce an attractive rhetoric that may be subsequently used for control purposes. Of course, metaphors always carry an analytic potential, but in this case, they are used to discourage analysis—a shiny, new cover for somewhat fatigued, old contents. Culture was "the way we do things around here," and it was good to be able to find names that would make this "way" attractive and acceptable.

"Policies" and "strategies" smacked of cold rationality, of something imposed from above, and was both temporary and superficial. "Values" were what everybody had and are deep and emotionally supported. But this is my interpretation. Deal and Kennedy put it differently:

> Values are not "hard," like organizational structures, policies and procedures, strategies, or budgets. Often they are not even written down. And

when someone does try to set them down in a formal statement of corporate philosophy, the product often bears an uncomfortable resemblance to the Biblical beatitudes—good and true and broadly constructive, but not all that relevant to Monday morning. (Deal & Kennedy, 1982, p. 21)

And those values, shared "by all the people who work for the company—from the lowest production worker right through to the ranks of senior management" (p. 22), distinguished one organization from another and therefore should become an object of special care for managers.

"Manager," however, was another boring word from the traditional organizational dictionary. Sometimes they were called "leaders," but if in some audiences this name was associated with all that is admirable and desirable, others immediately started thinking about Hitler. "Heroes" were to replace them.

If values are the soul of culture, then heroes personify those values and epitomize the strength of the organization. Heroes are pivotal figures in a strong culture. (Deal & Kennedy, 1982, p. 37)

Heroes were antidotes for the rational, "scientific" managers who had run institutions since the 1920s. They did not make decisions, but had visions; they did not apply incentives, but led the people; they did not motivate, but infected with enthusiasm.

The most boring part of organizational life was, by definition, *standard operating procedures*. These, presumably, could not be removed, but could be balanced by rites and rituals, also standard operating procedures, but of an expressive, not instrumental character. (That is, not directly instrumental; their instrumentality lies in their power of expression, as Cohen explained to us.)

And finally, the set of organizational roles (head of personnel department, chief engineer, secretary) was replaced with a set of characters for an organizational drama (story teller, priest, spy, cabal).

What was the result? The boring, down-to-earth annual report changed into a poem; robot-like figures turned into intriguing characters; and the everyday life routine turned into a fascinating plot. An abstract sketch in a positivist framework was replaced by a color movie. In short, the rhetoric followed completely different aesthetic criteria.

At this junction, I cannot resist inserting Weick's little joke at the expense of organizational culture. Readers are asked to fill in the first word in all sentences:

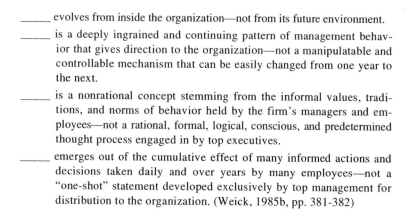

_____ evolves from inside the organization—not from its future environment.

_____ is a deeply ingrained and continuing pattern of management behavior that gives direction to the organization—not a manipulatable and controllable mechanism that can be easily changed from one year to the next.

_____ is a nonrational concept stemming from the informal values, traditions, and norms of behavior held by the firm's managers and employees—not a rational, formal, logical, conscious, and predetermined thought process engaged in by top executives.

_____ emerges out of the cumulative effect of many informed actions and decisions taken daily and over years by many employees—not a "one-shot" statement developed exclusively by top management for distribution to the organization. (Weick, 1985b, pp. 381-382)

Anybody who answered *organizational culture* failed the test. The proper word is *strategy*.

Therefore, one may conclude that what we witness is a major change in organizational rhetoric: from militant to cultural. As such, it is a rather pleasant change. However, as stated at the outset, the brand new set of metaphors was not meant for analytic purposes. On the contrary, it carried a whole set of traits that were not inspected. Thus corporate culture was based on a deep consensus. (Possible subcultures varied only in terms of function-specific behaviors, such as an R&D department contrasted with a production unit.) Organizations were pleasantly irrational, just like people, and therefore it was easy to achieve cooperation. Organizations were presented as creating fun, joy, and excitement. Just as Cohen said, organizations offer solutions to all existential problems, and one has to admit that this cooing has never before been so convincing.

A Mythology for Our Times

Graduate students who read *Corporate Cultures* told me that the book reminded them of a *Reader's Digest* version of Greek mythology. Indeed, Deal and Kennedy's book can be seen as a popular mythology of organizations. It tells of people who believed in their ideas when no one else did and who then succeeded spectacularly, of bigger-than-life bosses who created industrial empires with their bare hands, of sellers who could foretell a change in demand from the wind.

The students liked the stories, but did not take them very seriously. It all sounded like high-life gossip. Indeed, readers of airline journals have undoubtedly noticed that business folk have joined royalty and show business people: We get an opportunity to know what they eat and where they go on vacation. And the phenomenon is not limited to the Western hemisphere; allegedly, there are four different translations of Peters and Waterman's book in the People's Republic of China.

What are the cultural origins of this organizational mythology? The United States is the first answer, but some point to Japan as the first promoter of the shared values and common rituals behind the organizational grind. A further look reveals that a very similar mythology was in use in the Soviet Union of the 1950s. "Heroes of work," like Stachanov, were leading the collective/family to unthinkable achievements in productivity and activity. If anything, they tended to play their roles of hero, spy, traitor, and priest (propaganda officer) more seriously.

Deal and Kennedy read like Agatha Christie, but, in addition, they offer a peaceful conscience to anyone who wants to dedicate even their travels to the good of the company. And here we come back to rhetoric: No matter how intensely and effectively researchers ridicule the folk wisdom of corporate culture books, no alternative message will come through if it is not packaged in an equally enticing rhetoric. In 1968 Roger Brown noted the trend to take elaborate rhetoric as a sign of propaganda and dullness as a proof of sincerity. Similarly, the more complicated the study, the more it is taken as a hallmark of the scientific method. The tide has turned, however; rich rhetoric is back, and complicated dullness does not have a chance when competing with a colorful story. The antidote to kitsch is not a treatise on taste, but art.

Cultural Elements of Corporate Life

A new rhetoric is not the only way of using corporate culture for purposes of control. Another is noticing, and including in the mainstream of organizational life, actions and events that before were considered unimportant, irrelevant, or downright dysfunctional in major organizational processes.

Organizational myths, legends, stories, and sages are a focus of interest for a great many researchers, of whom Joanne Martin is perhaps the best known (Martin, 1982; Martin, Feldman, Hatch & Sitkin, 1983). She used anthropological literature as a starting point for further analysis of these elements, within a socio-psychological, experimental paradigm, searching for a causal relationship between storytelling and commitment to an organization's policies and philosophy of management.[1] Insofar as such a relationship can be established, her study might be used as a guide for practitioners willing to manipulate organizational culture. From the point of view of research, she provided an interesting analysis of previously neglected aspects of organizational life. In that sense, Martin's research is an example of a fruitful transfer of a study topic from one discipline to another.

Other examples of research that tackle only some aspects of culture could be found in what is jokingly referred to as "coffee-drinking studies." Alvesson (1985) complains about the triviality of culture studies in the following manner:

> Organization theorists have located new aspects of organizational life and its function to study during the second half of the decade. Among these we can find jokes, coffee breaks, how people are dressed, how they behave at the corporation's Christmas party, how they sit at meetings, how they get fired (the "rite" of getting fired), what stories about present and former figures of authority are told, and so on. . . . It could be argued that these are of marginal importance compared to, for example, the organization's hierarchy and the ways in which work is organized, controlled, and carried out. (p. 108)

Coffee-drinking studies, it seems to me, can be seen—and carried out—from different perspectives. First, there are undoubtedly some studies dealing with random events. As Alvesson points out, a persistent joke might have to do with the idiosyncratic behavior of some person or extraordinary event, and organizational parties in small organizations may be initiated and dominated by one or a few people who are otherwise insignificant. But the fact that every such piece of organizational life is collected as if it were a precious gem, seems to indicate the strength of the shared values assumption.

Second, the coffee-drinking studies (those that criticize it, as well as those that advise how to organize it) might be seen as an illustration of the increasing scope of organizational control, a phenomenon noted already by Etzioni in 1965. Anybody in a Swedish organization who tried to refuse to join common lunches would immediately experience sanctions against such deviant behavior—lunches are high points of socialization and indoctrination.

Third, the role of ceremonies and rituals is indeed very important. I do not agree with Alvesson when he doubts whether a Christmas party influences the remaining 225 working days. It is enough to see the care with which Deal and Kennedy (1982) advise management to design their rituals to reflect the significance of ceremony in organizational life as it is more seriously analyzed, for example, by Trice, Belasco, and Alluto (1969) or Burnett (1969). In addition, the methodological gain of observing a dramatized version of the most important messages, as Cohen (1974) demonstrated, is not to be neglected.

Nevertheless, the final recommendation formulated by Alvesson (1985) on how to discern trivia from nontrivia is fully acceptable: "One possible way of finding criteria of some general use is to proceed from what is significant for organizational members in their working life" (p. 110). This requires a change of perspective—culture, not as a tool of management, but as an organizational way of life, or rather, its symbolic aspect. The final sections of this chapter are dedicated to this perspective. But before we move to these, some rounding up of the instrumental perspective is due.

Gaining Control of the Corporate Culture

A collection of papers gathered by Kilmann, Saxton, Serpa, et al. (1985) can be seen as an optimistic manifesto for "culture controllers." Through theories, case studies, and the advice of consultants, the final conclusion is reached: "Managing corporate cultures is now possible" (p. 431). Although the articles are many and differentiated, several threads seem to recur more or less systematically.

First, culture is what used to be called the informal structure of an organization: The actual ways of doing things as contrasted to those prescribed in documents, decisions, and regulations. Second, "like most organizational research, the study of organizational culture is mainly from a managerial standpoint. . . . This emphasis is understandable. The prospect of changing the corporate culture has exciting implications for improving organizational performance" (p. 163). This dominating managerial concern provokes a worry that, perhaps, studies of organizational cultures only skim the culture that surrounds the top executives; therefore, studies of "lower-level cultures" are done and recommended (managing culture at the bottom). Third, "culture-related concepts are seen as very powerful both for apologetic and critical purposes" (corporate taboos). Fourth, the basic functionalist metaphor of an organization—"organism"—remains unchallenged. It is only that the *body* now has acquired a *soul,* similarly obsessed with the survival issue.

And finally, five steps for closing culture-gaps, using six organizational rites to change culture, and arriving at four cultures by managing the reward system were described. This gives us, presumably, 120 combinations that are all put to the service of American organizations. "There is a religious side to American industry. It is forever seeking salvation, never sure what form the messiah will take" (p. 421).

All in all, even for skeptics, the book is a very interesting presentation of approaches revolving around the idea of control through culture. However, the authors' conclusion can be seen as biased because of the results desired.

Can Organizational Culture Be Managed?

A more critical standpoint must be introduced to address this question, and Walter R. Nord expressed it very well (1985). Although he stated his original question as in the title above, he subsequently restated it in terms more convergent with my original intentions: "Culture is of interest as a tool to achieve some desired outcomes through an organization" (p. 189). In order to control through culture, one had to be able to control culture first. Or, perhaps, when culture was under control, the major source of behavioral variation was under control, too.

The answer was: "to an extent." There were many constraints, such as "life cycles, conflicting interests, a lack of willingness on the part of some actors, different salience attached to issues, different meanings, poor communication, lack of subordinate development, bad timing, a leader getting trapped by his or her own rhetoric, and complexity" (Nord, 1985, p. 193). Standard constraints to control and change, one cannot but notice. The difference may lie not in constraints, but in the way control through culture succeeds. On the one hand, it is very imprecise, as compared to conventional methods of control. On the other, it is very effective, as compared to the same. The "man proposes, God [culture] disposes" type of control. Nord (1985) made a significant observation:

> [S]ystematic, continuing attention to the components (of culture) may one day have a major impact on the knowledge and management of organizations. Attention to culture may, via deviation amplification, produce major changes—not immediately, but over an extended time period. In a sense, if we view culture as a tool, it may inform theory in important ways. (p. 193)

This *feed-forward* role of researchers and of theory is achieving more and more attention (R. H. Brown, 1977). Would organizations have become scientifically managed without Taylor? Will organizations become culturally managed because of culture studies?

Finally, Nord pointed out the weaknesses typical of studies that view culture as a managerial tool. One was the basic assumption of harmony and the consequent neglect of countercultures in large, complex organizations. Another was that culture could be understood using conventional research methods, even if they were clinical and qualitative, rather than routine and quantitative. Finally, Nord commented that if we treated Jung's notion of archetypes seriously, then they had to be taken as incomprehensible to the human mind. The ultimate paradox of research would have to be confronted, so to speak.

I do not wish to go that far. Nevertheless, the fact is that there are clear tendencies in *culture-as-managerial-tool* studies to attempt as little methodological change as possible. There will be new names, new labels, some softening of positivist criteria, but no dramatic changes in the paradigm. This is different, though, in most studies that see culture as a new, promising analytical metaphor for organization.

Organizations as Symbolic Orders

The era of organizational symbolism is often seen as beginning with Barry A. Turner's *Exploring the Industrial Subculture* (1971). I omitted organizational symbolism as professed by Dandridge, Mitroff, and Joyce (1980), because it essentially fits the culture-as-management-tool perspective. Nor did I include semiotic analyses (see e.g., Manning, 1979, or Broms & Gamberg, 1982) on the assumption that ethnomethodology represents a more distinct contribution to the analysis of language and conversation. I will examine the idea of organizations as "multicultures" and close with a discussion on the relationships between organizational culture studies and anthropologies of complex organizations.

Exploring the Industrial Subculture

Barry A. Turner's attempt to describe and analyze the culture of British industry (understood as part of national culture, thus subculture) is reported here not on historical grounds alone. The analysis made of empirical materials followed the rules of Glaser and Strauss's constant comparative analysis (1974); the general frame of reference was supplied by Alfred Schütz's phenomenological sociology (1964a); and Edmund Leach served as a guide to anthropological concepts. In short, the present attempt at an anthropology of complex organization shares almost all intellectual inspirations with *Exploring the Industrial Subculture*. Even the mistrust of the concept of *culture as a thing apart* is shared: "Although there are cultural differences between industry and the wider society, it is important not to reify the notion of these differences in a way which leads to fruitless pursuit of *the* definite industrial subculture" (Turner, 1971, p. ix).

Culture as a Set of Shared Meanings

Culture (or subculture, in this case) is a distinctive set of meanings shared by people whose actions are similar to each other and different from those of other cultures. Together with this definition, Turner removed the assumption of shared values (one can hold very different values from those of a culture and still be an accepted member), and generally weakened the concept of *sharing* so that it might finally be interpreted as "recognizing" or even "put into use without conviction." Indeed, one of the most interesting definitions of culture contained in the book is that it "may be regarded as an aggregation of definitions of those situations in which the members of the culture may expect to find themselves" (Turner, 1971, p. 55).

Turner commented on the fact that culture, in an organizational context, was noticed very early (Burns & Stalker, 1961; Jaques, 1951), but taken for granted. Indeed, although Jaques subsumed all his analysis under the concept of culture, he never wondered where it came from (presumably, from the past) and how it was sustained. These are two interesting questions to ask, and to answer, in learning how culture is understood by organizational actors.

Industry as Subculture

Turner's method consisted of reviewing important concepts from anthropology and ethnomethodology against the body of his empirical knowledge, from which he presented illustrations (contexts of those notions in the industrial culture). In a sense, his was *The Social Construction of Industry* type of work, and therefore interesting in the present context. Although the ethnography was, in Geertz's terms, thin, and many traditional organizational concepts came through (this criticism may in itself be evidence of a change in the conventional rhetoric of organization theory), the book discusses a variety of interesting issues that were worth studying in organizations. By applying alien concepts to an apparently well-known picture of organizational life, Turner managed to challenge their taken-for-grantedness in a very convincing way.

Speaking about rituals, Turner discussed well-known rites of passage, such as promotion or retirement. He tied them to the myth of constant upward progression and showed that this combination allowed people to cope with unpleasant situations such as demotion or lateral transfer, by subsuming them under the same positive event.

The punctuality ritual, claimed Turner, was one of the most amazing phenomena of modern life. According to him, even in industry there are very few people who really need to come and go at the same hour. However, the ritual celebrates the traditional industrial values and allows for a reflection of hierarchy by rules of exception. Rituals as supporting myths, and myths and rituals as supporting values that are seen as desirable, are phenomena that I find crucial for organizational control (Czarniawska-Joerges, 1988a).

What is interesting for the reader who encounters the book in the late 1980s is the fact that in 1971, Turner foresaw that the rational-technical ethos of industry and the accompanying rate of change would eliminate rituals in favor of more direct and open communication. He proved wrong in general terms. Nevertheless, the longevity and taken-for-grantedness of organizational rituals did decrease. Rituals, like furniture, are now made of plastic rather than oak and can easily be discarded.

While analyzing organizational talk, or communication, Turner turned to the naming[2] process, and in connection with this, analyzed the relationship between social and material worlds in organizations. This combination is very rare, with the notable exception of Berg, who proposed the notion of *techno-culture* (1985). Turner (1971) said:

> If material transformations are to be successfully achieved, the definitions which are used must come close to aspects of reality, within certain limits of tolerance, but the extent to which the constraints of the underlying material world limit the range of social definitions which can be "chosen from" will vary from item to item. In some cases it could be suggested that certain semantic divisions of the material world would be made in almost exactly the same place, regardless of the culture in which the items were found; in other cases, the constraints might be so undemanding as to allow considerable disagreement about definitions, so that there may even be an agreement to adopt a conventional definition, for reason of expediency. (p. 138)

Reasons of expediency, or pragmatic considerations, seemed to be the most important rule of naming or defining. Other things being equal (such as the power to define, to which I will return when speaking about social definitions), a good name was not necessarily the most accurate, but one that allowed action. It makes sense. "Tree" or "stone" is enough to decide whether to use a saw or a hammer; "fir" or "amethyst," albeit more accurate, do not improve the pragmatic advantage and may prove more costly in social terms (what if another person at the saw thought it was a pine and wanted to engage in a debate?). Naming seems to be a satisfying process, like any decision-making.

Focus on communication led Turner to observe the crucial role of translation between groups using different languages, and something even more interesting—a *joking mode*. The joking mode was a special mode of communicating that was used to test potential reactions, to soften a potentially threatening message, or to relieve tension.

One of the most interesting discussions concerned social definitions; in fact, Turner announced all that was to come under the label *management of meaning,* and more. He spoke about the social definitions of persons and nonpersons (secretaries, for example, being nonpersons), about the power to define, enactment of the environment, negotiations over meaning, challenging meaning, and accidental meaning. Although he did not develop his notions very far (indeed, the reader longs for more empirical examples), he sketched a magnitude of potential studies of symbolic elements of organizational life, many of them still neglected despite the blooming organizational culture studies, and he antedated many future trends: organizational identity, moral code, and organizational anecdotes.

Turner also considered the aspect of culture control under the eloquent title of "manipulation of the subculture." In relation to this, he discussed the management of space, introducing another aspect of the physical (or material) order to accompany the symbolic one. Another concept, management of awareness (based on the notion of *awareness contexts,* Glaser & Strauss, 1965), promises an interesting means of analyzing the distribution of power in organizations.

A Shopping List for an Anthropologist of Complex Organizations

Apart from admiring Turner's foresight concerning developments in organization theory, a potential student of complex organizations, worried perhaps by the lack of theoretical guidance, can use Turner as a checklist of concepts to be used in analysis. These concepts are characterized by two important attributes: They are reality tested (it is already known that they have referents in organizational reality), and at the same time, they are open (they do not preclude any possible result of subsequent analysis).

Another exceptional trait of Turner's work is his joint treatment of the symbolic and physical order of organizational reality. It is interesting that although the political order underlies his analysis, it is not explicitly described. This "gentle" approach to the political aspects of organizations (as compared to Burawoy, Cohen, or even Perrow) is also characteristic of the next perspective presented.

Organizations as Multicultures

Occupational Communities

John Van Maanen and Stephen R. Barley (1984) proposed the notion of *occupational community* as an alternative to organization, as a frame of reference that permits an understanding of people's actions in the workplace. They started with the assumption that the fundamental problem of management was controlling the labor process, and the occupational structure was of greater relevance here than, for example, in a mechanical hierarchy. Occupations were proposed as categories proper to highlight conflict and deviance in the workplace, and as more likely sources of identity than organizations. And it was occupations, not organizations, that were characterized by work cultures.

> Any outsider who observes naturally occurring conversation among self-defined members of an occupational community would quickly discover that members who have not previously met and who are of different ages, geographic regions, sexes, ethnic origins, or educational backgrounds are able to converse over a wide range of topics indecipherable to outsiders. Such is a manifestation of a shared culture. (Van Maanen & Barley, 1984, p. 32)

Culture was not, however, a variable: It was what a given occupational community was; it was what made it into an occupational community. It was a system of meaning. In that sense, it was also a source of self-control. Organizations could impose—or try to impose—working orders on their members, but within the occupational community it was the members who decided in accordance with, or against, organizational rules.

Some organizations fostered opportunities for self-control of occupational groups (for example, large R&D laboratories that could buy equipment individuals could not dream of buying) and some hindered it. Some supported certain occupational communities and suppressed others. The status of a given occupational community depended on its uniqueness and, obviously, on the demand for its work: "The more self-control possessed by an occupational community, the more distinct and self-perpetuating its culture" (Van Maanen & Barley, 1984, p. 44).

Three types of relationships between occupational communities and organizations were mentioned. The first type was an occupational community that organized itself in order to promote its interests. (There was a scale here, beginning with a professional association and ending with a cooperative.) Second, an organization might employ only, or mainly, the members of a given occupational community and more or less gear its interests to theirs (as in R&D laboratories and academic institutions). Third, and most common, was an organization that employed members of many different occupational communities. Although it might have favored some over others, it was not committed to promoting the interests of any of them. In such a case we are dealing with a *multicultural* organization. Some cultures might be strong and have a clear external focus (for example, a professional association or a union); some may not. Inevitably, this gives rise to conflicts among the cultures, and between cultures and management. The dynamics of these relationships are worthy of study.

"Tech": Organizational Culture as Managerial Ideology

The dynamics of the relationships between organizational culture and occupational culture, between mainstream culture and the margin, was the main topic of the study by Gideon Kunda, pupil to both Van Maanen and Schein (Kunda, 1986).

Tech, or the organization that was the site of the study, was the fruit of an occupational community, that is, computer engineering. The rapid growth of the company, however, began to speak in favor of another occupational community, professional management, although also technically educated.

Tech claimed to have an organizational culture, which was perceived by insiders and outsiders alike as

> . . . matrix management, multiple dotted lines, dense, almost indecipherable networks of informal relations, and an aura of ambiguity that, depending on context, is either celebrated as a source of creativity, or seen as a pain in the neck. As a result, formal and informal organization are not readily distinguishable. Informal organizing is formally prescribed and acknowledged. For many, "culture" replaces "structure" as an organizing principle to explain reality and guide action. (Kunda, 1986, p. 21)

Kunda's ethnographic description concerned mostly one group in the organization—a very visible product group in the engineering division that dealt with advanced products. The occupational groups involved were engineers, managers, wage class two (mostly female secretaries), and temporary workers (from free-lance engineers to cleaning people). The Tech culture did not aspire to include this last group.

Kunda first analyzed the phenomenon of organizational culture that was made explicit and therefore turned into a managerial ideology. Tech fed outside observers with the truth about itself, which could then be fed back.[3]

Researchers described Tech as a family, a group of autonomous people tied by emotional bonds, who discovered truth through conflict. Consultants repeated the same, but in more dramatic terms; to them, it was more a fanatic sect than a family. In addition, they claimed causative relationships: This tight culture led to economic success and was created on purpose by managers. Finally, journalists beheld the appearance of criticism, but it was made to sound temporary and a happy ending was announced (for example, "after a stormy period Tech is out again"). Generally, the message was the same: tight culture, with top management (or in plain terms, the president) in the lead, and engineers and managers as the workers at Tech. More critical attempts were easily censored from the internal, everlasting press conference at Tech.

The external image was strongly supported by the internal image, evidenced by documents, newsletters, and internal studies. What was striking about the contents of this image was the cleverness with which the conventional and the fashionable were blended. A picture of a "family" was at the same time a picture of a "controlled anarchy." Put in my terms, the ideology of organizational culture was firmly anchored in the cultural context of organizing, in myths of the past and visions of the future, and in present fashions (Czarniawska-Joerges, 1988a).

Kunda then moved to observing the rituals by which the ideology was enacted, more specifically, to the "presentations." Presentations were events at which one actor spoke to the group and explicitly referred to the organizational ideology, for example, top management presentations, training workshops, or work group meetings. These were minidramas, in which the ideology was explicated by various forms, including role-playing. In a top management presentation, for example, a manager would play a presenter and the engineers would play challengers, in a predictable, *comedia dell'arte* fashion. The ritualistic character of these events is best demonstrated by an example of a person who unexpectedly—for her and everyone else—breaks down and shows real emotions—to the horror of the audience, who does not know what to do. But usually, such emotions were used for deliberate purposes. Here, Kunda (1986) listens to an instructor in a training workshop:

> Balance your life. Don't say: "I'll work like crazy for four years then I'll get married." I heard this from a kid. But who will he marry? Don't let the company suck you dry; after nine or ten hours your work isn't worth much any way.
>
> She stops in the center of the room. All eyes are on her. After a pause for dramatic effect she says quietly: "What kind of company do you think allows me to be saying these things to you?" I feel moved myself. (p. 121)

All through that training workshop, the engineers played the role of challengers. They preferred hard facts to the fluff of cultural analysis. Instead of a business module, they got a technology module.

Kunda ended his study with an analysis of the consequences of this state of affairs for individuals. I shall try to summarize the study from the point of view of the organization as a whole. The main occupational community was that of engineers. However, it was the managers who promoted the organizational culture ideology. The relationship between the two groups was complicated. The organization was created around the engineering community, and was, for the most part, acting in their interest, leaving them a great deal of room for self-management. In addition, they reestablished this right for self-management by ridiculing and challenging the contents of the leading ideology. In doing so, however, they actually did managers a favor by exemplifying the supposed freedom of thought and right to conflicting ideas. One could imagine the future break between the overly business-like managers and the overly technology-minded engineers (as in the British wool industry, Chapter 6), but not yet. The group most fully controlled by the organizational culture ideology was secretaries, who could hardly count as an occupational community at all, considering the lack of their right to self-management. The extraculturals were actually in a better position, because they could ignore the ideology, which was not addressed to them anyway.

How Many Cultures Can an Organization Bear?

Van Maanen and Barley's (1985) answer was *many*. Segmentation was one process that separated occupational communities and their cultures from one another. Importation, due to mergers, acquisitions, or straightforward inclusion of other occupational groups was another. Technological innovation seemed to be creating new occupations before our eyes. Communities themselves might undergo an ideological differentiation. Finally, exclusion from a community or lack of opportunity to join one could lead to countercultures or small cliques.

I find the notion of a multicultural organization, with organizational culture as a possible managerial ideology, convincing. Organizing is embedded in a cultural context, from which certain traits are adopted by certain groups. This leads to clashes and conflicts. The notion of a uniformly shared organizational culture, on the other hand, seems to receive neither theoretical nor empirical support, only normative.

Organizations as Multiple Orders

Organizations as symbolic orders provide a very promising analytical frame of reference. Even if the authors presented here did not always formulate it explicitly, political and physical orders lurk behind every analysis. What to do? One can assume that organizational (sub)culture studies refer to only one aspect of an organization, the symbolic. Another possibility is to subsume the symbolic, political, and physical orders under culture; then organizations are cultures.

The compromise is to avoid the elusive concept of culture, at least in binding statements. Linda Smircich (1985) proposes very much the same, based on Abner Cohen's dictum: "Focus on symbols, not culture" (p. 66).

What, then, is an organizational culture? It can be an umbrella concept for clinical-minded researchers. Further, it can be a new control rhetoric, or even a managerial ideology. Alternatively, culture can be an analytical concept to use in organizations, but then it rarely appears with the adjective "organizational." Although organizational culture is a label that attracts all that has to do with culture and organization, the undesired result is that contrary approaches are subsumed under the same name. Its positive aspect is that the slogan "pluralism in research" begins to sound as if it were really possible.

Notes

1. Parallel to this, she also tries deconstructionist approaches from a feminist perspective, see Martin (1990).

2. I would call it *labeling* (Czarniawska-Joerges & Joerges, 1988).

3. One can observe the same phenomenon in the Swedish social sciences. Researchers inform colleagues from other countries, especially the United States, of their insights into Swedish society. These become published and then quoted by the very same researchers as objectified, or coming from impartial observers.

8

Toward an Anthropology
of Complex Organizations

Where, Who, and How to Study

Objects and Phenomena Under Study

The object of study, generally speaking, is a complex organization.[1] Organizations, it is assumed, are nets of collective action distinguished by artifacts and meanings related to that action. An anthropology of complex organizations should study the construction of meanings and artifacts typical (or unique) to complex organizations for the benefit of the actor and spectators alike.

How should one proceed in order to be able to grasp processes that are by definition complex? How much time and effort must be put into describing IBM, as compared to Samoa? Must not anthropological approaches be limited to small and simple ("primitive") organizations?

One can imagine that a complete description of IBM[2] would take the lifelong efforts of a substantial number of researchers. Or, to put it into a feasible frame, a study of an average complex organization, assuming intensive participation and a multimethod approach, would require a team of 5-10 people, fully employed for about five years (judging from Tavistock's experiences, and also from my own; see Beksiak & Czarniawska, 1977). Such studies must be done whenever possible. But it is rare that one can combine access, resources, and a committed team of people in the same time and space. An alternative is to view the anthropology of complex organizations as a cumulative science, in which various elements and partial studies contribute to a growing understanding of that crucial phenomenon in contemporary Western culture, the complex organization.

There are two ways of limiting a study: One can choose certain subnets of action, or focus on certain phenomena. In research practice, the most common approach is combining these two choices: Selected phenomena are linked with selected actions (for example, managerial *sagas*). This can be further justified by the fact that nets of collective action are forever overlapping; even a complex organization is only a construct helping to (arbitrarily) locate the center of a net. But equally important is tracing the connections that extend beyond the given net into political nets, professional nets, sociocultural nets, and so on.

Choice of these partial nets must, however, be guided by the specific complex organization. Such organizations are, as a rule, characterized by action called centralized control. This action and its connections (or lack of them) to various other nets of action inside (production) and outside the organization (norm-building) seem to be natural objects for study.

Shop floor activities, dealing with complex procedures of a technical or bureaucratic kind and far removed from top management, are other obvious partial nets of action. One could say, after Izraeli and Jick (1986), that the anthropological studies of life at the shop floor are relatively abundant. There are some studies that could be classified as anthropological studies of life at the managerial floor (see Kotter, 1982; Mintzberg, 1973). But the specificity of large organizations is what happens between floors, in the middle management level, the "thick waist" of complex organizations. The actions of this middle class of workers in complex organizations have as yet failed to attract much attention.[3]

Two other partial nets in large organizations are professional or occupational action systems and the construction of gender. Although the first is easier to detect because its net of action overlaps with a group of people, the other, which permeates to some degree all other actions, is taken for granted and is therefore very difficult for actors and observers to detect.

As for phenomena worth studying, they need not be analogies or functional equivalents to what has been studied in primitive societies (such as coming of age in General Electric), but those that are crucial and typical for complex organizations. Symbolic uses of ritual can be studied, if needed, but not rain dances (unless they prove to be an enriching metaphor).

What is important to remember is that analytical concepts cannot be studied. One cannot study power (although one can study people's use of power), value systems, or ideologies in any direct way. One can study a way of life, or a way to act, and use these concepts to interpret them.

Some phenomena relate naturally to certain nets of action: group decision-making to actions of top management, or a new technology to the shop floor net of action. But many can be studied from all or several viewpoints, thereby contributing to a more complete picture of complex organizations.

Almost inevitably, this requires a meso-perspective: not an individual one, and not that of macro-structures, but that most social perspective as experienced by us in the taken-for-granted, everyday life. Organizational reality must be seen as socially constructed by actors within and outside the system of collective action, which in its turn can be related to individual (e.g., deviant) realities and to societal (petrified) constructions.

A Social Meso-Perspective

Contemporary organization theory, lavished with approaches and overflowing with tolerance, still has inherent problems with grasping the idea of *social*. And it is no wonder, social psychology has the same problem, whereas sociology tries to equate it with "societal." Whenever organizations are not mechanisms, organisms, or something of the sort, they are usually aggregates of persons (as in organizational psychology) or else supra-persons, who decide, learn, and interpret (Daft & Weick, 1984). Although we know that organizations are not really people, for all practical purposes they are treated as such.

Yet the social character of organizations is, in my opinion, the key to understanding them. Here anthropology is most helpful, perhaps due to its overconcern with small societies and, at the same time, its lack of close contact with individuals populating them (because it is forced to focus on the social character of life).

In Chapter 6, I proposed to treat *social* as an interplay of the practical, the symbolic, and the political. This was inspired mainly by Abner Cohen who, however, neglected the material aspect of social life. Rom Harré (1979), on the other hand, proposes that

> [t]he public and collective aspects of human life are to be treated as products generated by an interplay between a *practical order,* concerned with the production of the means of life, and an *expressive order* concerned with honour and reputation. (p. 4, emphasis added)

Although I find this definition of expressive order peculiarly masculine (I would speak about dignity and meaningfulness), I agree with this interpretation, and also with the addition that "for most people at most times the expressive order dominates or shapes the practical order" (p. 4).

Harré did not propose a political order, but ended by suggesting "a political psychology of social action" (p. 398). For him, this meant introducing a moral element into analysis—and especially into praxis—of practical and expressive orders. The political aspect was a feature of social change, a type of action rather than its aspect.

I shall stay with Cohen on that matter and, combining both thoughts, continue to see this particular system of complex action, the complex organization, as a composition of practical, symbolic, and political dimensions. So the stage is set for an organizational drama. It also reflects a wider societal drama with its three positive heroes: the Rich, the Politician, and the Artist. All three have their equivalents in organizations, and so do their negative counterparts: the Poor,

the Powerless, and the Menial Worker.[4] Their many possible combinations confirm their interrelatedness.

While toiling to meet their practical and expressive needs, people
produce relationships among themselves that persist irregardless of
social and organizational action. Think, if you will, of the political aspect as a relatively static product, a result of the interaction between
the practical and the expressive. Harré saw it the other way around:
the practical and expressive orders being relatively stable in a given
time and space, and the politics involving the change. The version
one chooses depends on personal beliefs, especially those concerning
politics, and on one's understanding of organizations (which Harré
saw as people-structures and not action-structures). But the three
must remain together if the whole of organizational life is to be
portrayed.

This method of reasoning about organizations necessarily puts the
analysis between the macro- and micro-levels, between individuals
and social structures, on a *meso-*, or middle-range level. Leaving the
micro-level is necessary if we assume that a collective (or a group) is
able to perform actions impossible for any of its parts to achieve indi-
vidually, and this indeed is an assumption on which organizations are
built. But what about social classes, economic systems, and historical
forces?

Harré's analysis (1981) dealt on all levels with people, from individuals to societies. The difference between micro, meso, and macro
was originally the difference in numbers. His reasoning can, however,
be extended to these cases in which organizations are seen as systems
of action and not groups of people. Harré's argument was, in short,
that macro-groupings had no structural properties (relations between
elements that were not properties of elements themselves), and therefore could be seen, at best, as taxonomic groupings (every member
shares the same property, for example, blue eyes or a Swedish pass-
port) and treated as rhetorical devices. In the same vein, Abner Cohen
said that "classes are figments of the imagination of sociologists"
(1974, p. 17).

Harré claimed that the only way to study collectives was by applying an ethogenic methodology, which "involves assembling members'

understandings and interpretations of the institution and the events which make up its life, and negotiating these with an outside observer's ethnography" (1981, p. 151). The name is new but the content should, by now, be well known. This is the method that this book is about and, in fact, an early book by Harré and Secord (1972) was one of the early inspirations in my search for a different method.

The problem is that of scale. Although I agree with Harré on macro entities, we have different ideas as to what constitutes meso. His argument is well grounded in the sense that it is obviously easier to apply such a method to small collectives, such as families and small organizations. Should large organizations then be counted as figments of the imagination of organization theorists? Are they rhetorical figures? Are they taxonomic groupings, or can they be tackled at a truly interpretive level, as a way of life?

> [I]t is a central doctrine of the macro-collective approach that there are ramifying systems of unintended consequences, and that it is these that, as systems, are constitutive of the non-taxonomic aspects of a large-scale collective. (Harré, 1981, p. 153)

This is a significant statement, because "unintended consequences" is a key concept in the life of complex organizations. Are we then getting into a paradox? If, as stated at the outset, complex organizations are systems of action that are incomprehensible for the actors, what sense does it make to ask actors for accounts of what they do?

This apparent paradox is, for me, the main challenge and a main promise in studying complex organizations. I see it as bridging microscale, intelligible action, as seen by the actors, with the vastness of unintended consequences that we as spectators watch every day on our televisions, paralyzed with incomprehension.[5]

What is proposed here is to start with an intersubjective understanding of social action and to take it to its logical conclusion— within complex organizations. *Bridge* is an optimistic metaphor. Maybe there is nothing more than an abyss over there. Nevertheless, following this lead seems more promising than keeping individuals and macro-structures apart and/or mechanically connected.[6]

Gathering Insights
(Formerly Known as Data Collection)

Access

When all is said and done, there is one main obstacle to the emergence of an anthropology of complex organizations: access. Organizations do not particularly like being observed, if I may use this anthropomorphic expression. Or, as it is sometimes jokingly formulated, there are two kinds of organizations: those that are interesting, and those that permit access.[7]

What, then, is the secret of studies that were actually carried out? Was it effort, chance, or luck? Which allowed Dalton to do his amazing study, and which led Burawoy's cousin to be employed in the company where Roy had conducted his research?

Rosalie Wax (1974) went so far as to claim that one had to rely on luck even in such matters as research assistants: Their abilities become known only in the process, and no formal degree and no amount of training will help. It sounds fatalistic, but it is actually very obvious, even though it is ignored. People whose hands shake do not attempt to become surgeons, and people without talent are not successful writers. However, it sometimes seems that an act of will is all that is needed to become a social scientist. This is patently untrue; what is more, there are many subskills and subtalents within the practice of social science. Not everyone can be an interviewer and not everyone can produce a sound theory, just as not everyone can produce a soufflé. So what is the conclusion? There are several.

First, as much needed as an anthropology of complex organizations is, there are and should be many other fruitful ways of studying organizations. Field studies are not everybody's piece of cake and everyone has a right to establish their own diet. Second, a variety of individual skills and talents can be effectively employed in teamwork. Formal evaluation criteria within the social sciences are against such solutions, but common sense, the exigencies of field work, and the complexity of large organizations all point that way. Third, and finally, access can be defined as a lucky fit between the object being studied and the student. Researchers as individuals can be obstacles to access.

The Amount of Initial Structuring

There is a holy war going on in this matter, with complete pre-structuring on one side and the tabula rasa on another. Complete pre-structuring makes empirical study redundant, at least from the point of view of theory building. As to tabula rasa—first, it is quite obvious that none of us is a tabula rasa in any sense of the word, and the only way to counteract these biases and initial expectations is to self-account for them, as deeply and honestly as it is possible without boring the readers too much. Second, there is the issue of how much information an anthropologist needs before entering the organization. If one were to take literally the "total newcomer" approach, the first few days of anthropological inquiry would be spent on tracing footsteps around the building, in the hope of locating the entrance.

> In practice, observers steer a middle path between the two extreme roles
> of total newcomer (an unattainable ideal) and that of complete partici-
> pant (who in going native is unable usefully to communicate to his com-
> munity of fellow observers). (Latour & Woolgar, 1979/1986, p. 44)

Where the middle path is depends on the more or less random development of events (an anthropologist forced to listen to a thorough introduction by an overzealous organization member can hardly cover her ears) and a combination of the conscious and unconscious preferences of the researcher. It is like traveling: Some people will not depart without complete knowledge of the place they are going. I usually know the name of the place and the plane departure time. After having returned, I begin to devour information that helps me make sense of my experience. When all is said and done, anthropology might, after all, be seen as a frame of mind.

A Mini-Immigration

A field study is, in many ways, an experience similar to that of immigration. One similarity lies in the fact that field workers, like immigrants, have to be resocialized. They have to undergo a process that is much more painful than that of the original socialization, because it inevitably means a clash between different social rules. From that follows another similarity: Personal identity, taken for granted by successfully functioning adults, is challenged. A student of organization, like an immigrant, perceives that the new people she meets try to reconstruct her image and classify her personality, which encourages a conscious monitoring of self-presentation and a generally increased self-reflection, operations that, one had hoped, were safely put away together with other memories of adolescence. Finally, the feeling of "being dumb," of continuously running into glass walls is, if less acute in a study compared to the immigration experience, also basically the same.

Many researchers who consider themselves empirical students of organizations may not recognize this picture at all. In numerous cases that can be due to a successful employment of defense mechanisms protecting the exposed egos. Like immigrants who return to their families looking for relics of the old culture, researchers retreat (much more easily) into their own culture and forget about the discomfort caused by the encounter with aliens. Nonanthropological, "aerial" methods of data gathering facilitate this evasion. A telephone interview spares one from seeing the horrified face of the interlocutor as one makes a terrific blunder, and strange noises can be blamed on line failure. The sheer necessity of meeting an interlocutor twice provides researchers with personal feedback that they might wish to avoid.

Everything that is most acutely felt by those residing in and, so to speak, earning their daily social bread in an organization, also happens to some extent in any type of direct and repetitive contact. Some researchers are lucky enough to cut off the feeling of estrangement completely; the question arises as to whether their studies profit to the same degree. The psychological discomfort of estrangement that must be overcome seems to me a necessary price of learning. The bonus is in gaining extra knowledge about oneself.

On the Importance of Studying Social Representations

Let us assume that the threshold of access has been overcome; a researcher is in, tuned to an organizational reality. But now the problem of access is repeated: Reality, as accessible by one's senses, is not enough. In order to understand others' ways of life as they are observed, an observer must see reality as others see it. Or, to put it bluntly, in order to be able to observe a reality we must understand it.

Why can reality not be approached directly? Because

> ... we are never provided with any information which has not been distorted by representations "superimposed" on objects and on persons which give them a certain vagueness and make them partially inaccessible. When we contemplate those individuals and objects, our inherited genetic predispositions, the images and habits we have learned, the memories of them which we have preserved and our cultural categories all combine to make them such as we see them. (Moscovici, 1984, p. 6)

When approaching a cultural setting we are confronted with two alternatives only: One is to approach it through our own set of representations; another is to try to reach the representations held by the natives. Each has its advantages and disadvantages. The first is often regarded as more objective, because it is supposedly free from involvement. But it is free from involvement of one type only—the one that the actors have. Otherwise, we bring in all the ballast of our private and social prejudices. That ballast might, of course, be much better and nobler than the values and prejudices of the natives. Nevertheless, the actors involved act upon *their* representations and not ours, however biased the former and correct the latter might be. In order to understand their actions we must understand their representations.[8]

But is this not impossible by definition? What we can reach is ultimately only our representations of their representations, because our representations are the last link in a chain of perceptions, opinions, and concepts. What is accessible to our cognition is our own distortion of other people's distortions. How can we understand what they mean? And what do they know about their own reality, perceived through the taken-for-grantedness of their representations? The answer lies in the intersubjectivity of the social world, which guarantees that the meanings of others can be understood (Silverman, 1972).

This intersubjectivity is the basis of the common core of representations held by actors involved in the same collective action, the core of meanings they share. This core determines what their common reality is—the object of the researchers' curiosity and interest. This curiosity can be satisfied not only due to the intersubjectivity of the social world, but also due to the fact that representations appear to us and others

> . . . almost as material objects, insofar as they are the product of our actions and communications. . . . Individuals and groups create representations in the course of communication and cooperation. . . . Once created, however, they lead a life of their own, circulate, merge, attract, and repel each other, and give birth to new representations, while old ones die out. . . . [Representation] ceases to be ephemeral, changing and mortal and becomes, instead, lasting, permanent, almost immortal. In creating representations, we are like the artist who bows down before the statue he has sculpted and worships it as a god. (Moscovici, 1984, pp. 12-13)

Due to the fact that social representations become reified, researchers of organization have a chance to grasp something that is ephemeral and intangible. Due to the fact that they are treated as "real" by those who act upon them, the competing representations of researchers and the academic community will never have the same weight as those that originate with the actors. Their value, as we shall see later, is as a supplement and not a replacement.

The notion of social representations is helpful in at least two crucial points. First, it helps us understand the fragility of the borders between reality and fiction, ideas and things, owing to the fact that the only objects of our cognition are our representations. Second, it helps us understand the idea of collective thought or, in Douglas's version, the thought worlds, as distinct from aggregate thought.

The next question, then, is how to study social representations, and the answer is obvious: with anthropological methods. But what do we consider to be anthropological methods?

On Techniques: Anthropology and the Interview

> The method of the social scientist . . . must take dramatic account of the social cultural world—the complex of actors and their plots as they live and dream on the stage of society. (Bruyn, 1966, p. xiv)

Bruyn goes on to say that research techniques are needed that help grasp the social drama as it appears to the actors, their views of their roles and their assumptions about the unfolding plot. And the most obvious way of doing that is via participative observation.[9] In the case of organization research, it means that the researcher assumes the role of an organizational member (or, sometimes, the other way around). This was the method adopted by Melville Dalton, Michael Burawoy, and Göran Palm (a Swedish author who worked at LM Ericsson).

It is clear, though, that such studies are limited to two situations: a lucky access situation or a working place that does not require particular qualifications. But even the latter requires some luck or special dispositions. I could not possibly work as a radial drill operator, and my only factory job, in a preservatives factory, was brought to an end by a dramatic stomach indisposition after having eaten too much fruit. Working as a waitress, a job I often held in the past, would make me into a native in no time at all: I would simply stop being a researcher and plunge into waiting tables instead. It is difficult to obtain the state of "detached involvement" that Bruyn (1966) declares is the ideal state for a participant observer when dropped in the midst of an alien culture. One needs time, and this is a serious impediment to organization studies—much more serious than the need for money.

These limitations are one of the main reasons that there are so few anthropological studies of complex organizations. Torn between anthropological orthodoxy and organizational realities, researchers tend to choose other approaches. At the risk of sounding heretical, I propose to abandon orthodoxy in order to be able to adopt anthropology as the study of ways of life. Anthropological method recommends immersing oneself in the flood of alien cultures in order to grasp the direction of the stream and to feel the temperature of the water. But there are, or at least should be, many ways of doing that.

The first possible relaxation of the rules is the requisite for researchers to act as nonparticipating observers. In other words, they are allowed to be around, look, and ask, but they are not required to act in the organizational drama.[10] This approach was used by Henry Mintzberg, Bruno Latour, and Gideon Kunda. Marianella Sclavi (1989), inspired by Truman Capote, calls it a shadowing technique.

But such access demands even more luck. And as this is not a book on luck and how to command it, more viable possibilities must be considered. One of them is what I call observant participation, a method I proposed and introduced in a study of a consumer goods management system in Poland (Beksiak & Czarniawska, 1977; Czarniawska, 1980). The study was carried out in several stages: In each stage, actors (from 10 to 25 at a time) in chosen organizations, under our guidance, collected systematic observations of events over a period of 18 months. We would never have achieved an introduction of 25 researchers into organizations in the same branch. And if we had, we might have waited 18 months for them to be acculturated enough to be able to start observation.

I still use this method with variations, because it has proved fruitful. A common variation can be called, after Stephen Barley (whose study is presented in the section "The power of irony"), ethnographic interviews: repetitive, open, and extensive interviews aimed at achieving a representation of people's work and organization.

But there is a very serious mistrust of interviews within the anthropological method. By interviewing people we learn about the reality of interviewing, and not about some other reality behind, let us say, the ethnomethodologists. By interviewing people we create an artificial reality that does not relate to the "real" reality, that is, the ethnographers'. And by interviewing people *about* something we miss an authentic insight, that of the phenomenologists.

All this is true, but exaggerated. Giving answers to the interviewers, as long as it reveals a pattern, is a part of making sense in (and of) organizations. In other words, if organizational actors lie, and they do it in a repetitive way, this common lie is more informative than an idiosyncratic truth. There may be no other reality behind the interview, but the interlocutors believe there is, and the purpose is to reconstruct their beliefs. Finally, enriching as the observation might be, it will never be comprehensive without the actors' accounts, and what are interviews if not provoked accounts?

According to Scott and Lyman (1968), an account is

> . . . a linguistic device employed whenever an action is subjected to valuative inquiry . . . a statement made by a social actor to explain unanticipated

or untoward behavior—whether that behavior is his own or that of others, and whether the proximate cause for the statement arises from the
actor himself or from someone else. (p. 46)

I am not sure whether Scott and Lyman would agree, but in my view, almost all behavior is unanticipated for someone in an anthropological
frame of mind, and therefore an account of organizational action can le-
gitimately be demanded. Usually the actors understand this estrangement
and willingly produce desired accounts (although they do say sometimes,
"Don't they teach you that at your business school?" thus refusing to acknowledge the researcher's lack of social competence).

My claim that interviews are provoked accounts is based on the fact
that organizational action, from the perspective of lay persons or the
rules of everyday life, appears peculiar, and therefore has to be accounted for, usually in terms of rationality (whereas everyday accounts
are more often formulated in terms of morality). In addition, this need to
account for one's actions might not be so natural in conversation with
participant observers who, by virtue of participation, are supposed to
share the same values and norms, at least to some degree. Actually, the
old anthropologists were not really participants; they were spectators,
and as such, they were permitted to demand accounts and to obtain them.
One can say with Hannah Arendt (as quoted in Young-Bruehl, 1982),
who was speaking from personal and social experience:

> In matters of theory and understanding, it is not uncommon for outsiders
> and spectators to gain a sharper and deeper insight into the actual mean-
> ing of what happens to go on before or around them than it would be
> possible for the actual actors or participants, entirely absorbed as they
> must be in the events. (p. xi)

The point is trivial really, because all techniques have advantages and
disadvantages. Because the interview can be seen as the most accessible technique for research in organizations, our interest lies in maxi-
mizing the advantages and minimizing the disadvantages. The most
dangerous pitfall is, of course, language.

> Any social group, to the extent that it is a distinctive unit, will have to
> some degree a culture differing from that of other groups, a somewhat

different set of common understanding around which action is organized, and these differences will find expression in a language whose nuances are peculiar to that group and fully understood only by its members. . . . In interviewing members of groups other than our own, then, we are in somewhat the same position as the anthropologist who must learn a primitive language, with the important difference that . . . *we often do not understand that we do not understand* and are thus likely to make errors in interpreting what is said to us. (Becker & Geer, 1957, p. 29, emphasis added)

A continuous comparative analysis, discussed in the next section, helps to deal with this problem by using successive interviews as texts in decoding the meanings of words and concepts used repetitively. The commonsensical reaction of asking when one does not understand is, of course, of enormous use, but I will not go further into the psychosocial aspects of interviewing, well described in almost all books on techniques.

My unwillingness to engage in this sort of prescription stems also from the fact that, as much as I believe in the possibility of *improving* one's interviewing skills, those skills must be there from the beginning in order to improve them. In that, I agree with Rosalie Wax when she says:

I am convinced that the ability to conduct a good interview involves a particular kind of adeptness at relating to other human beings—to the respondent and to the person for whom the interview is being done. It has very little to do with formal education or even with instruction and training. . . . With interviewing, the proof of the pudding is only in the eating. (Wax, 1974, p. 294)

This does not mean that poor interviewers must give up hope of doing decent field research. In observing my students who take method courses, I noticed that some have enormous talents for observation and not for interviewing, or the other way around. The problem is that it is rarely recommended that people try their technical aptitude before engaging in a serious field study. Everybody is supposed to be able to do everything, which is patently untrue.

Another problem has nothing to do with the interview as a technique, but with the most common way of using it, which is as a single encounter with a given interlocutor. The result is a paralyzing feeling of lack of familiarity on both sides, which produces resistance in interlocutors and prevents interviewers from reading various cues that become visible only after some time. Repeated interviews, possibly over a longer time period to ensure coverage of various changes of mood and opinion (in fact, a simulation of observation), can help remedy this problem.

The main trap is still the "reality of interviewing" as opposed to the "reality beyond the interview." Even if we know that what we reach are only representations, how do we know that these are the representations that guide the action and not just the representations produced for our benefit during the interview? We do not know, and we never will. Perfect controllability is the dream of the simplistic positivist (of whom there are not many) and the nightmare of the humanistically oriented researcher. It is up to the interlocutors' will and cultural custom to choose what they say. The least we can do is help them by not asking about hypothetical realities (for example, "What would your company do if the market changed?") if it is not these that we want. We usually want to know what they do and why, so this is what we, observers and interviewers alike, should ask.

I would gladly avoid the dichotomy of the two realities by moving the discussion to the level of methods rather than techniques. Conversation (subject-to-subject) is the main method of the social sciences. It can take all forms, from body language through barter to a formalized interview. In that sense, all observations are participatory; it is only the degree of participation that differs.

Observation (subject-to-object) is the main method of the natural sciences. At one extreme, natural scientists can even kill the objects of their study in order to observe them better. At the other, they can treat their objects of study with the respect and openness that will make them closer to subjects than objects (and this applies to machines as well as to animals).

These definitions indicate that the border between the two methods is not sharp. Conversation and observation are two extremes of the same dimension ("contact") and both natural and social research can be placed in between. Indeed, many computer hackers handle their computers with greater respect than some psychologists treat their subjects ("Ss"). Natural scientists anthropomorphize, social scientists reify; both operations are considered erroneous from the point of view of the conventional ideal of science.

In my opinion, actors and their accounts are and will remain the main source of whatever knowledge we can obtain about organization theory. After all, it is *their* way of life, the system of collective action where *they* act as subjects, that is interesting. Nevertheless, this does not release the researchers from their obligations. Severyn Bruyn, who I quoted at the beginning of this section, saw participant observation as much more than just a field technique. He envisaged it as a metaphor for the researcher's task, dictated by a humanist obligation:

> The social scientist cannot understand people scientifically in any adequate sense unless he understands them in particular, and for their own sake. This is part of the human perspective which now must be understood as a part of the scientific culture of man. It is a "participant requirement" for the researcher who seeks to know his subjects adequately. There is another requirement, however, for the researcher to fulfill. The culture and organization of people in society should be subjected to objective analysis. This is an "observer requirement." *And this is done as part of the purpose of understanding people in particular and valuing their individual existence.* (Bruyn, 1966, p. 122)

What Bruyn meant by "objective" is something other than intersubjective reality as it appears to the actors involved. Some ethnomethodologists would like to stop there, because, in their opinion, this reality can be explained in self-referential terms and without reference to the constructs of an observer. The world of common sense is complete, and any search for "objective causality" destroys the genuine reality of the world as we perceive it. To which Silverman responds:

> If, however, we do not wish to go beyond lived experience, we would do best to rely upon what a person has to say for himself or, although it is clearly dangerous, a sophisticated journalist. The role of sociologist must be to go beyond this position in order to understand the logic that underlies it. While the sociologist must *begin* from the first-order constructs of the participants themselves, his work necessarily involves a distortion of their experience as he seeks to idealize and formalize, to talk about

typical where there is ultimately a number of unique cases. (Silverman, 1972, p. 191-192)

Distorted as it might be, an account of accounts is needed, in order to make the intersubjective reality of the actors more open to others.

An Account of Accounts

One or Many Accounts

Gilbert and Mulkay (1984) provided us with the following sarcastic description of a typical way of analyzing qualitative "data":

1. Obtain statements by interview or by listening to or observing participants in a natural setting.
2. Look for broad similarities between the statements.
3. If there are similarities which occur frequently, take these statements at face value, that is, as accurate accounts of what is really going on.
4. Construct a generalised version of these participants' accounts of what is going on, and present this as one's own analytical conclusion. (p. 5)

As an alternative, they proposed a discourse analysis (how the accounts are constructed) and promised to move to action analysis as a next step. But, as we know from the classic ending of most papers, entitled "Further Research," such promises are rarely kept. At any rate, a recent publication by one of the authors (Mulkay, 1985) indicates that he is still busy with discourse analysis, and therefore we are left alone with our task, which is the analysis of action. Therefore, I propose to retain both discourse and its topic as the focus of analysis. This gives us a double perspective, the how and the what; in addition, the actors provide us with differing versions of reality. I agree with Gilbert and Mulkay (1984), that

> ... sociologists' attempts to tell *the* story of a particular social setting or to formulate *the* way in which social life operates are fundamentally unsatisfactory. Such "definite versions" are unsatisfactory because they imply unjustifiably that the analyst can reconcile his version of events

with all the multiple and divergent versions generated by the actors themselves. (p. 2)

My strategy, then, is as follows:

1. Obtain actors' accounts; they must be detailed and coherent enough to serve as a basis for action for someone with the same standpoint[11] as a given actor.
2. Look for similar accounts; try to understand why they are similar. Concentrate on holistic accounts, ways of seeing the world and not just particular opinions or judgments on a particular matter. Try to track down the reasoning behind the accounts through the way the accounts are formed.
3. Do the same for differences.
4. Attempt a story (not a history) of a phenomenon. Try to tie together various versions, actors, situations, and accounts so that they make sense even if they contradict each other. The result should be a multifaceted magnifying glass, showing a picture that is wholly visible but fuzzy from a distance, and that becomes sharp but incomplete when viewed through one of the facets.
5. Avoid any one version of events, including your own, to lead the narrative. Use concepts as a frame into which different facets of the magnifying glass can be slotted.

The challenge is in presenting the complexity of a situation as it is perceived simultaneously by different actors (and the researcher), in the hope that this same complexity will help both actors and observers to understand the reasons and effects of actions undertaken by actors when they are looking through one facet only. They see a fairly clear picture, yet do not realize that looking through another facet will produce a similarly clear but different picture. Simply adding one more picture, that of the researcher (as is done in conventional studies) will multiply the realities even further.

Theories, it is claimed, are simplifications of reality. This is true, if they are to serve as grounds for action; or false, if they are to serve as grounds for reflection. Interpretive theories attempt to simulate the complexity of social reality in order to make people aware of this very complexity. Provided that we strive for both action *and* reflection, we need both theories: simplifications, that is, correspondence theories that stand for reality; and problematizations, that is, representative theories that discard the taken-for-grantedness of everyday action.

Constant Comparative Analysis

Constant comparative analysis, as advised by the proponents of grounded theory, beginning with the classic text by Barney G. Glaser and Anselm Strauss (1974) and further developed by Barney G. Glaser (1978), Barry A. Turner (1981, 1983; with Patricia Y. Martin, 1986), and Derek Layder (1982), is a commendable way of representing multiple realities without getting lost in the jungle of differing accounts. Constant comparative analysis is basically an inductive method of categorizing events ("incidents," as Glaser & Strauss call them) on the strength of their similarities and differences. Events are contained in the accounts obtained by interviews, participant observation, or whichever techniques the researcher uses. Names for categories (derived from the field or proposed by the researcher), compose a hierarchy of increasing abstraction, constituting the building blocks of an emerging theory that is held in place by the relationship between them.

In a study of control over central public agencies in the Swedish public sector, the Directors General that I interviewed mentioned many incidents of control attempts on the part of the Ministries, told me their reactions to that and described their notions of ideal control, including historical and modern concepts of public control. I had, therefore, a collection of various classes of events—actual control, actual countercontrol, desired control, myth of public control, and emerging ideals of control—some of which pertained to a "reality beyond" (e.g., the Ministry's attempts at actual control), whereas others were typical of the "reality of interviewing" (e.g., desired control, as presented to me by my interlocutors). Differences and similarities within, between, and among classes led to the emergence of categories and properties of categories: tight actual control, negotiated control, desire for tightened control, and so on. These relationships and categories comprised a modest but substantial theory—that the control of public agencies in Sweden is based on a shared myth of agencies' independence, which allows for a variety of actual control relationships. An economic and political crisis disturbed the existing balance, provoking a search for a new stabilizing myth (Czarniawska, 1985).

The main difference between constant comparative analysis and conventional qualitative analysis is the fact that it is *constant*. Instead of collecting innumerable events (a year in the field) and then trying to acquire some understanding, the researcher starts comparative analysis at the second interview, and each continuing step in "gathering insights"[12] is guided by previous analyses. Even when a theory is complete, and new events arrive, the analysis must be continued.

> Using the constant comparative method makes probable the achievement of a complex theory that corresponds closely to the data, since the constant comparisons force the analyst to consider much diversity in the data. . . . *To make theoretical sense* of so much diversity of his data, the analyst is forced to develop ideas on a level of generality higher in conceptual abstraction than the qualitative material being analyzed. (Glaser & Strauss, 1974, p. 114, emphasis added)

In other words, analysts do not have to choose one version of reality as correct or introduce their own version as the right one; instead, one learns to deal with diversity by trying to understand its roots. (All kinds of control happen in reality, but how do the interlocutors explain the kind they are confronted with?)

In all fairness, it must be noted that the strategy of grounded theory is, in part, a systematization of what was already being done. (It must take an especially trained or especially hapless researcher not to do any analysis during "the year in the field"; in fact, accounts of field work like those of Rosalie Wax [1974] or Nigel Barley [1983, 1986, 1988] show that constant comparative analysis is almost a matter of unconditioned reflex.) On the other hand, even if meant as an honest reconciliation with the realities of research as opposed to unattainable ideals, the grounded theory approach is still unfeasible in its pure form. No sponsor will give money to a project that will end only when the theoretical satiation point is reached. The realities of academia make comparative analysis less constant than one would wish. Research is a series of compromises; nevertheless, it is good to know which ideals to follow even if one errs.

What to Compare

It is easy to compare incidents, or events, that are already accounted for, but first and last, we must decide where to demand accounts. Glaser and Strauss tell us to select comparison groups according to their theoretical relevance, that is, according to the degree to which their observation might help us understand a phenomenon in question (the one whose theory is emerging). In other words, we know that a given phenomenon takes place in a given group (I could not study central control in large organizations by observing a nuclear family); the choice of the next group then either minimizes the differences (the group is almost the same as the first group; does the theory still hold?) or maximizes them (the group is very different; does the theory still hold?). The end of a constant comparative analysis is marked by theoretical satiation: At least temporarily (theories never cease to emerge) we seem to understand the phenomenon in question. But what does it mean in terms of complex organizations?

In the comparative studies tradition, complex organizations can be compared across cultures (as in Hofstede's study, 1980), across time (as in Chandler's study, 1977), or with noncomplex organizations (as when Perrow [1972/1986] compared a bureaucratic organization with Gouldner's Gypsum Plant).

As to comparing organizations across cultures, the assumption seems to be, as Giorgio Inzerilli (1981) pointed out, that organizations are treated as rational instruments whose characteristics are universal in nature; therefore the sociocultural environment is either disregarded or treated as an intervening, distorting variable. As Karlene H. Roberts (1970) sarcastically put it, this tradition of comparative studies

> . . . is paralleled in American organizational research where one group of workers has been interested in people without the organizations and another group in the organizations without people. (p. 329)

In other words, instead of studying large organizations *against* a given background, "organizations must be understood as isomorphic representations of their sociocultural environments" (Inzerilli, 1981 p. 11).

As to time-based comparisons, they are always of value because of their unique dynamic aspects, but are always scarce because of practi cal difficulties. Finally, comparing complex organizations with non complex organizations is a somewhat deceitful endeavor in that the comparison of distinct instances in each category (such as IBM and a family restaurant) are nonsensical, whereas comparing those that dif fer only slightly creates more problems in the effort to distinguish them than the eventual illumination is worth.

Provided we succeed in finding subsequent comparative groups there is always the problem of where to stop. Comparative complete ness, says Barney G. Glaser, is never possible because there will al ways be another group or unit that would be worthwhile to include The same is valid for descriptive or ethnographic completeness which is never reached because there is always something more to de scribe—as a study extends in duration, the original descriptions be come obsolete. The only hope lies in *theoretical* completeness, which Glaser defines in somewhat old-fashioned social science rhetoric as the stage when the analyst "explains with the fewest possible con cepts, and with the greatest possible scope, as much variation as pos sible in the behavior and problem under study" (Glaser, 1978, p. 125). I would rather say that theoretical completeness is reached when we can tell a story of the phenomenon that makes sense to us and to our readers, and leaves no questions open (for the time being). In aes thetic terms, to which we shall return, this is called cogency, consis tency, and economy (R. H. Brown, 1977). But before we move to the issue of theory evaluation, we must formulate the theory. What re mains then, is the problem of story writing.

The Story Is Told

For an overview of alternative ways of writing ethnographic stud ies, I refer the reader to the recent books by Clifford Geertz, *Works and Lives: The Anthropologist as Author* (1988) and John Van Maanen, *Tales of the Field* (1988). Here I shall tackle only a few problems that are, in my opinion, of crucial importance: "thick description" versus "thin theory," the choice of narrative, and the choice of rhetoric.

As to the first of these, Clifford Geertz advised everybody to engage in thick description, a rich narrative of ethnographic data, which would prove to be more illuminating than any theory could. Although Geertz himself seems to prove the point, most others fail to do so. Anthropologists point out that "other people's ethnography is often very dull" (Leach, 1976, p. 3; see also Pratt, 1986). Caustic commentators speak about monographs that are thick on description but thin on theory, and counsel beginners to return to the old tradition, where a thick theory was sparsely illustrated by carefully chosen or, even better, thought up examples. Commonsense-oriented researchers cannot avoid the feeling that some middle way must exist. This is what Abner Cohen recommends:

> [T]he more analytically advanced an anthropological study is, the more "oversimplified" its conclusions in the final presentation seem to be. A poorly analyzed body of field data presents a confused account, cluttered with a great deal of irrelevant and superficial detail. At best, it gives a "naturalistic" picture, presenting a mechanical reflection of appearances. An analytical account of the same data on the other hand is like a sketch, showing a few bold lines here and there, and weeding out much irrelevant detail. (1974, p. 47)

Before producing the sketch, however, we must first decide what tradition to use and then which means to employ. As to the former, many students choose the case narrative as the easiest or perhaps most appealing, irrespective of their study method. A case study can be written in the form of a problematic discussion, and a grounded theory study can be written in the form of several case studies; the form of narration (the reporting mode) does not have to be the same as the method of study. A word of caution, however: Many said of Joyce that the main reason for his revolutionary approach to the novel was that he could not write like Tolstoy. And, indeed, a chronological account, especially when many versions are involved, requires at least a Flaubert or other master of narrative. Some researchers can manage this, but those who cannot are safer in the haven of traditional, problem-focused theoretical discussion. (I assume here that description is presented jointly with the analysis, that, indeed, there is no such thing as a "pure description.")

Donald McCloskey (1990) claimed that economics[13] has two things to offer: stories and models (metaphors). A similar categorization is taken up by Leach (1976) in his conceptualization of the analysis of rituals. The meaning, he claimed, lies in transformations between metaphors and metonymies (of which causal chains of events are a type). The choice of the final form depends more or less on individual preferences—some people are better at stories, some at metaphors. What is more, some stories sound better when told chronologically, and some when metaphorically transformed.

This brings us, finally, to rhetoric. My point here is very simple: Any rhetoric might do, if consciously used and acknowledged. Even an "illegitimate" rhetoric is acceptable when presented as a conscious exercise in style (see Michael Pacanowsky's attempt at fiction as a reporting mode, "A Small-Town Cop Story," Pacanowsky, 1983). Lack of reflection on rhetoric is, in some cases, a more or less conscious attempt to hide some values or manipulative intentions (on rhetoric in economics, see McCloskey, 1985; on rhetoric in management theory, see Calàs & Smircich, 1987). In other cases, it may just be carelessness, resulting in mixed metaphors and confused styles.

For a while, it was bad style to write in a good style; now it is no longer so. But the focus on rhetorics and the permission to use metaphors begin to produce another exaggeration. Pinder and Bourgeois (1982) warn against the excessive use of tropes. Indeed, when one reads that population ecologists in organization theory are looking for organizational "genes," one begins to wonder where the frontier is between a metaphor and a definition. There is none, some say; all is metaphor. This might be true, etymologically, but at the moment of inquiry, one deals with metaphors, as there is not yet familiarity with the phenomenon under study. Each metaphor has a nonapplicable aspect that the researcher must be aware of as a prophylactic against misuse. In what sense are complex organizations not elephants? They are not animals; they do not have ears or trunks. In what sense are not all organizations theaters? Their performance might not be visible. In what sense are organization theories not holograms? Theories are verbal and holograms are visual. Beware of your favorite metaphors.

To sum up, one can say, with Rosaldo, that

> anthropologists aspire to describe other cultures in ways that render them familiar (or at any rate intelligible and humanly plausible) without losing sight of their differences. Good descriptions neither bring other people so close that they become just like ourselves nor so distance them (in the name of objectivity) that they become objectified and dehumanized. (Rosaldo, 1987, p. 89)

Rosaldo was speaking not only about the formal characteristics of a description but also about its contents: a theory. Is theory the same as rhetoric, or is it something else? In other words, is there good rhetoric with bad theory, and good theory with bad rhetoric?

Anything Goes? A Normative Obligation

In order to decide whether theory and rhetoric are one, we must ask another question: What is a good theory and what is a bad one? Is there any way to tell? Is it important? This section deals with matters that were traditionally discussed under the headings *reliability* and *validity*. These standards of evaluations are no longer paramount because other concepts and aspects have been introduced.

The Credibility of Grounded Theory

Because the recommended way of theory building is that of a grounded theory, it is only fair to refer to its authors when speaking of theory evaluation. Glaser and Strauss (1974) state explicitly that the clarity and integration of a theory (which I take to be the traits of its rhetoric) increase the credibility of that theory. But, in reality, the proof of the theory is in its applicability.

> The practical application of grounded sociological theory . . . requires developing a theory with (at least) four highly interrelated properties.

The first requisite property is that the theory must closely *fit* the substantive area in which it will be used. Second, it must be readily *understandable* by laymen concerned with this area. Third, it must be sufficiently *general* to be applicable to a multitude of diverse daily situations within the substantive area, not to just a specific type of situation. Fourth, it must allow the user partial *control* over the structure and process of daily situations as they change through time. (p. 237)

A good theory must fit, must be relevant, and must work. There is no doubt as for the first two, but what is meant by saying that it *must* work? Glaser (1978) expands on this theme by saying that

a theory should be able to explain what happened, predict what will happen and interpret what is happening in an area of substantive or formal inquiry. (p. 4)

With all respect to my methodological forebears, this statement contains a postpositivist mirage. The very critique of positivism, to which Glaser and Strauss contributed substantially, started by pointing out that human actions cannot be explained in the same way as natural events, neither can they be predicted: Possibly, they could be interpreted and understood. Instead of "explanation by cause or universal law," we arrive at a hermeneutic understanding of particular wholes, usually by means of interpretation of rules and motives (R. H. Brown, 1977, p. 10).

We can help the practitioners to rationalize what has happened, and we can diminish the shock of surprise, which comes inevitably with the future, by widening their understanding, but we cannot explain and predict social phenomena. So, the theory must fit and be relevant. But how do we know that it will? We learn that from "the man in the know," as Glaser calls him.

What the man in the know does not want is to be told what he already knows. What he wants to be told is how to handle what he knows with some increment in control and understanding of his area of action. The sociologist as theorist provide[s] this theoretical traction in many ways when his theory is grounded, that is, when it fits, works, and is relevant. (Glaser, 1978, p. 13)

Another apology is due, but this is a completely apolitical view of the man in the know. The man in the know understands the value of a clever form and might prefer it to relevance and workability (on what managers want to hear, see Sevón, 1986; on what consultants offer, see Czarniawska-Joerges, 1990a). In this sense, a theory might work beautifully just because it does not fit reality.

In addition, the man in the know is often committed to his position, which means that he might refuse a theory because it fits too well, that is, because it convincingly shows the rationale of those who are against him.

Glaser and Strauss's views on credibility are strongly influenced by the so-called Socratic-rational view of social processes: People confronted by truth humbly succumb to its appeal. Organizational realities show a more complex side. The theory must fit and be relevant, yes; the actors involved must have a say in it, true; but it is not yet the whole story.

The Trustworthiness of Naturalistic Inquiries

Because the anthropological approach proposed here has many aspects in common with the naturalistic paradigm (Guba, 1981; Lincoln, 1985), we can follow Egon G. Guba's discussion concerning the trustworthiness of such studies. Trustworthiness is in itself composed of four elements: truth value, applicability, consistency, and neutrality. Within the rationalistic (positivist) paradigm, these are called internal validity, external validity and generalizability, reliability, and objectivity. Within the naturalist paradigm, the terms are credibility, transferability, dependability, and confirmability.

Guba's argument is that trustworthiness is more a matter of trying than of evaluation. The moral duty of the researcher is to do everything possible to increase the trustworthiness of the results. This is witnessed not by the results themselves but by the way they are obtained. In order to increase credibility, researchers should extend their stay in the field, collect insights from various sources, alternate between field and nonfield experiences, and do "member checks," that is, confront the actors with the results, while collecting insights and while writing the report. Guba is not naive about this method:

> An inquirer must be aware, of course, that audience members may choose to label the data and interpretations as noncredible for reasons of their own. (1981, p. 85)

Actors can dupe themselves as well as inquirers; they might do it on purpose or unconsciously. What is to be done then? The political and moral duty, says Lincoln (1985), is to negotiate the results with the actors.

> Research results are not to be ripped off like priceless cultural artifacts from unsophisticated and primitive peoples. . . . The naturalist checks his or her constructions of information and patterns against those that are held by respondents; if those perspectives are not in agreement, additional sharing is called for so that the meanings and values are understood, respected, and represented appropriately by the inquirer. (p. 153)

Both Guba and Lincoln provide a detailed list of practices that increase the trustworthiness of naturalistic research, so there is no need to repeat them here. But even they stop at the point of trying and do not reach the final point: Which theories are good?

Truth Is Beauty: Symbolic Realism

> Correspondence theories of science and art focus on ways in which these symbolic forms copy or resemble some reality internal to them. Formalist or cogency theories, in contrast, tend to deal with the internal properties of the scientific theory or work of art. Both these views are transcended yet integrated in symbolic realism. . . . In this view one does not speak of internal versus external properties. Instead, when the scientific theory or art object is successful, both the internal and the external come to be seen as elements of a single structural system. (R. H. Brown, 1977, p. 24)

Symbolic realism, proposes Richard H. Brown, is the way to reconcile and transcend both scientific realism and romantic idealism (or, we may add after Bernstein [1983], objectivism and relativism, science and hermeneutics) in light of the growing understanding that "adequate social theory must be both objective *and* subjectively meaningful; it must yield understanding of persons' consciousness and agency as well as explanations of social forces beyond their immediate control" (R. H. Brown, 1977, p. 27).

What are the concrete consequences of such a stance? In the first place, researchers (like artists) are *makers* of the reality they study. Therefore, the criterion of resemblance—for either truth or beauty— is irrelevant. "Realism" is, in fact, a name for a currently dominating mode of representation. The "realism" of Rubens's pictures has nothing to do with the "realism" of modern photography; and, at the same time, modern photography is a pioneer in the most "unrealistic" representations.

Where the scientific realists proposed to reduce the multiplicity of visions, the symbolic realists propose to preserve them for the same purpose: to render as much as possible of reality or, rather, realities. The problem in accepting such a seemingly paradoxical stance might be better understood by pointing out the historical status of the two terms:

> The confinement of interpretive analysis in most of contemporary anthropology to the supposedly more "symbolic" aspect of culture is a mere prejudice, born out of the notion, also a gift of the 19th century, that "symbolic" opposes to "real" as fanciful to sober, figurative to literal, obscure to plain, aesthetic to practical, mystical to mundane, and decorative to substantial. (Geertz, 1980, pp. 135-136)

If, however, we abolish this dichotomy, "symbolizations" (which amount to the same as expressions of social representations) can then be judged not on their correspondence to "reality," but on the extent to which they enhance our perception and understanding of the phenomenon in question.

In this perspective, our original question concerning the relationship between the rhetoric and its contents, between the theory and its form, does not make sense. Form and content cease to be opposites; it is more useful to speak about "structurings of content" and "embodiments of form." Bad form damages the content. Good form enhances the content to a point that opens the field for demagogues. But bad form is not the way to exorcise demagogues, nor does it enhance the purity of intentions.

The Power of Irony

According to Brown's cognitive aesthetic theory of truth, credibility enhances beauty, and beauty enhances credibility. Truth is not correspondence between a representation and a reality, but a credibility of representation, in terms of motivational plausibility (we understand why actors act as they do) and practical feasibility (we believe that they could do as they did in the story). But it is the *inevitable interdependency of incongruous opposites,* the paradox, or, as Brown calls it, irony, that keeps our attention and makes a theory or a work of art attractive.

In order to illustrate this aesthetic power of explanation, let us contrast two presentations of the same reality—funeral homes in America—as presented in fiction by Evelyn Waugh and in organization theory by Stephen Barley. (I have chosen the latter author because of his semiotic approach and his proficiency in using language, making his work comparable to that of a novelist.)

Stephen Barley toured various funeral homes and conducted intensive, ethnographic interviews with funeral directors (S. R. Barley, 1980, 1983a, 1983b) in order to reach and reproduce funeral directors' understanding of funeral work. The semiotic analysis led him to conclude that *smoothness* was the strategic concept describing funeral work. Corpse, mourners, workers, and technical equipment all had to contribute and cooperate in an appropriate way so as to make a funeral smooth. The obstacles were many, and their major source was the fact that a majority of the actors were incompetent, because a funeral is an unusual event.

> Although death and dying were once familiar events in the daily lives of Americans, during the 20th century death has become a more distant phenomenon as death rates (especially infant mortality rates) have declined, as the practice of holding wakes in private homes drifted to the funeral parlor, and as hospital care for the terminally ill became common. (S. R. Barley, 1983a, p. 10)

In Waugh's novelette, *The Loved One* (1948), a young English poet arrives in Hollywood, and because his film career does not proceed as he wishes, he is forced to accept a job at Happier Hunting Ground, a funeral home for pets. Thus Waugh establishes an advantageous starting point: Being English, Dennis automatically becomes an anthropologist in a foreign country, and the Happier Hunting Ground symbolizes the peculiarity of its customs. Being a pet's mortician, his role is exactly the one described by Barley—smoothness is the key concept of his work. The death of a friend makes him expand his professional expertise by putting him in contact with a funeral home for people, Whispering Glades, which is, actually, a large and complex organization.

> Dennis sought and obtained leave of absence from the Happier Hunting Ground for the funeral and its preliminaries. Mr. Schultz did not give in readily. He could ill spare Dennis; more motor cars were coming off the assembly lines, more drivers appearing on the roads and more pets in the mortuary; there was an outbreak of food poisoning in Pasadena. The icebox was packed and the crematorium fires blazed early and late.
>   . . . "It is really very valuable experience for me, Mr. Schultz," Dennis said, seeking to extenuate the reproach of desertion. "I see a great deal of the method of Whispering Glades and am picking up all kinds of ideas we might introduce here." (Waugh, 1948, p. 50)

Basically, both descriptions tell the same story. The motives of the actors are plausible and their actions feasible (although in Dennis's case, the plausibility and feasibility were due to the genre; Barley's interlocutor could not dream of doing the same things). In terms of economy, Waugh told us much more than Barley did, and this was due to the intensity of communication possible through irony.

The Loved One can be seen as a better anthropological report, due to its power of expression. The question is, then, had Barley a right to use irony in his study? In other words, what is the morality of aesthetics? In my opinion, there is nothing to prevent a social scientist from being ironic (Philip Slater, for example, is a very ironic anthropologist). Irony seems to be an excellent device for unmasking, and showing the interdependency and dialectical resolutions of opposites, which are the major tasks of the social sciences.

> No moralistic name calling is required; indeed, the moral absolutism of the reform is as inelegant as the "nothing but" reductionism of positivist defenders of the status quo. Unlike the hypocrite who hides the evil in a

cloak of virtue, or the reformer who strips away the cloak, the ironist is sufficiently distanced to enter into *either* of these roles, often simultaneously. That is, he is just as pleased to find goodness hiding within evil as he is to unmask evil posing as good. (R. H. Brown, 1977, p. 185)

Irony *at the expense of one's interlocutors* would be morally unacceptable. But if a report is negotiated, that can be avoided. When a negotiation is fruitless, the researcher might decide to act—for instance, demasking an evil person or a corporate crime. But this is not research, this is life (or, as Brown would say, conduct).

What, then, are the differences between literature and social science? The first is that one is fiction and the other is nonfiction: The basis for telling the story is different. However, this is relative. There are many writers who use factual events for their novels and many social scientists who use fictitious reality to illustrate their theses (for example Berger & Luckmann, 1966/1971). The second is that social scientists are obliged to be systematic, that is, to demonstrate a method, which is also relative. Writers often have a very systematic method. (It is said that Alistair MacLean has a veritable research institute at his disposal.) The third is the presence or lack of aesthetic expression, and this is a difference that, following R. H. Brown (1977, 1987), I propose to abolish.

What about nonfiction, for example a journalist's report as compared to a social scientist's? Let us take as an example a story used commonly in organizational teaching, *The Soul of a New Machine* by Tracy Kidder (1981). Kidder described the history of a technical invention, the construction of a powerful new computer. But no description is just a description; there is always a judgement involved, although it can be clear and authorized, or hidden and muddy.

In Kidder's case, the reviewers decided for him. According to the book jacket, this is a modern, Western hero story. Kidder said nothing himself. Is it possible that it is a horrid story of senseless power- and ego-driven manipulation of young people into a limited system of meanings, which truncated their lives? That we do not know. The problem lies in the interpretation of the aesthetic forms used. Which formal effects belong to the story and which to the author? Does the kitschy atmosphere of the melodramatic introduction ("hero on the boat") come from Kidder's own soul, or is it ultimately an irony, a way of showing the surrounding social and cultural climate of "mushroom culture"? And finally, is mushroom culture a metaphor for unlimited growth, or for life limited to a cellar and "eating shit"? Or did Kidder wish to be ambiguous?

Both the writer and the social scientist have the right to use magic, but while the former can collect applause and withdraw behind the curtain with an enigmatic smile, the latter must stay and submit all the rabbits, hats, and tricks to public scrutiny. Open reflection on the form must become a duty as the originality of the form becomes a new custom.

Is there a difference between social science and fiction, and social science and journalism? Which is more than mere convention? The difference is the literary genre that all three use (on science as literary genre, see Rorty, 1982, 1989). It is not a mere convention because it is conventions that regulate most of our conduct. It is a literary convention because social science, like all other types of literature, busies itself with interpretations of the world.[14] Therefore, the question of whether technical realism shows me more of the world than symbolic realism can be asked equally well of works by population ecologists and organizational symbolists, as of works by Tom Wolfe and Julio Cortazar.

Truth Is in Experience Fit

But how shall we proceed if we are willing to engage in an action? Or how do we advise somebody who does? We said already that theories for action must be simplified and not problematic. Among many interpretations, we must choose one. But which one is right? According to Lakoff and Johnson (1980),

> We understand a statement as being true in a given situation when our understanding of the statement fits our understanding of the situation closely enough for our purposes. (p. 179)

Lakoff and Johnson call this "an experientialist account of truth." It contains elements of correspondence theory (fit), but not in its naive, mirror reflection view. It has relations to coherence theory because it stresses the need for coherence with a broader conceptual system (as in "This can't be true!"). It is a pragmatic theory because it assumes that understanding is grounded in experience and tested in successful performances.

Finally, truth joins both realism and relativism—realism because things are and people are, and they constantly interact. But it is not the classical, objective realism: Objects do not have inherent properties (to be discovered), only *interactional* properties (emerging from experience). It joins relativism in the sense that truth is relative to the context and experience. Meaning and truth are based on understanding. Theories of meaning and truth must therefore be theories of understanding.

Like Richard H. Brown, Lakoff and Johnson look for a reconciliation of objectivism and subjectivism, positivism and romantism, and find it in an experientialist alternative. Like Bernstein (1983), they see praxis as a way out of the dilemma. Symbolic realism and experientialism seem to be two sides—reflective and active—of the same pragmatic solution.

Last but Not Least: The Academic Community

Although many authors working within the interpretive paradigm claim that in terms of the value of the theory, the opinion of the academic community is immaterial; this claim certainly does not fit our experience. In order to be able to reach more than a private audience, one has to publish, and publishing rules are constructed by the academic community. Hence, we must consider the community's opinions regarding the validity and credibility of theories.

Peter Sederberg (1984) points out that in order to get their findings accepted, social scientists must demonstrate the descriptive validity of the findings (that is, correspondence to empirical evidence, as in the natural sciences); their interpretive adequacy (that is, acceptance of the actors); and critical authenticity (that is, deep analysis and self-reflection). In other words, they must prove that their work is nonfiction, that it has some use and that it makes a contribution to the science. But both descriptive validity and interpretive adequacy are often questioned on the grounds of lacking critical authenticity, which in itself can be challenged endlessly. Where is the limit to self-deception, or, alternatively, to self-reflection?[15]

Therefore, claims Sederberg (1984), social science cannot reach a consensus on what are relevant social facts, who should decree this relevance, and how they should go about it:

> The emergence of such a consensus is under a form of social control, specifically the dominant criteria used to establish acceptability. (p. 17)

> In order to participate in a community of inquiry, a person must submit to the dominant procedural ideology. (p. 20)

Researchers negotiate their results with the actors and their method with the research community. A method must be systematic and explicit, but also much more: It must be open for debate and the influence of fashions and politics.

This is not a common picture of the process, however. The social science community is guilty of several hypocrisies concerning its own conduct. One is the claim that there are objective and external criteria of acceptability; although one might allow for "pluralism," one never admits "politics of meaning." The result is a strong conviction that a good method unerringly leads to good results, whereas in fact the two are negotiated in two different and separate arenas. A good method gives at least a decent result, but not always a very good one, and sometimes good results are achieved by a faulty method. The two are loosely coupled.

Another hypocrisy is that the heroes of the field never follow the prescriptions of the field. Weber, Marx, and Freud were truly poets; students are advised to write uninspiring prose.[16] Moreover, students are encouraged to follow existing methods and schools of thought, whereas the laurels go to those who abolish them.

And, finally, students are directed toward findings and facts, whereas it is only ideas that count and stay. According to Amelia Oksenberg Rorty, this tradition was initiated by Descartes himself, who "despite his austere recommendations about the methods of discovery and demonstration . . . hardly ever followed these methods, hardly ever wrote in the same genre twice" (after Nelson, Megill, & McCloskey, 1987, p. 7).

How does one accomplish a good theory, then? By trying, with the help of the heuristics of the field, and with the awareness that these are not algorithms and therefore there is no recipe to be followed.

On Theaters, Elephants, and Holograms

The message of this book can be represented by three main metaphors: a theater, an elephant, and a hologram. The theater represents complex organizations as such and symbolizes the essence of the object under study. The elephant symbolizes the difficulty of studying such an object and the reductionist approaches to the problem. The hologram, finally, is a recently proposed solution to the problem. Up to now the elephant has received most of the attention. It is time to evoke theaters and holograms by way of summary.

The hologram metaphor stresses primarily one property of holograms: that of containing a whole in each part. As Misia Landau put it, all influential metaphors are like "narrative holograms, carrying within a single image a beginning, middle, and an ending" (1987, p. 114). This aspect is of importance in the present context, in the sense that organization studies that concentrate on certain phenomena must still reflect the whole organization. However, there are also several other important aspects.

One is that a hologram represents reality but does not correspond to it. This suggests the differentiation between organizational reality and organization study, as its reflection is misleading. The process of studying and describing organizational reality is a reality in itself, a separate reality, whose product attempts to simulate certain aspects of organizational reality. Maybe this is a normative postulate; after all, organization studies should give an understanding, an "as if I were there" feeling to those who read them.

Another property of a hologram is that the hologram changes with the point from which it is seen, simulating the changes that would take place if the viewer went around the object depicted in the hologram. Similarly, a study of an organization must provide the reader with a picture that is consistent yet changing, depending on the perspective. The reader should be able to see that although an organization viewed from the top looks different than it does from the bottom, it is nevertheless one and the same organization, and that there is no standpoint that gives the true picture of it.

Fascinating as it is, the art of holography suffers at present from serious limitations. For example, there is as yet no camera that can take a holographic picture of such a large object as an elephant. But size is not the only, or not the real problem. If organizations were elephants, all we would have to do is wait for the next generation of holographic cameras (or produce them ourselves). The real problem lies in the complexity and intangibility of such concepts as "nets of collective action." This is why theater is a better metaphor for complex organizations than is the elephant.

Theater is, in fact, a synecdoche: a part that stands for the whole. Theater is an organization; but its specificity allows us to understand the essence of complex organizations. This is, of course, not an original idea. It can be traced back to Goffman (1959, 1981), Geertz (1980), Turner (1982), Mangham and Overington (1987), and even Shakespeare, but as Robert K. Merton shows in his *On the Shoulders of Giants* (1965), one can always go even further back in the history of ideas and find the same ones again and again. Let us then assume that theater is a very old metaphor that is by now common property and have a closer look at it.

What is a theater? It is a play, a stage, actors, a director, the public, an administration, a board of trustees, money, and costumes. All these ingredients are theater, but they do not become theater until they contribute to performance, which is, in turn, a result of a repetitive cycle of preparation and performing. But even this is not all of it. Activating these ingredients into a performance is possible due to the existence of theater as an institution, with various professions, systems of knowledge, and its own history coupled to it. The ingredients may well stand for the practical, performance for the symbolic, and institution for the political aspect of organization. John Kenneth Galbraith used the same metaphor when speaking of large corporations:

> The modern corporation is socially a theater of all the conflicts that might be expected when hundreds and thousands of highly charged, exceptionally self-motivated, and more than normally self-serving people work closely and interdependently together. (1986, p. 14)

But if we have problems with holograms of elephants, can we make holograms of theaters? How can we grasp something that is both large *and* complex?

It so happens that holograms are used in theater to simulate props, and with time, animated props are expected. A "real" house will be built in front of the spectators. Holograms, like organization theory, began with simulating physical aspects of reality. Political and symbolic aspects will follow, and, one hopes, the practical will not be lost again.

The End (In a Manner of Speaking)

This is a very tentative and temporary ending, and in fact, more a beginning than anything else. The book is an attempt to sketch a line of research that promises much in terms of our understanding of large, complex organizations. The proposal itself is a study in eclecticism. In a postmodern spirit, I opened the old box with dichotomies such as positivism and romanticism, realism and idealism, objectivism and relativism, and chose and put together those that fitted my purpose at hand, in a pragmatist spirit. I took seriously C. W. Mills's invocation that each man be his own methodologist (1959), assumed that it referred to women, too, and picked out from various traditions what made sense to me. What is presented here is not so much a pattern to follow as an example that it can be done.

Going through the literature was as if I were in a whirlpool of labels and concepts threatening to become a maelstrom to those who succumb to the temptation of discovering "what they really meant by that." I tried to keep to the surface, remembering that my life task is in organizations and not in the methodology of social science. The experience was fascinating, and if it can be of use to anyone else but me, I shall be happy.

Notes

1. This simple introductory statement illustrates very well the metaphoric traps our language sets upon us. For more than 200 pages I argued that organizations are *not*

objects, but here I call organizations objects, using a conventional metaphor in order to be understood. This kind of difficulty abounds: When on our way to grasp an interesting new aspect of meaning, we are constantly blocked by conventional expressions that deny our aim. The radical solution—to abandon them all—would lead to total incomprehension. The hermeneutic spiral builds the new via the old, that is certain. But how does one reach a constructive balance?

2. In a manner of speaking. Considering that organizations (as cultures and societies) are not things apart, a complete description of IBM could well aim at a theory of the universe. . . .

3. Maybe because, like middle classes in general, they are perceived as dull: Their actions (or rather, the renditions of their actions) lack the drama typical of accounts from the upper and lower floors.

4. In an essay-interview with Ivan Klima, Philip Roth says with emphasis that during the times of harshest political persecution, Klima and many other Czech and Slovak artists were forced to work as construction workers, street cleaners, etc., facing a daily horror of meaningless, hard, menial work (*New York Review of Books*, April 12, 1990). I am sure that both Klima and Roth were completely unaware of the impression it produces, but one cannot but wonder, what about all those whose life is and will be spent in these jobs?

5. On different strategies of micro and macro integration, see Marcus (1986).

6. For an alternative procedure within the same perspective, which reverses my proposal by going from macro-structures to actors' accounts, see Gowler and Legge (1982).

7. Those interested in the adventures of researchers trying to enter the organizational "field" will enjoy a book by Colin Brown, Pierre Guillet de Monthoux, and Arthur McCullough called *The Access-Casebook* (1976).

8. The adjective *social* is usually added to differentiate the kind of representations discussed here from mental representations which, in the Cartesian tradition, are the mind's reflections of the world outside (Rabinow, 1986).

9. For a classical text on the technique, read Becker and Geer (1957).

10. This does not mean that they never do. The modern theater tends to involve the spectators in the spectacle itself.

11. The concept of *standpoint* comes from Dorothy Smith (1990).

12. As Laing (1967) put it, "The 'data' (given) of research are not so much given as *taken* out of a constantly elusive matrix of happenings. We should speak of *capta* rather than data" (p. 62). Thus my expression "gathering insights," which even further softens what we do to reality.

13. I would extend this claim to the rest of the social sciences (with my apologies to economists who do not like to be counted as social scientists).

14. Expressed in everyday language, as opposed to various kinds of formal languages used, for example, in mathematical interpretations of the world. I thank Marilyn Mehlmann for this suggestion.

15. Experimenting with new forms brings us papers that are written by two egos of the same author (Pinch & Pinch, 1988) or where the author as critic renders the story told by the author as author (Travers, 1990).

16. Freud himself, when awarded a Goethe Award by the German Academy, felt deeply hurt—after all, he was a scientist and not a mere writer!

Bibliography

Abravanel, H. (1982). Mediatory myths in the service of organizational ideology. In
L. R. Pondy, P. J. Frost, G. Morgan, & T. C. Dandridge (Eds.), *Organizational
symbolism* (pp. 273-293). Greenwich, CT: JAI.

Acker, J., & Van Houten, D. (1974). Differential recruitment and control: The sex
structuring of organizations. *Administrative Science Quarterly, 19,* 152-163.

Aldrich, H. E. (1980). Technology and organizational structure: A reexamination of the findings of the Aston group. In A. Etzioni, & E. W. Lehman (Eds.), *A sociological reader
on complex organizations* (pp. 233-250). New York: Holt, Rinehart and Winston.

Allport, F. H. (1962). A structuronomic conception of behavior: Individual and collective. *Journal of Abnormal and Social Psychology, 64,* 3-30.

Alvesson, M. (1985). On focus in cultural studies of organizations. *Scandinavian Journal of Management Studies, 2*(2), 105-120.

Asplund, J. (1971). *Om undran inför samhället* [Wondering about society]. Stockholm:
Argos Förlag AB.

Bailyn, L. (1977). Research as cognitive process: Implications for data analysis. *Quality and Quantity, 11,* 97-117.

Barley, N. (1983). *The innocent anthropologist.* Harmondsworth, UK: Penguin.

Barley, N. (1986). *A plague of caterpillars.* London: Penguin.

Barley, N. (1988). *Not a hazardous sport.* London: Penguin.

Barley, N. (1989). *Native land.* London: Penguin.

AUTHOR'S NOTE: This bibliography contains positions which, although not directly
quoted, substantially influenced the text.

Barley, S. R. (1980). *Taking the burden: The strategic role of the funeral director* (Working Paper No. 1129-80). Cambridge: MIT Sloan School of Management.

Barley, S. R. (1983a). Codes of the dead: The semiotics of funeral work. *Urban Life, 12*, 3-31.

Barley, S. R. (1983b). Semiotics and the study of occupational and organizational cultures. *Administrative Science Quarterly, 28*, 393-413.

Barnard, C. I. (1980). Organizations as systems of cooperation. In A. Etzioni and E. W. Lehman (Eds.), *A sociological reader on complex organizations* (pp. 11-13). New York: Holt, Rinehart and Winston. (Original work published 1938)

Barney, J. B. & Ouchi, W. G. (Eds.). (1986). *Organizational economics.* San Francisco: Jossey-Bass.

Becker, H. S. & Geer, B. (1957). Participant observation and interviewing. *Human Organization, 16*(3), 28-32.

Beksiak, J. & Czarniawska, B. (1977). Enterprise response patterns under the socialist management system. *Oeconomica Polona, 2*, 211-228.

Benedict, R. (1948). Anthropology and humanities. *American Anthropologist, 50*(4), 585-593.

Benson, J. K. (1980). The interorganizational network as a political economy. In A. Etzioni & E. W. Lehman (Eds.), *A sociological reader on complex organizations* (pp. 349-368). New York: Holt, Rinehart and Winston.

Berg, P.-O. (1979). *Emotional structures in organizations.* Lund: Studentlitteratur.

Berg, P.-O. (1985). Techno-culture: The symbolic framing of technology in a Volvo plant. *Scandinavian Journal of Management Studies, 1*(4), 237-256.

Berg, P.-O. (Ed.). (1986). Organizational symbolism [Special issue]. *Organization Studies, 7*(2).

Berger, L. A. (1989). Economics and hermeneutics. *Economics and Philosophy, 5*, 209-233.

Berger, P. (1970). The problem of multiple realities: Alfred Schütz and Robert Musil. In T. Luckmann (Ed.), *Phenomenology and sociology* (pp. 343-367). Harmondsworth, UK: Penguin.

Berger, P. L. & Luckmann, T. (1971). *The social construction of reality.* Harmondsworth, UK: Penguin. (Original work published 1966)

Bernstein, R. J. (1983). *Beyond objectivism and relativism.* Oxford: Basil Blackwell.

Bion, W. R. (1961). *Experiences in groups.* London: Tavistock.

Bittner, E. (1965). The concept of organization. *Social Research, 31*, 240-255.

Britan, G. M. & Cohen, R. (Eds.). (1980). *Hierarchy and society: Anthropological perspectives on bureaucracy.* Philadelphia: Institute for the Study of Human Issues.

Broms, H. & Gamberg, H. (1982). *Mythology in management culture.* Helsinki: The Helsinki School of Economics and Business Administration.

Brown, C., Guillet de Monthoux, P., & McCullough, A. (1976). *The access-casebook.* Stockholm: THS.

Brown, D. S. (1982). *Managing the large organization.* Mt. Airy, MD: Lomond.

Brown, R. H. (1977). *A poetic for sociology.* Cambridge: Cambridge University Press.

Brown, R. H. (1978). Bureaucracy as praxis: Toward a political phenomenology of formal organizations. *Administrative Science Quarterly, 23*(3), 365-382.

Brown, R. H. (1987). *Society as text.* Chicago: Chicago University Press.

Brunsson, N. (1985). *The irrational organization.* London: Wiley.

Bruyn, S. (1966). *The human perspective in sociology: The methodology of participant observation.* Englewood Cliffs, NJ: Prentice-Hall.

Burawoy, M. (1979). *Manufacturing consent.* Chicago: Chicago University Press.

Burawoy, M. (1981). Terrains of contest: Factory and state under capitalism and socialism. *Socialist Review, 58,* 83-124.

Burawoy, M. (1985). Piece-rates, Hungarian style. *Socialist Review, 79,* 42-69.

Burawoy, M. & Lukacs, J. (1985, December). Mythologies of work: A comparison of firms in state socialism and advanced capitalism. *American Sociological Review, 50,* 723-737.

Burke, K. (1954). *A grammar of motives.* Englewood Cliffs, NJ: Prentice-Hall.

Burnett, J. H. (1969). Ceremony, rites and economy in the student system of an American high school. *Human Organization, 28*(1), 1-10.

Burns, T. & Stalker, G. M. (1961). *The management of innovation.* London: Tavistock.

Burrell, G. & Morgan, G. (1979). *Sociological paradigms and organizational analysis.* Aldershot, UK: Gower.

Calàs, M. B. & Smircich, L. (1987). Reading leadership as a form of cultural analysis. In J. G. Hunt, D. R. Baliga, H. P. Dachler, & C. A. Schriesheim (Eds.), *Emerging leadership vistas* (pp. 201-226). Lexington, MA: Lexington Books.

Castaneda, C. (1986). *The teachings of don Juan: A Yaqui way of knowledge.* Harmondsworth, UK: Penguin. (Original work published 1968)

Chandler, A. D., Jr. (1977). *The visible hand: The managerial revolution in American business.* Cambridge: Harvard University Press.

Cicourel, A. V. (1974). *Cognitive sociology: Language of meaning in social interaction.* New York: Free Press.

Clark, D. L. (1985). Emerging paradigms in organizational theory and research. In Y. S. Lincoln (Ed.), *Organizational theory and inquiry: The paradigm revolution* (pp. 43-78). London: Sage.

Clegg, S. (1987). The language of power and the power of language. *Organization Studies, 8*(1), 61-70.

Clegg, S. & Dunkerley, D. (1980). *Organization, class and control.* London: Routledge and Kegan Paul.

Clifford, J. (1986). Introduction: Partial truths. In J. Clifford & G. E. Marcus (Eds.), *Writing cultures: The poetics and politics of ethnography,* (pp. 1-26). Berkeley: University of California Press.

Cohen, A. (1974). *Two-dimensional man: An essay on the anthropology of power and symbolism in complex society.* Berkeley: University of California Press.

Cohen, A. (1981). *The politics of elite culture.* Berkeley: University of California Press.

Cohen, M. D., March, J. G., & Olsen, J. P. (1980). A garbage can model of organizational choice. In A. Etzioni and E. W. Lehman (Eds.), *A sociological reader on complex organizations* (pp. 144-159). New York: Holt, Rinehart and Winston. (Original work published 1972)

Cohen, P. S. (1969). Theories of myth. *Man, 4,* 337-353.

Crozier, M. (1964). *The bureaucratic phenomenon.* Chicago: Chicago University Press.

Czarniawska, B. (1980). Metody badan i usprawnien procesu zarzadzania organizacjami gospodarczymi [Methods for studying and improving management processes in economic organizations]. *IOZDiK, Materialy i Studia, 15,* pp. 1-28.

Czarniawska, B. (1985). The ugly sister: On relationships between the private and the public sector in Sweden. *Scandinavian Journal of Management Studies, 2*(2), 83-103.

Czarniawska-Joerges, B. (1988a). *Ideological control in non-ideological organizations.* New York: Praeger.

Czarniawska-Joerges, B. (1988b). Power as an experiential concept. *Scandinavian Journal of Management,* 4(1/2), 31-44.

Czarniawska-Joerges, B. (1989). *Economic decline and organizational control.* New York: Praeger.

Czarniawska-Joerges, B. (1990a). Merchants of meaning: Management consulting in the Swedish public sector. In B. A. Turner (Ed.), *Organizational symbolism* (pp. 139-150). Berlin: de Gruyter.

Czarniawska-Joerges, B. (1990b). *In the eyes of the innocent: Students of an organizational power.* Uppsala: The Study of Power and Democracy in Sweden.

Czarniawska-Joerges, B. (in press). Rationality as an organizational product. *Finnish Public Administration Studies.*

Czarniawska-Joerges, B. & Joerges, B. (1988). How to control things with words: Organizational talk and control. *Management Communication Quarterly,* 2(2), 170-193.

Czarniawska-Joerges, B. & Joerges, B. (1990). *Organizational change as materialization of ideas.* Uppsala: The Study of Power and Democracy in Sweden.

Daft, R. L. & Weick, K. E. (1984). Toward a model of organizations as interpretation systems. *Academy of Management Review,* 9(2), 284-295.

Dalton, M. (1959). *Men who manage: Fusions of feeling and theory in administration.* New York: Wiley.

Dalton, M. (1964). Preconceptions and methods in "Men who manage." In P. Hammond (Ed.), *Sociologists at work* (pp. 44-86). New York: Basic Books.

Dandridge, T. C., Mitroff, I., & Joyce, W. F. (1980). Organizational symbolism: A topic to expand organizational analysis. *Academy of Management Review,* 5(1), 77-82.

Daun, A. (1989). *Svenskt mentalitet* [The Swedish mentality]. Stockholm: Raben & Sjögren.

Davis, K. (1959, December). The myth of functional analysis as a special method in sociology and anthropology. *American Sociological Review,* 24, 757-772.

Deal, T. E. & Kennedy, A. A. (1982). *Corporate cultures: The rites and rituals of corporate life.* Reading, MA: Addison-Wesley.

de Mille, R. (1990). *The don Juan papers.* Belmont, CA: Wadsworth.

DiMaggio, P. J. & Powell, W. W. (1983). The iron cage revisited: Institutional isomorphism and collective rationality in organizational fields. *American Sociological Review,* 48, 147-160.

Donnellon, A., Gray, B. & Bougon, M. G. (1986). Communication, meaning and organized action. *Administrative Science Quarterly,* 31(1), 43-55.

Douglas, M. (1986). *How institutions think.* Syracuse, NY: Syracuse University Press.

Ebers, M. (1985). Understanding organizations: The poetic mode. *Journal of Management,* 11(2), 51-62.

Eco, U. (1979). *The role of the reader: Explorations in the semiotics of texts.* London: Hutchinson.

Edelman, M. (1971). *Politics as symbolic action.* New York: Academic Press.

Edelman, M. (1977). *Political language: Words that succeed and policies that fail.* New York: Academic Press.

Etzioni, A. (1961). *A comparative analysis of complex organizations.* New York: The Free Press of Glencoe.

Etzioni, A. (1965). Organizational control structure. In J. G. March (Ed.), *Handbook of organizations* (pp. 650-677). Chicago: Rand McNally.

Etzioni, A. (1980). Compliance structures. In A. Etzioni & E. W. Lehman (Eds.), *A sociological reader on complex organizations* (pp. 87-100). New York: Holt, Rinehart and Winston.

Etzioni, A. (1986). Rationality is anti-entropic. *Journal of Economic Psychology, 7,* 17-36.

Etzioni, A. (1988). *The moral dimension: Toward a new economics.* New York: The Free Press.

Etzioni, A. & Lehman, E. W. (Eds.). (1980). *A sociological reader on complex organizations* (3rd ed.). New York: Holt, Rinehart and Winston.

Farr, R. M. (1987). Social representations: A French tradition of research. *Journal for the Theory of Social Behaviour, 17*(4), 343-369.

Farr, R. M. & Moscovici, S. (Eds.). (1984). *Social representations.* Cambridge: Cambridge University Press.

Follett, M. P. (1949). *Freedom and coordination.* London: Management Publications Trust.

Frankl, V. E. (1973). *Man's search for meaning.* New York: Simon and Schuster.

Friedan, B. (1963). *The feminine mystique.* New York: Dell.

Galbraith, J. K. (1986, April 10). Behind the wall. *The New York Review of Books,* pp. 11-13.

Garfinkel, H. (1967). *Studies in ethnomethodology.* Englewood Cliffs, NJ: Prentice-Hall.

Garfinkel, H., Lynch, M., & Livingston, E. (1981). The work of a discovering science construed with materials from the optically discovered pulsar. *Philosophy of the Social Sciences, 11,* 131-158.

Geertz, C. (1964). Ideology as a cultural system. In D. Apter (Ed.), *Ideology and discontent* (pp. 47-76). New York: The Free Press of Glencoe.

Geertz, C. (1973). *The interpretation of cultures.* New York: Basic Books.

Geertz, C. (1980). *Negara: The theatre state in nineteenth-century Bali.* Princeton, NJ: Princeton University Press.

Geertz, C. (1983). *Local knowledge.* New York: Basic Books.

Geertz, C. (1988). *Works and lives: The anthropologist as author.* Stanford, CA: Stanford University Press.

Geertz, C. & Hofstede, G. (Eds.). (1986). Organizational culture and control [Special issue]. *Journal of Management Studies, 23*(3).

Giddens, A. (1981). Agency, institution and time-space analysis. In K. Knorr-Cetina & A. V. Cicourel (Eds.), *Advances in social theory and methodology* (pp. 161-174). Boston: Routledge and Kegan Paul.

Giddens, A. (1984). *New rules of sociological method.* London: Hutchinson.

Gilbert, G. N. & Mulkay, M. (1984). *Opening Pandora's box: A sociological analysis of scientists' discourse.* Cambridge: University of Cambridge Press.

Giroux, N. & Taylor, J. R. (1987, June). *Organizational meaning through communication: A text-oriented approach.* Paper presented at the 3rd International Conference on Organizational Symbolism and Corporate Culture, Milan.

Glaser, B. G. (1978). *Theoretical sensitivity.* Mill Valley, CA: The Sociology Press.

Glaser, B. G. & Strauss, A. (1965). *Awareness of dying.* Chicago: Aldine.

Glaser, B. G. & Strauss, A. (1974). *The discovery of grounded theory: Strategies for qualitative research.* Chicago: Aldine.

Goffman, E. (1959). *The presentation of self in everyday life.* New York: Doubleday.

Goffman, E. (1961). *Asylums.* Harmondsworth, UK: Penguin.

Goffman, E. (1980). The characteristics of total institutions. In A. Etzioni & E. W. Lehman (Eds.), *A sociological reader on complex organizations* (pp. 319-340). New York: Holt, Rinehart and Winston. (Original work published 1957)

Goffman, E. (1981). *Forms of talk.* Oxford, UK: Basil Blackwell.

Gould, S. J. (1990). *Wonderful life: The Burgess shale and the nature of history.* New York: Norton.

Gouldner, A. W. (1954). *Patterns of industrial bureaucracy.* New York: Free Press.

Gouldner, A. W. (1970). *The coming crisis of Western sociology.* London: Heinemann.

Gouldner, A. W. (1976). *The dialectics of ideology and technology: The origins, grammar and future of ideology.* London: Macmillan.

Gowler, D. & Legge, K. (1982). The integration of disciplinary perspectives and levels of analysis in problem-oriented organizational research. In N. Nicholson & T. D. Wall (Eds.), *The theory and practice of organizational psychology* (pp. 63-101). London: Academic Press.

Guba, E. G. (1981). Criteria for assessing the trustworthiness of naturalistic inquiries. *Educational Communication and Technology Journal, 29*(2). 75-91.

Hall, R. H. (1980). Closed-system, open-system and contingency-choice perspectives. In A. Etzioni & E. W. Lehman (Eds.), *A sociological reader on complex organizations* (pp. 23-43). New York: Holt, Rinehart and Winston. (Original work published 1977)

Harré, R. (1979). *Social being.* Oxford, UK: Basil Blackwell.

Harré, R. (1981). Philosophical aspects of the macro-micro problem. In K. Knorr-Cetina & A. V. Cicourel (Eds.), *Advances in social theory and methodology* (pp. 140-172). Boston: Routledge and Kegan Paul.

Harré, R. (1982). Theoretical preliminaries to the study of action. In M. von Cranach & R. Harré (Eds.), *The analysis of action: Recent theoretical and empirical advances* (pp. 136-160). Cambridge: Cambridge University Press.

Harré, R. & Secord, P. F. (1972). *The explanation of social behaviour.* Oxford: Basil Blackwell.

Heritage, J. (1984). *Garfinkel and ethnomethodology.* Oxford: Polity Press.

Heydebrand, W. (1980). Organizational contradictions in public bureaucracies: Toward a Marxian theory of organizations. In A. Etzioni & E. W. Lehman (Eds.), *A sociological reader on complex organizations* (pp. 56-73). New York: Holt, Rinehart and Winston.

Hickson, D. J., Hinnings, C. R., Less, C. A., Schneck, R. E., & Pennings, J .M. (1971). A strategic contingencies theory of intraorganizational power. *Administrative Science Quarterly, 16,* 216-229.

Hickson, D. J., Pugh, D. S., & Pheysey, D. C. (1980). Operations technology and organizational structure: An empirical reappraisal. In A. Etzioni & E. W. Lehman (Eds.), *A sociological reader on complex organizations* (pp. 208-232). New York: Holt, Rinehart and Winston.

Hirschman, A. O. (1967). *Development projects observed.* Washington: The Brookings Institution.

Hofstede, G. (1978). The poverty of management control philosophy. *The Academy of Management Review, 3*(3), 450-461.

Hofstede, G. (1980). *Culture's consequences.* London: Sage.

Hofstede, G. (Ed.). (1986). Organizational culture and control [Special issue]. *Journal of Management Studies, 23* (3).

Hofstede, G. (1988). Mary Douglas: How institutions think. *Organization Studies, 9*(1), 122-124.

Inzerilli, G. (1981). Some conceptual issues in the study of the relationships between organizations and societies. *International Studies of Management and Organization, 10*(4), 3-14.

Izraeli, D. M. & Jick, T. D. (1986). The art of saying no: Linking power to culture. *Organization Studies, 7*(2), 171-192.

Janowitz, M. (1963). Anthropology and the social sciences. *Current Anthropology, 4*(2), 139, 149-154.

Jaques, E. (1951). *The changing culture of a factory.* London: Tavistock.

Joerges, B. (1975). *Beratung und Technologietransfer* [Consultancy and technology transfer]. Baden-Baden, Germany: Nomos Verlagsgesellschaft.

Joerges, B. (1988). Technology in everyday life: Conceptual queries. *Journal for the Theory of Social Behaviour, 18*(2), 219-237.

Joerges, B. (1989). Soziologie und Maschinerie [Sociology and machinery]. In P. Weingart (Ed.), *Technik als Sozialer Prozess* [Technology as a social process] Frankfurt, Germany: Suhrkamp.

Kanter, R. M. (1977). *Men and women of the corporation.* New York: Basic Books.

Kanter, R. M. (1980). Women and tokenism in organizations: Some effects of proportions on group life. In A. Etzioni & E. W. Lehman (Eds.), *A sociological reader on complex organizations* (pp. 461-476). New York: Holt, Rinehart and Winston.

Kaplan, R. & Tausky, K. (1980). Humanism in organizations: A critical appraisal. In A. Etzioni & E. W. Lehman (Eds.), *A sociological reader on complex organizations* (pp. 44-55). New York: Holt, Rinehart and Winston. (Original work published 1977)

Kidder, T. (1981). *The soul of a new machine.* Harmondsworth, UK: Penguin.

Kilmann, R. H., Saxton, M. J., Serpa, R., et al. (1985). *Gaining control of the corporate culture.* San Francisco: Jossey-Bass.

Kluckhohn, C. & Kelly, W. H. (1945). The concept of culture. In R. Linton (Ed.), *The science of man in the world crisis* (pp. 78-106). New York: Columbia University Press.

Konecki, K. (1990). Dependency and worker flirting. In B. A. Turner (Ed.), *Organizational symbolism* (pp. 55-56). Berlin: de Gruyter.

Kotter, J. P. (1982). *The general managers.* Glencoe: Free Press.

Kunda, G. (1986). *Engineering culture: Control and commitment in a high-tech organization.* Philadelphia: Temple University Press.

Kundera, M. (1984). *The unbearable lightness of being.* London: Faber and Faber.

Laing, R. D. (1967). *The politics of experience.* New York: Ballantine Books.

Lakoff, G. & Johnson, M. (1980). *Metaphors we live by.* Chicago: University of Chicago Press.

Landau, M. (1987). Paradise lost: Terrestriality in human evolution. In J. S. Nelson, A. Megill, & D. N. McCloskey (Eds.), *The rhetoric of the human sciences: Language and argument in scholarship and public affairs* (pp. 112-126). Madison: The University of Wisconsin Press.

Latour, B. (1986). The powers of association. In J. Law (Ed.), *Power, action and belief: A new sociology of knowledge?* (pp. 264-280). London: Routledge & Kegan Paul.

Latour, B. & Woolgar, S. (1986). *Laboratory life: The construction of scientific facts.* Princeton, NJ: Princeton University Press. (Original work published 1979)

Layder, D. (1982). Grounded theory: A constructive critique. *Journal for the Theory of Social Behaviour, 12*(1), 103-123.

Lazarsfeld, P. F. & Menzel, H. (1980). On the relation between individual and collective properties. In A. Etzioni & E. W. Lehman (Eds.), *A sociological reader on complex organizations* (pp. 508-521). New York: Holt, Rinehart and Winston.

Leach, E. R. (1961). *Rethinking anthropology.* London: University of London, The Athlone Press.

Leach, E. R. (1968). Ritual. In *The International Encyclopedia of the Social Sciences.* New York: Free Press.

Leach, E. R. (1976). *Culture and communication.* Cambridge: Cambridge University Press.

Leach, E. R. (1982). *Social anthropology.* Oxford: Oxford University Press.

Leach, E.R. (1985, November 29). Observers who are part of the system. *The Times Higher Education Supplement,* pp. 15-18.

Levine, S. & White, P. E. (1980). Exchange as a conceptual framework for the study of inter-organizational relationships. In A. Etzioni & E. W. Lehman (Eds.), *A sociological reader on complex organizations* (pp. 256-268). New York: Holt, Rinehart and Winston.

Lewin, K. (1951). *Field theory in social science.* New York: Harper.

Lieberson, S. & O'Connor, J. F. (1980). Leadership and organizational performance: A study of large corporations. In A. Etzioni, and E. W. Lehman (Eds.), *A sociological reader on complex organizations* (pp. 284-299). New York: Holt, Rinehart and Winston.

Lincoln, Y. S. (1985). The substance of the emergent paradigm: Implications for researchers. In Y. S. Lincoln (Ed.), *Organizational theory and inquiry: The paradigm revolution* (pp. 137-160). Beverly Hills, CA: Sage.

Lindblom, C. E. (1980). Capitalism, socialism and democracy. In A. Etzioni & E. W. Lehman (Eds.), *A sociological reader on complex organizations* (pp. 477-479). New York: Holt, Rinehart and Winston.

Litwak, E. & Hylton, L. F. (1980). Interorganizational analysis: A hypothesis on coordinating agencies. In A. Etzioni & E. W. Lehman (Eds.), *A sociological reader on complex organizations* (pp. 269-283). New York: Holt, Rinehart and Winston.

MacKay, D. M. (1964). Communication and meaning—a functional approach. In F. S. C. Northrop & H. H. Livingston (Eds.), *Cross-cultural understanding: Epistemology in anthropology* (pp. 162-179). New York: Harper and Row.

Malinowski, B. (1926). *Zwyczaj i zbrodnia. Zycie seksualne dzikich* [Crime and custom: The sexual life of savagery]. Warszawa: PWN.

Malinowski, B. (1967). *A diary in the strict sense of the term.* Stanford, CA: Stanford University Press.

Mangham, I. L. & Overington, M. A. (1987). *Organizations as theatre: A social psychology of dramatic appearances.* Chichester, UK: Wiley.

Manicas, P. T. & Rosenberg, A. (1988). The sociology of scientific knowledge: Can we ever get it straight? *Journal for the Theory of Social Behaviour, 18*(1), 51-76.

Manning, P. K. (1979). Metaphors of the field: Varieties of organizational discourse. *Administrative Science Quarterly, 24,* 660-671.

March, J. G. & Olsen, J. P. (1976). *Ambiguity and choice in organizations*. Bergen: Universitetsforlaget.

March, J. G., & Simon, H. A. (1958). *Organizations*. New York: Wiley.

March, J. G. & Simon, H. A. (1980). The theory of organizational equilibrium. In A. Etzioni & E. W. Lehman (Eds.), *A sociological reader on complex organizations* (pp. 16-21). New York: Holt, Rinehart and Winston. (Original work published 1958)

Marcus, G. E. (1986). Ethnography in the modern world system. In J. Clifford & G. E. Marcus (Eds.), *Writing culture: The poetics and politics of ethnography* (pp. 165-194). Berkeley: University of California Press.

Marsh, N. (1982). *Light thickens*. London: William Collins.

Martin, J. (1982). Stories and scripts in organizational settings. In A. Hastrof & A. Isen (Eds.), *Cognitive social psychology* (pp. 255-305). New York: North Holland-Elsevier.

Martin, J. (1990). Deconstructing organizational taboos: The suppression of gender conflict in organizations. *Organization Science, 1*(4), 339-359.

Martin, J., Feldman, M. S., Hatch, M. J., & Sitkin, S. B. (1983). The uniqueness paradox in organizational stories. *Administrative Science Quarterly, 28*(3), 438-453.

Martin, P. Y. & Turner, B. A. (1986). Grounded theory and organizational research. *The Journal of Applied Behavioral Science, 22*(2), 141-157.

McCloskey, D. N. (1985). *The rhetoric of economics*. Brighton, UK: Harvester.

McCloskey, D. N. (1990) *If you are so smart. . . . The narrative of economic expertise*. Chicago: University of Chicago Press.

McGee, M. C. & Lyne, J. R. (1987). What are nice folks like you doing in a place like this? In J. S. Nelson, A. Megill, & D. McCloskey (Eds.), *The rhetoric of the human sciences: Language and argument in scholarship and public affairs* (pp. 375-386). Madison: The University of Wisconsin Press.

McLuhan, M. & Quentin, F. (1967). *The medium is the message*. New York: Bantam Books.

Mead, M. (1949). *Male and female*. Harmondsworth, UK: Penguin.

Melischek, G., Rosengren, K-E., & Stappers, J. (Eds.). (1984). *Cultural indicators*. Wien: Verlag der Österreichischen Akademie der Wissenschaften.

Merelman, R. M. (1969). The dramaturgy of politics. *The Sociological Quarterly, 10*, 216-241.

Merton, R. K. (1965). *On the shoulders of giants: A Shandean postscript*. New York: Harcourt Brace Jovanovich.

Merton, R. K. (1980). Bureaucratic structure and personality. In A. Etzioni & E. W. Lehman (Eds.), *A sociological reader on complex organizations* (pp. 22-31). New York: Holt, Rinehart and Winston. (Original work published 1957)

Métraux, R. & Mead, M. (1954). *Themes in French culture*. Stanford, CA: Stanford University Press.

Meyer, J. W. (1985, August). *Decentralization and legitimacy in public organization*. Paper presented at the seminar *Organization and economy of local government in change*. Vattnahalsen, Norway.

Meyer, J. W. & Rowan, B. (1980). Institutionalized organizations: Formal structure as myth and ceremony. In A. Etzioni & E. W. Lehman (Eds.), *A sociological reader on complex organizations* (pp. 300-318). New York: Holt, Rinehart and Winston. (Original work published 1977)

Meyer, J. W. & Scott, W. R. (1983). *Organizational environments: Ritual and rationality.* Beverly Hills, CA: Sage.

Milgram, S. (1963). Behavioral studies of obedience. *Journal of Abnormal and Social Psychology, 67,* 371-378.

Miller, E. J. (1959). Technology, territory and time: The internal differentiation of complex production systems. *Human Relations, 12,* 243-273.

Mills, C. W. (1959). *The sociological imagination.* Harmondsworth, UK: Penguin.

Mintzberg, H. (1973). *The nature of managerial work.* New York: Harper and Row.

Mintzberg, H. (1987). Crafting strategy. *Harvard Business Review, 4,* 66-77.

Morgan, G. (1980). Paradigms, metaphors and puzzle solving in organization theory. *Administrative Science Quarterly, 25*(4), 605-622.

Morgan, G. (1981, October). Paradigm diversity in organizational research: Threat or opportunity? York, UK: York University Faculty of Administrative Studies Working Paper Series.

Morgan, G. (1983). More on metaphor: Why we cannot control tropes in administrative science. *Administrative Science Quarterly, 28,* 601-607.

Morgan, G. (1986). *Images of organization.* Newbury Park, CA: Sage.

Moscovici, S. (1984). The phenomenon of social representation. In R. Farr & S. Moscovici (Eds.), *Social representations* (pp. 3-69). Cambridge: Cambridge University Press.

Mulkay, M. (Ed.). (1985). *The word and the world: Explorations in the form of sociological analysis.* London: George Allen and Unwin.

Mullins, N. C. (1973). *Theories and theory groups in contemporary American sociology.* New York: Harper and Row.

Musil, R. (1953). *The man without qualities.* New York: Coward-McCann.

Nelson, J. S., Megill, A., & McCloskey, D. (1987). Rhetoric of inquiry. In J. S. Nelson, A. Megill, & D. McCloskey (Eds.), *The rhetoric of the human sciences: Language and argument in scholarship and public affairs* (pp. 63-82). Madison: The University of Wisconsin Press.

Nord, W. R. (1985). Can organizational culture be managed? In P. J. Frost, L. F. Moore, M. R. Louis, C. C. Lundberg, & J. Martin (Eds.), *Organizational culture* (pp. 187-196). Newbury Park, CA: Sage.

Northrup, H. R. (1980). Codetermination: A critique. In A. Etzioni & E. W. Lehman (Eds.), *A sociological reader on complex organizations* (pp. 496-487). New York: Holt, Rinehart and Winston.

Olsen, J. P. (1970). Local budgeting: Decision making or a ritual act? *Scandinavian Political Studies, 5,* 85-118.

Ouchi, W. (1981). *Theory Z: How American business can meet the Japanese challenge.* Boston: Addison-Wesley.

Pacanowsky, M. (1983). A small-town cop story. In L. Putnam & M. Pacanowsky (Eds.), *Communication and organizations* (pp. 261-282). Beverly Hills, CA: Sage.

Palm, G. (1977). *The flight from work.* Cambridge: Cambridge University Press.

Palmer, R. E. (1969). *Hermeneutics.* Evanston, IL: Northwestern University Press.

Parsons, T. (1949). *Essays in sociological theory.* Glencoe, IL: The Free Press.

Parsons, T. (1980). Goals or functions. In A. Etzioni & E. W. Lehman (Eds.), *A sociological reader on complex organizations* (pp. 116-117). New York: Holt, Rinehart and Winston.

Perrow, C. (1980a). Technology. In A. Etzioni & E. W. Lehman (Eds.), *A sociological reader on complex organizations* (pp. 116-117). New York: Holt, Rinehart and Winston.

Perrow, C. (1980b). Zoo story or life in the organizational sandpit. In G. Salaman & K. Thompson (Eds.), *Control and ideology in organizations* (pp. 259-277). Cambridge: MIT Press.

Perrow, C. (1986). *Complex organizations: A critical essay* (3rd ed). New York: Random House. (Original work published 1972)

Peters, T. J. & Waterman, R. H., Jr. (1982). *In search of excellence.* New York: Harper and Row.

Pfeffer, J. (1977). The ambiguity of leadership. *Academy of Management Review, 2,* 104-112.

Pinch, T. & Pinch, T. (1988). Reservations about reflexivity and new literary forms or why let the devil have all the good tunes? In S. Woolgar (Ed.), *Knowledge and reflexivity. New frontiers in the sociology of knowledge* (pp. 178-187). London: Sage.

Pinder, C. C. & Bourgeois, V. W. (1982). Controlling tropes in administrative science. *Administrative Science Quarterly, 27,* 641-652.

Pitkin, F. M. (1972). *Wittgenstein and justice.* Berkeley: University of California Press.

Polanyi, M. (1958). *Personal knowledge.* London: Routledge & Kegan Paul.

Potter, J. & Wetherell, M. (1987). *Discourse and social psychology: Beyond attitudes and behaviour.* London: Sage.

Pratt, M. L. (1986). Fieldwork in common places. In J. Clifford & G. E. Marcus (Eds.), *Writing culture: The poetics and politics of ethnography* (pp. 27-50). Berkeley: University of California Press.

Putnam, L. L. & Pacanowsky, M. (Eds.). (1983). *Communication and organizations: An interpretive approach.* Beverly Hills, CA: Sage.

Rabinow, P. (1986). Representations are social facts. In J. Clifford & G. E. Marcus (Eds.), *Writing culture: The poetics and politics of ethnography* (pp. 234-261). Berkeley: University of California Press.

Rice, A. K. (1987). *Productivity and social organization: The Ahmedabad experiment.* London: Tavistock. (Original work published 1958)

Riesman, D. (1950). *The lonely crowd.* New York: Anchor/Doubleday.

Riesman, D. (1954). *Individualism reconsidered.* New York: Anchor/Doubleday.

Roberts, K. H. (1970). On looking at an elephant: An evaluation of cross-cultural research related to organizations. *Psychological Bulletin, 74*(5), 327-350.

Rohlen, T. P. (1973). "Spiritual education" in a Japanese bank. *American Anthropologist, 75,* 1542-1562.

Rohlen, T. P. (1974). *For harmony and strength: Japanese white-collar organization in anthropological perspective.* Berkeley: University of California Press.

Rorty, R. (1979). *Philosophy and the mirror of nature.* Princeton, NJ: Princeton University Press.

Rorty, R. (1982). *Consequences of pragmatism.* Minneapolis: University of Minnesota Press.

Rorty, R. (1989). *Contingency, irony and solidarity.* Cambridge: Cambridge University Press.

Rosaldo, R. (1987). Where objectivity lies: The rhetoric of anthropology. In J. S. Nelson, A. Megill, & D. N. McCloskey (Eds.), *The rhetoric of the human sciences:*

Language and argument in scholarship and public affairs (pp. 83-91). Madison: The University of Wisconsin Press.

Rosaldo, R. (1989). *Culture and truth: The remaking of social analysis.* Boston: Beacon Press.

Roth, P. (1990, April 12). A conversation in Prague. *The New York Review of Books,* p. 8.

Rotter, J. B., Rafferty, J. E. & Schachtitz, L. (1949). Validation of the Rotter incomplete sentences blank for college screening. *Journal of Consulting Psychology, 13,* 348-356.

Roy, D. (1952). *Restrictions of output in a piecework machine shop.* Unpublished doctoral dissertation, University of Chicago, Chicago.

Sabel, C. & Piore, M. (1984). *The second industrial divide.* New York: Basic Books.

Sabini, J. & Silver, M. (1982). *Moralities of everyday life.* New York: Oxford University Press.

Salaman, G. (1980). Organizations as constructors of social reality. In G. Salaman & K. Thompson (Eds.), *Control and ideology in organizations* (Vol. 2, pp. 237-258). Milton Keynes, UK: The Open University Press.

Sanday, P. R. (1979). The ethnographic paradigm(s). *Administrative Science Quarterly, 24*(4), 527-538.

Sayles, L. R. (1962). The change process in organizations: An applied anthropology analysis. *Human Organization, 21,* 62-67.

Scarry, E. (1985). *The body in pain: The making and unmaking of the world.* New York: Oxford University Press.

Schein, E. H. (1961). *Coercive persuasion.* New York: Norton.

Schein, E. H. (1969). *Process consultation.* Reading, MA: Addison-Wesley.

Schein, E. H. (1978). *Career dynamics: Matching individual and organizational needs.* Reading, MA: Addison-Wesley.

Schein, E. H. (1985). *Organizational culture and leadership.* San Francisco: Jossey-Bass.

Schein, E. H. (1987). *The clinical perspective in fieldwork.* Beverly Hills, CA: Sage.

Schumacher, E. F. (1973). *Small is beautiful: A study of economics as if people mattered.* London: Abacus.

Schütz, A. (1964a). *Collected papers: The problem of social reality.* (1st ed.). The Hague: Martinus Nijhoff.

Schütz, A. (1964b). *Collected papers: Studies in social theory.* (2nd ed.). The Hague: Martinus Nijhoff.

Sclavi, M. (1989). *A una spanna da terra* [Close to the ground]. Milan: Feltrinelli.

Scott, M. B. & Lyman, S. M. (1968). Accounts. *American Sociological Review, 33,* 46-62.

Scott, R. W. (1981). *Organizations: Rational, natural and open systems.* Englewood Cliffs, NJ: Prentice-Hall.

Sederberg, P. C. (1984). *The politics of meaning.* Tucson: The University of Arizona Press.

Selznick, P. (1957). *Leadership in administration.* New York: Harper and Row.

Selznick, P. (1966). *TVA and the grass roots: A study in the sociology of formal organizations.* New York: Harper and Row. (Original work published 1949)

Sevón, G. (1986). Handling och reflektion [Action and reflection]. *Hallinnon tutkimus, 2,* 301-315.

Silverman, D. (1971). *The theory of organizations.* New York: Basic Books.

Silverman, D. (1972). Methodology and meaning. In P. Filmer, M. Phillipson, D. Silverman, & D. Walsh (Eds.), *New directions in sociological theory* (pp. 183-200). London: Collier-Macmillan.

Silverman, D. (1975). *Reading Castaneda: A prologue to the social sciences.* London: Routledge & Kegan Paul.

Silverman, D. & Jones, J. (1976). *Organizational work: The language of grading, the grading of language.* London: Collier Macmillan.

Silverman, D. & Torode, B. (1980). *The material word: Some theories of language and its limits.* London: Routledge & Kegan Paul.

Skinner, B. F. (1948). *Walden Two.* New York: Macmillan.

Slater, P. (1970). *The pursuit of loneliness: American culture at the breaking point.* Boston: Beacon Press.

Slater, P. (1974). *Earthwalk.* New York: Anchor Press/Doubleday.

Smelser, N. J. (Ed.). (1988). *Handbook of sociology.* Newbury Park, CA: Sage.

Smircich, L. (1983). Concepts of culture and organizational analysis. *Administrative Science Quarterly, 28*(3), 339-358.

Smircich, L. (1985). Is the concept of culture a paradigm for understanding organizations and ourselves? In P. J. Frost, L. F. Moore, M. R. Louis, C. C. Lundberg, & J. Martin (Eds.), *Organizational culture* (pp. 55-72). Newbury Park, CA: Sage.

Smircich, L. & Morgan, G. (1982). Leadership: The management of meaning. *The Journal of Applied Behavioral Science, 18*(3), 257-273.

Smircich, L. & Stubbart, C. (1985). Strategic management in an enacted world. *Academy of Management Review, 10*(4), 724-736.

Smith, D. (1990). *The conceptual practices of power: A feminist sociology of knowledge.* Toronto: University of Toronto Press.

Spybey, W. A. (1982). *The rationality of the business organisation in advanced capitalist society.* Unpublished doctoral dissertation, Bradford University, Bradford, UK.

Spybey, W. A. (1984). Traditional and professional frames of meaning in management. *Sociology, 18*(4), 550-562.

Thompson, J. D. (1967). *Organizations in action.* New York: McGraw-Hill.

Thompson, J. D. & McEwen, W. J. (1980). Organizational goals and environment. In A. Etzioni & E. W. Lehman (Eds.), *A sociological reader on complex organizations* (pp. 136-143). New York: Holt, Rinehart and Winston.

Thompson, K. (1980). Organizations as constructors of social reality. In G. Salaman & K. Thompson (Eds.), *Control and ideology in organizations* (Vol. 1, pp. 216-236). Milton Keynes, UK: The Open University Press.

Tilly, C. (1984). *Big structures, large processes, huge comparisons.* New York: Russell Sage Foundation.

Travers, A. (1990). Seeing through: Symbolic life and organizational research in a postmodern frame. In B. A. Turner (Ed.), *Organizational symbolism* (pp. 271-280). Berlin: de Gruyter.

Trice, H. M., Belasco, J., & Alluto, J. A. (1969). The role of ceremonials in organizational behavior. *Industrial and Labor Relations Review, 21*(1), 40-51.

Turner, B. A. (1971). *Exploring the industrial subculture.* London: Macmillan.

Turner, B. A. (1981). Some practical aspects of qualitative data analysis: One way of organizing the cognitive processes associated with the generation of grounded theory. *Quality and Quantity, 15,* 225-247.

Turner, B. A. (1983). The use of grounded theory for the qualitative analysis of organizational behaviour. *Journal of Management Studies, 20*(3), 333-348.

Turner, R. H. (1962). Role-taking: Process versus conformity. In A. Rose (Ed.), *Human behavior and social process* (pp. 20-40). Boston: Houghton Mifflin.

Turner, V. (1982). *From ritual to theatre: The human seriousness of play.* New York: Performing Arts Journal Publications.

Tyler, S. A. (1986). Post-modern ethnography. In J. Clifford & G. E. Marcus (Eds.), *Writing culture: The poetics and politics of ethnography* (pp. 122-140). Berkeley: University of California Press.

Van Maanen, J. (1974). Working the street: A developmental view of police behavior. In H. Jacob (Ed.), *The potential for reform of criminal justice* (pp. 83-130). Beverly Hills, CA: Sage.

Van Maanen, J. (1979). The fact of fiction in organizational ethnography. *Administrative Studies Quarterly, 24*(4), 539-550.

Van Maanen, J. (1981, August 2). *Some thoughts (and afterthoughts) on context, interpretation and organization theory.* Paper presented at the Academy of Management Annual Meeting, San Diego, CA.

Van Maanen, J. (1988). *Tales of the field.* Chicago: Chicago University Press.

Van Maanen, J. & Barley, S. R. (1984). Occupational communities: Culture and control in organizations. In B. M. Staw & L. L. Cummings (Eds.), *Research in organizational behavior* (Vol. 6, pp. 287-365). Greenwood, CT: JAI Press.

Van Maanen, J. & Barley, S. (1985). Cultural organization. In P. J. Frost, L. F. Moore, M. R. Louis, C. C. Lundberg, & J. Martin (Eds.), *Organizational culture* (pp. 31-53). Newbury Park, CA: Sage.

Van Maanen, J. & Schein, E. H. (1979). Toward a theory of organizational socialization. In B. Staw (Ed.), *Research in organizational behavior* (Vol. 1, pp. 209-264). Greenwich, CT: JAI Press.

Vickers, G. (1972). *Freedom in a rocking boat.* London: Penguin.

Waldo, D. (1961). Organization theory: An elephantine problem. *Public Administration Review, 21,* 210-225.

Waugh, E. (1948). *The Loved One.* Harmondsworth, UK: Penguin.

Wax, R. (1974). *Doing fieldwork: Warnings and advice.* Chicago: The University of Chicago Press.

Weber, M. (1980). The three types of legitimate rule. In A. Etzioni & E. W. Lehman (Eds.), *A sociological reader on complex organizations* (pp. 4-10). New York: Holt, Rinehart and Winston. (Original work published 1922)

Weick, K. E. (1969). *The social psychology of organizing.* Reading, MA: Addison-Wesley.

Weick, K. E. (1977). Reward concepts: Dice or marbles? In T. H. Hammer & S. B. Bacharach (Eds.), *Reward systems and power distribution in organizations: Searching for solutions* (pp. 33-55). Ithaca: NYS School of Industrial and Labor Relations, Cornell University.

Weick, K. E. (1983). Organizational communication: Toward a research agenda. In L. L. Putnam & M. E. Pacanowsky (Eds.), *Communication and organizations: An interpretive approach* (pp. 13-30). Beverly Hills, CA: Sage.

Weick, K. E. (1985a). Sources of order in underorganized systems: Themes in recent organization theory. In Y. S. Lincoln (Ed.), *Organizational theory and inquiry* (pp. 106-136). Beverly Hills, CA: Sage.

Weick, K. E. (1985b). The significance of corporate culture. In P. J. Frost, L. F. Moore, M. R. Louis, C. C. Lundberg, & J. Martin (Eds.), *Organizational culture* (pp. 381-390). Newbury Park, CA: Sage.

Whyte, W. H. (1956). *The Organization Man.* New York: Simon and Schuster.

Wilcock, K. D. (1984). *The corporate tribe*. New York: Warner Books.

Wildavsky, A. B. (1984). *A nurturing father: Moses as a political leader*. Birmingham: The University of Alabama Press.

Wilensky, H. L. (1980). Blockages to organizational intelligence. In A. Etzioni & E. W. Lehman (Eds.), *A sociological reader on complex organizations* (pp. 134-206). New York: Holt, Rinehart and Winston.

Wilkins, A. L. & Ouchi, W. G. (1983). Efficient cultures: Exploring the relationship between culture and organizational performance. *Administrative Science Quarterly, 28*(3), 468-481.

Wolf, E. R. (1966). Kinship, friendship, and patron-client relations in complex societies. In M. Banton (Ed.), *The social anthropology of complex societies* (pp. 1-22). London: Tavistock.

Young-Bruehl, E. (1982). *Hannah Arendt: For the love of the world*. New Haven, CT: Yale University Press.

Zelditch, M., Jr. (1980). Can you really study an army in the laboratory? In A. Etzioni & E. W. Lehman (Eds.), *A sociological reader on complex organizations* (pp. 531-539). New York: Holt, Rinehart and Winston.

Zey-Ferrell, M. (1981). Criticism of the dominant perspective on organizations. *The Sociological Quarterly, 22,* 181-205.

Zimbardo, P. G., Haney, C., Banks, W. C., & Jaffe, D. (1974). Psychology of imprisonment. In Z. Rubin (Ed.), *Doing unto others* (pp. 61-73). Englewood Cliffs, NJ: Prentice-Hall.

Zinoviev, A. (1983). *Homo Sovieticus*. Paris: Juillard.

Author Index

Subject Index

Accounts, 36-37, 44, 48-49, 64, 94, 117-138, 147, 152-153, 155-157, 191, 198-204, 207-209, 220, 225

Aesthetics, 214-219

Anthropological frame of mind, 73, 193

Anthropology, 2, 4, 7, 23, 35, 40-74, 75-77, 93, 113-116, 130, 140-141, 144, 160, 189, 197, 215

   cognitive, 117, 124, 127

   cultural, 52, 140

   of complex organizations, 23, 28, 32, 35, 71-72, 93, 120, 130, 136, 140, 147, 150, 176-180, 186-225

   political, 4, 139-158

   social, 4, 40-42, 52, 140, 146

Anthropomorphism, 19, 29, 57, 80, 152, 192, 202

Anxiety, 93, 142

Artifacts, 32-33, 45, 186, 214

Bracketing, 34, 48, 158

Bureaucracy, 18-19, 26-29, 48, 71, 90, 95, 187, 207

Clinical approach, 86, 163-167, 175, 185

Collage, 5

Collective action, 10, 18-19, 32-34, 37, 45, 54, 57, 61, 72, 96, 126-127, 152, 162, 186-188, 195, 202, 223

Communication, 10, 14, 43-44, 126-127, 145, 148, 163, 166, 175, 178-179, 196, 217

Comparative studies, 15, 42, 76-77, 95-97, 108, 114, 150, 207

Complex organizations, 2, 4-7, 8-39, 48, 50, 56, 61-62, 63, 70-72, 78, 85, 93, 95-96, 98-99, 102-103, 106-107, 112, 120-124, 127, 131-132, 136, 140, 145, 154, 175, 186, 188-189, 191, 207-208, 210, 224

   definitions of, 9, 13-14, 18-20, 26-30, 32-33, 36-38, 69, 74, 104, 137, 153, 166, 168, 178-179, 186, 210

   metaphors of, 17, 19, 20, 24, 27-31, 42, 44, 52-54, 62, 64, 66, 67-69, 74, 75, 80, 82, 86, 101, 104, 126-127, 130, 137, 153, 155, 160, 168, 170,

About the Author

Barbara Czarniawska-Joerges, Ph.D., is Professor of Business Administration at Lund University, Sweden. Her research focuses on control processes in complex organizations. She has published widely in Polish (her native language), as well as in Swedish and English, in the area of business administration. Her books include *Controlling Top Management in Large Organizations* (1985), *Ideological Control in Nonideological Organizations* (1988), and *Economic Decline and Organizational Control* (1989). Her articles have appeared in *Economic and Industrial Democracy; Scandinavian Journal of Management Studies; Organization Studies; Journal of Management Studies; Accounting, Organizations and Society; Management Communication Quarterly;* and *Consultation.*

DATE DUE

MAR 4 '92	
FEB 17 '93	
JUN 1 5 '93	

BRODART, INC.   Cat. No. 23-221